MINITAB
Student Handbook

Thomas A. Ryan, Jr.
Pennsylvania State University

Brian L. Joiner
University of Wisconsin

Barbara F. Ryan
Pennsylvania State University

DUXBURY PRESS
Boston, Massachusetts

PWS PUBLISHERS

Prindle, Weber & Schmidt · 🐾 · Willard Grant Press · **wg** · Duxbury Press · ♠
Statler Office Building · 20 Providence Street · Boston, Massachusetts 02116

ISBN 0-87150-359-X

(previously ISBN 0-87872-116-9)

PWS Publishers is a division of Wadsworth, Inc.

MINITAB Student Handbook was prepared for composition by Irene Rubin. Interior design was provided by Dorothy Booth. The cover was designed by Garrow Throop.

L.C. Cat. Card No.: 75-41977

Printed in the United States of America

12 – 82

Contents

Preface

This HANDBOOK is intended as a supplementary text for a first or second course in statistics (pre- or post-calculus). It is designed to be used along with Minitab, a computing system specifically developed to relieve students of the computational drudgery usually associated with statistics, so that they can focus on important concepts. *The book emphasizes topics not normally given due attention in standard elementary statistics texts.* These include aspects of statistics that are particularly appropriate to computer use, such as the application of standard methods to real data, in-depth exploration of data, the creative use of plots, simulation as a learning tool, and regression, including polynomial regression, multiple regression, and transformations.

The HANDBOOK includes numerous examples and exercises which show step-by-step how to use the computer to explore data. Many of these examples and exercises were obtained by the authors while consulting with researchers from a wide variety of application areas, and are presented in sufficient detail to provide the students with an idea of the scope and importance of the problems amenable to statistical treatment. Obviously, the computer does not replace handwork. Some problems are best done by hand, and others involve a mixture of hand and computer work. This mixture is emphasized throughout the HANDBOOK.

The chapters and sections are designed to be as independent of each other as possible. Once the main points of Chapters 1 (Introduction to Minitab) and 2 (Descriptive Statistics) have been covered, other chapters may be covered in almost any desired order. This flexibility extends itself even to the ordering of sections within most chapters.

Notes on the Minitab Statistical Computing System

Minitab is designed to allow students in introductory statistics courses to "speak" to the computer in commands similar to English sentences. These commands generally correspond to the major steps a student might follow in solving a problem by hand. For example, to do a paired t-test, a student tells Minitab to READ the data, SUBTRACT one variable from the other, then do a single-sample TTEST on the differences.

Minitab was originally developed for an introductory pre-calculus statistics course given at Penn State. Each year over 1200 students take this course. About one hour of the first week is spent giving the students a brief introduction to Minitab, showing them how to use keypunches, and how to run a job. Little additional class time is spent on Minitab, per se. As new statistical concepts are taught, the appropriate Minitab commands are introduced. Typically, one homework assignment per week involves Minitab. These assignments usually require the student to link together several Minitab commands in an "outline" of the analysis, to make a few passes on the computer, to interact with the output, to combine hand and computer work, and to interpret results. Once the students have gotten started, the instructor can run a program, then hand out duplicated copies of the computer output for discussion or as part of an exercise.

The Minitab system is not limited to use in elementary courses. Many students use it in courses in fields of application, for term papers, theses, and other projects. It is also useful in more advanced data analysis courses, particularly in regression. The system is one of the most frequently used tools of the Penn State and Wisconsin statistical consulting laboratories, and is used in business, industry, and government as well.

The Minitab system also provides an excellent introduction to the use of other packages, such as SPSS, BMD, SAS, and more specialized programs.

The Minitab system is available to anyone for a nominal charge to cover costs. It is written in standard FORTRAN IV and has been easily implemented on a wide variety of medium to large size computers. It may be used in either batch or interactive mode. The cost of running a Minitab program is quite minimal. For further information about the system, write

Professor T. A. Ryan, Jr.
Statistics Department
215 Pond Laboratory
The Pennsylvania State University
University Park, Pa. 16802

Acknowledgements

Minitab began as a student-oriented adaptation of the National Bureau of Standards' "Omnitab" system. We have benefited considerably by being able to use their basic command structure and their copious documentation.

We are grateful for the many suggestions we have received from colleagues and students at Penn State, University of Wisconsin, and elsewhere during the development of the Minitab system. Particular mention is due Cynthia Mable, Del Scott, and Alfred Rademaker for their help with programming; to Robert Kohm of Alcoa Laboratories, who was the first person to give us extensive comments on the use of Minitab on an interactive system; and to Lawrence Klimko of Bucknell University for his careful and extensive criticisms; and to Peggy J. Burris for her help in distributing the system.

We are grateful to the Pennsylvania State University for partial support in writing this book through a course improvement grant. Thomas P. Hettmansperger provided extensive suggestions, particularly in the nonparametric statistics chapter. Reference is made throughout the book to those who have kindly made their data available to us. To them and to Peter Nemenyi go our special thanks. We also wish to express our appreciation to Bonnie Henninger, Cheryl Schweitzer, and Linda Lower for their help with the manuscript. Finally, we wish to acknowledge the advice which we received from reviewers of the manuscript: Professor M. D. Butler, University of California-Irvine; Professor Robert Johnson, Monroe Community College; Professor Elmo Keller, California State Polytechnic Institute; Professor Jerome H. Klotz, University of Wisconsin; Professor George McCabe, Purdue University; and Professor Donald McIsaac, University of Wisconsin.

1

Introduction to Minitab

Minitab is an easy-to-use general purpose statistical computing system. It is a flexible and powerful tool that has been designed especially for students and researchers who have no previous experience with computers. In this chapter we discuss how Minitab works and, in the chapters that follow, we will show how Minitab can be used to solve various types of statistical problems.

1.1 A Simple Example

A study was done to see how blood cholesterol level changes following a heart attack. Part of the data on 12 patients is given below. The first measurement of cholesterol level was made 2 days after the heart attack. The second measurement was made 4 days after the attack.

Cholesterol Level 2 Days After	Cholesterol Level 4 Days After
270	218
236	234
210	214
142	116
280	200
272	276
160	146
220	182

226	238
242	288
186	190
266	236

(a) Calculate how much the cholesterol level of each patient changed from the second to the fourth day. (b) Find the average change for the 12 patients. (c) Make a histogram of the 12 changes.

A Minitab program that performs these operations is shown in Exhibit 1.1. Each line corresponds to one punched card, or if you're using a typewriter-like terminal, to one typed line. Notice that Minitab commands are given in English, just about the same way you'd tell someone to do the calculations by hand. Minitab stores the data in a worksheet it maintains in the computer. The first command

READ THE FOLLOWING DATA INTO COLUMNS C1 AND C2

tells the computer to take the data from the lines that follow the READ command and put those data into the first and second columns of the worksheet. After the data have been read, the worksheet will look like the following (where ... always means that we haven't taken the trouble to write in all of the numbers):

Col. 1	Col. 2	
270	218	
236	234	
210	214	
142	116	
.	.	
.	.	
.	.	
266	236	

EXHIBIT 1.1

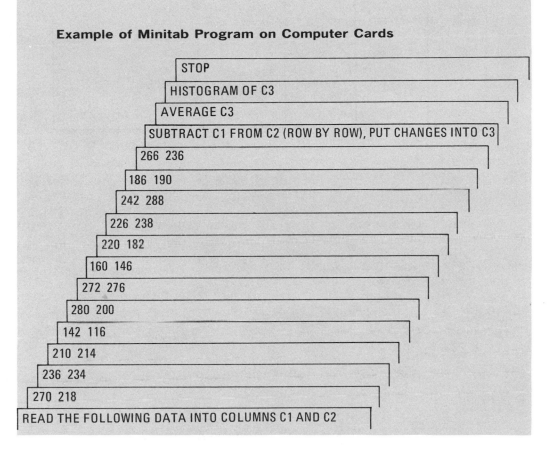

Example of Minitab Program on Computer Cards

```
                              │STOP
                            │HISTOGRAM OF C3
                          │AVERAGE C3
                        │SUBTRACT C1 FROM C2 (ROW BY ROW), PUT CHANGES INTO C3│
                   │266  236
                 │186  190
               │242  288
             │226  238
           │220  182
         │160  146
       │272  276
     │280  200
   │142  116
 │210  214
│236  234
│270  218
│READ THE FOLLOWING DATA INTO COLUMNS C1 AND C2
```

The next command

SUBTRACT C1 FROM C2 (ROW BY ROW), PUT CHANGES INTO C3

says to subtract column 1 of the worksheet from column 2 and store the difference in column 3. After this has been done, the worksheet will look like this:

Col. 1	Col. 2	Col. 3	
270	218	−52	
236	234	−2	
210	214	4	

142	116	−26	
.	.	.	
.	.	.	
.	.	.	
266	236	−30	

EXHIBIT 1.2

Output From the Minitab Program Shown in Exhibit 1.1

```
-- READ THE FOLLOWING DATA INTO COLUMNS C1 AND C2
     COLUMN C1    C2
     COUNT   12   12
ROW
    1        270. 218.
    2        236. 234.
    3        210. 214.
    4        142. 116.
    . . .


-- SUBTRACT C1 FROM C2 (ROW BY ROW), PUT CHANGES INTO C3
-- AVERAGE C3
     AVERAGE =    −14.333
-- HISTOGRAM OF C3
     MIDDLE OF  NUMBER OF
     INTERVAL   OBSERVATIONS
       −80.       1    *
       −60.       1    *
       −40.       1    *
       −20.       3    ***
         0.       4    ****
        20.       1    *
        40.       1    *
-- STOP
```

Column 3 now contains the change in cholesterol level for each patient. The next command

AVERAGE C3

says to calculate the average of the numbers in column c3 and print out that average. The next command

HISTOGRAM OF C3

says to print out a histogram of the numbers in c3. The last command

STOP

says you are finished with Minitab. The output from this program is shown in Exhibit 1.2.

Exercise

1-1   (a) Run the program in Exhibit 1.1.

       (b) Try to interpret the output.

1.2 Basic Rules

The following rules concerning Minitab programs are important:

(a) Minitab reads a command, looks up the command in its dictionary (of about 100 names), checks for errors, carries out the command, and then goes on to the next command.

(b) Minitab has a dictionary of command names it recognizes. Only the (first 4 characters of the) command name and the numerical arguments are used by the computer. All other text is simply for the reader's benefit. (This extra text, however, may not contain any numbers.) All commands and data are free format. That is, all values may be put anywhere on the line just so long as they're in the right order. Thus the first command in our example could have been written

READ DATA INTO COLUMNS C1 AND C2

or simply

READ C1 C2

(c) Each command must be on a separate line.

(d) Ordinarily, the worksheet has 50 columns, each of which can store up to 200 numbers. (This may be different on some computers. This can be changed with the DIMENSION command described on page 314.)

(e) In some commands, such as ADD and MULTIPLY, the computer needs to know whether you want to add a constant (e.g., 10.0) to a column or whether you want to add another column. Minitab uses the convention that column numbers must have a C in front. For example,

ADD C1 TO C2, PUT INTO C3

means add column 1 to column 2 and put the results into column 3, while

ADD 1 TO C2, PUT INTO C3

means add the value 1.0 to each entry in column 2 and put the results into column 3.

(f) Some commands store their answers, some print out answers, and some do both. As you become familiar with the commands, it will become easy to remember what each does.

(g) A list of consecutive column numbers may be indicated using a dash. For example, you could use

READ C2-C5

instead of

READ C2, C3, C4, C5

The dash can be used any time you have consecutive columns.

(h) Commands can be used any number of times in a program, and in any order (provided the order makes sense).

(i) Commas cannot appear within a number. For example, to write one thousand forty-one, use 1041, not 1,041.

1.3 Some Minitab Commands

The most important Minitab commands are described throughout this Handbook. Each description is set off in a box like this. A complete list of all commands is given in Appendix F (page 318). In addition, each command is listed alphabetically in the Index at the back of the book.

In the command descriptions the symbol **C** can be replaced by any column number, the symbol **K** by any constant, and the symbol **E** means you can use either a column number or a constant. As an example of this notation the general description of the AVERAGE command is written:

AVERAGE THE VALUES IN COLUMN **C**

The symbol **C** can be replaced by any column number. If you want to average the numbers in column c18, write

AVERAGE THE VALUES IN C18

The letters in boldface are the only necessary parts of the command. So you could write just

AVER C18

READ THE FOLLOWING DATA INTO COLUMNS

C, C,...,C, ROW BY ROW

This command is followed by rows of data. The numbers are put in the worksheet one row at a time.

Example

```
READ INTO COLS C2, C3, C5
1.0      3      10.5
3        0      11.5
2        4      5.2
7        5      4
```

Following this, the worksheet will look like

Col. 1	Col. 2	Col. 3	Col. 4	Col. 5	
	1.0	3.0		10.5	
	3.0	0.0		11.5	
	2.0	4.0		5.2	
	7.0	5.0		4.0	

The numbers can appear anywhere on a line, just as long as they're in the proper order.

(*More details about* READ *are given on page 20.*)

> ## SET THE FOLLOWING DATA INTO COLUMN C

This command also puts numbers into the Minitab worksheet. It differs from READ in that you can put as many numbers as you want on each line and they all go into the same column. Note that no data may be put on the SET line itself.

Example

SET FOLLOWING DATA INTO COL C7
1.0	10.5	3	3,11.5	2,12.5,4
5.2	6.8	7	4	5

Following this, column 7 will contain the thirteen numbers: 1.0, 10.5, 3.0, 3.0, 11.5, 2.0, 12.5, 4.0, 5.2, 6.8, 7.0, 4.0, and 5.0.

(*More details about* SET *are given on page 21.*)

> ## ADD E TO E, PUT INTO C

> ## SUBTRACT E FROM E, PUT INTO C

> ## MULTIPLY E BY E, PUT INTO C

> ## DIVIDE E BY E, PUT INTO C

Recall that E says that you can use either a column number (e.g., C2) or a constant (e.g., 5.31). Consequently the presence or absence of a C is crucial. ADD C1 TO C3 PUT IN C2 and ADD 1 TO C3 PUT IN C2 are quite different.

Example

ADD C1 TO C3 AND PUT IN C2

causes the worksheet to be changed as follows:

Col. 1		Col. 3		Col. 2
1.1		2.2		3.3
2.3	+	3.1	⟶	5.4
20.0		5.1		25.1

Here the two columns are added row by row. On the other hand,

ADD 1 TO C3 AND PUT INTO C2 causes the worksheet to be changed as follows:

		Col. 3		Col. 2
		2.2		3.2
1.0	+	3.1	⟶	4.1
		5.1		6.1

Here, since the 1 is not preceded by a C, Minitab uses it as a constant and the value 1.0 is added to every number in column 3.

(*More about* ADD *and* MULTIPLY *is given on page 77.*)

AVERAGE THE VALUES IN COLUMN C

This command tells the computer to find the average of the values and print out the result. Another version of this command is

---

AVERAGE VALUES IN COL **C**, PUT AVERAGE INTO COL **C**

This tells the computer to find the average, print out the average, and store the average in the indicated column.

Example

Suppose column 1 contains the numbers 1, 2, 3, 4. Then

AVERAGE C1

prints the average, 2.5, while

AVERAGE C1, PUT IN C2

prints the average and puts it into every row of column 2. Thus after this command, the worksheet will look like this.

Col. 1	Col. 2	
1	2.5	
2	2.5	
3	2.5	
4	2.5	
	2.5	
	2.5	
	.	
	.	
	.	
	.	
	.	
	.	
	2.5	

General Rule

Any time the result of a command is a single number answer, that answer is printed automatically.

SQRT OF E PUT IN C

Calculates square roots.

Example

SQRT OF C2, PUT IN C3

Col. 2	Col. 3
4.0	2.0
9.0 →	3.0
0.0	0.0
2.0	1.414...

Example

SQRT OF 2 PUT IN C1

Stores 1.414... in every row of column 1. (Since the answer is a single number, Minitab also prints it out.)

PRINT COLUMNS C, C,...,C

This command can be used to print out numbers that have been stored in the Minitab worksheet. One or more columns can be printed.

Example

PRINT COLS C1, C4, C5

Tells the computer to print out the contents of these three columns.

(*More details about* PRINT *are given on page 22.*)

STOP

This tells the computer you're finished with Minitab.

Exercises

1-2   The following program calculates the average improvement in reading scores for the 8 students in a reading improvement class. Each data line corresponds to one student, with the first number his "before" score and the second number his "after" score.

READ INTO C1, C2
   10   12
   10   14
    8   11

```
 6   15
 8   10
11   12
 8   12
12   15
SUBTRACT C1 FROM C2, PUT IN C3
AVERAGE C3
PRINT C1, C2, C3
STOP
```

(a) Pretend that you are Minitab and carry out all the steps of the program. Keep a worksheet as you go along. What does the worksheet contain at the end of the program? What is printed out?

(b) Run this program on the computer.

1-3 (a) Write a Minitab program to print out a table of squares and square roots of the integers from 1 to 20. Use SET to put the integers 1,2,3,...,20 into a column. Then use MULTIPLY and SQRT to calculate the squares and square roots. Print out the three columns.

(b) Run the program.

1-4 World records (as of September 1975) for men's track are given below.

Distance of Race		Record Time	
Miles	Yards	Minutes	Seconds
0	100	0	9.0
0	220	0	19.5
0	440	0	44.5
0	880	1	43.9
1	0	3	49.4
2	0	8	13.8
3	0	12	47.8
6	0	26	47.0
10	0	46	4.2
15	0	72	22.6

(a) Calculate the average speed (in miles per hour) for each of the 10 races. To do this, first read the data into 4 columns. Divide yards by 1760 and add to miles to get total distance in miles. In a similar way convert total time into hours. Then divide miles by hours to get speed in miles per hour.

(b) How does speed vary with the length of the race? Does it usually decrease? What about the speed for the 100-yard race? Can you explain why the 100-yard race might not follow the general pattern?

1-5 (a) Suppose you have the following data for the students in a small class:

Student Identification Number	Grade on Exam 1	Grade on Exam 2	Grade on Exam 3
23651	92	82	96
23658	84	84	80
23690	75	79	83
22100	98	60	72
23101	62	55	40
23400	79	72	81
23121	81	70	78

A student's grade in this course is simply the average of his 3 exam grades. Write a Minitab program which (1) prints out a list containing each student's identification number followed by his course grade, and (2) find the class average for each exam and for the course grades. (Why can the AVERAGE command be used in part 2, but not in part 1?)

(b) Run the program.

1-6 What's wrong with each of the following commands?

(a) READ 1ST SCORE INTO C1, 2ND SCORE INTO C2

(b) MULTIPLY C5 BY 2,431 PUT ANSWERS INTO C10

(c) SET DATA INTO COLUMNS C1 AND C2

(d) SUPTRACT C2 FROM C1, PUT INTO C4

(e) READ DATA INTO COLUMNS 1 AND 2

1-7 (a) Are the following two commands equivalent?
ADD C1 TO C2, PUT INTO C3
ADD C1-C3

(b) Will the following command work?

MULTTIPLE C1 BY C2, PUT INTO C3

1.4 Error Messages

Everyone who uses a computer makes mistakes—many mistakes. Usually, if you make a mistake using Minitab, you'll get an error message.
This message should help you discover what's wrong. You might deliber-
ately make some mistakes just to see what happens. For example, try
running the following program:

```
SET INTO C1
1, 2, 3, 4, 5, −1, −2
AVERAGE C1
SQRT C1, PUT INTO C2
PRINT C1, C2
PRINT C1, C2, C3
AVERAGE C4 PUT INTO C3
AVERAGE C1
AVARAGE C1 (NOTE AVERAGE MISSPELLED)
STOP
```

Of course, Minitab will not be able to detect all the mistakes you make.
For example, if you want to add 12 to column 5, but write ADD 2 TO C5,
PUT IN C6, Minitab has no way of knowing you wanted to write 12 instead
of 2. In the same way, if you ask Minitab to do a statistical analysis which
is not appropriate, Minitab cannot usually tell that the analysis is inappropriate.

Exercise

1-8   Run the above program and see if you can explain each of the error
       messages and relate them to the errors in the program.

1.5 Some More Minitab Commands

> | **SUM** THE VALUES IN **C**
>
> This command sums the values in the column, and prints the answer.
>
> **Example**
>
> If column C1 contains the four numbers 1.0, 2.0, 8.0, −2.0 and you use
> the command
>
> SUM THE VALUES IN C1
>
> Minitab prints out the answer, 9.
>
> | **SUM** THE VALUES IN **C** , PUT INTO **C**
>
> This version prints the sum of the values, and stores the sum in every
> row of the second column named.

> | **NOTE** COMMENTS CAN GO HERE
>
> This command doesn't do anything. It is just printed out along with the
> other commands in your program. Use it to help you remember what
> your program is supposed to do.

Example

NOTE TRACK TIMES ARE NOW IN C5, SPEEDS ARE IN C8

GENERATE THE FIRST K INTEGERS INTO COL C

This command puts 1, 2, 3,..., K into the column.

Example

GENERATE 5 INTEGERS INTO C8

Puts the numbers 1, 2, 3, 4, 5 into column c8.

GENERATE THE INTEGERS FROM K TO K, PUT INTO C

Example

GENERATE INTEGERS FROM −5 TO 3 INTO C1

Puts the numbers −5, −4, −3, −2, −1, 0, 1, 2, 3 into c1.

(*A more advanced form of* GENERATE *is described on page 319.*)

Exercises

1-9 (a) Pretend that you are Minitab and carry out the steps of the follow-
         ing program. What does the worksheet contain at the end of the
         program? What is printed out? What have you calculated?

         SET INTO C1
         5 3 4 1 6 2 1 2
         SUM C1, PUT IN C2
         DIVIDE C2 BY 8 PUT IN C3
         PRINT C3
         STOP

     (b) Run the program.

1-10 (a) The United States may soon convert to the metric system. Write a
          Minitab program which converts feet to meters. In particular, print
          a table which gives the distance in feet and the corresponding dis-
          tance in meters for 1, 2,...,50 feet. (Multiply the number of feet by
          0.3048 to get the number of meters.)

      (b) Run the program.

1-11 (a) Write a Minitab program which produces a table giving the temper-
          ature in degrees Fahrenheit (from 20° to 80° F) and the equivalent
          temperature in degrees Celsius. To convert from degrees Fahren-
          heit to degrees Celsius, first subtract 32. Then multiply this result
          by 5, then divide by 9. This is given by the formula $C = (F - 32)(5/9)$.

      (b) Run the program.

1-12 Consider the following Minitab program:

      SET INTO C1
      6, 4, 2, 1, 2
      AVERAGE C1 PUT INTO C2
      SUBTRACT C2 FROM C1, PUT DEVIATIONS INTO C3
      MULTIPLY C3 BY C3, PUT SQUARED DEVIATIONS INTO C4
      SUM C4, PUT SUM INTO C5
      DIVIDE C5 BY 4, PUT QUOTIENT INTO C6
      SQRT C6, PUT INTO C7
      PRINT C7
      STOP

      (a) Do the computation by hand. The command PRINT C7 will print out
          what number (or numbers)?

(b) Run the program to check your answer to part (a).

(c) Do you happen to know the statistical term for what you've cal-
     culated?

APPENDIX 1a
More About Reading and Printing Data

(Continued from page 8.)

> **READ** THE FOLLOWING DATA INTO COLUMNS **C, C ,...,C**

When data are read into the worksheet, the first number on each line
is put into the first column mentioned in the READ command, the second
number on each line is put into the second column mentioned on the READ
command, and so on. Extra numbers and any text are ignored.

Example

```
READ INTO C3-C5, C1
B. J. SMITH              2.1    3.2    1.9    28000    150    28
W. JOHNSON              2.0    3.8    1.4    31000    148
D. D. JONES             2.1    2.9    2.5    62000    151
F. A. BROWN             1.9    3.6    2.3    40000    155    14
```

After this, the worksheet will look as follows:

C1	C2	C3	C4	C5	
28000		2.1	3.2	1.9	
31000		2.0	3.8	1.4	
62000		2.1	2.9	2.5	
40000		1.9	3.6	2.3	

There are a few obvious restrictions on entering data: (1) numbers must be separated by blanks, commas, or other separators, (2) numbers themselves may not contain commas, (3) a data line may not begin with a legitimate command name. The first 4 rows of data read into the worksheet are automatically printed out for you to check (unless the command NOPRINT has been used).

(Continued from page 9.)

SET DATA INTO C

As in the READ command, data lines may contain text, the first 4 numbers are automatically printed out (unless NOPRINT has been used), and the same 3 restrictions also apply.

END OF DATA

For use mainly on interactive computers.* Use this command after you've entered all your data (either with a READ or SET command) and before you use another command. Using this command allows you to find out about any mistakes you've made in typing the data before you go on to further calculations. This command is optional.

*The difference between an "interactive" and a "batch" computer is described on page 307.

Example

```
SET C1
2  3  5  7  8  2  6
1  3  7  8
END OF DATA
ADD 1.5 TO C1 PUT IN C2
```

NOPRINT

Suppresses the automatic printing of data by READ and SET. It also suppresses the automatic printing of data simulated by IRANDOM, NRANDOM, BTRIALS, SAMPLE, DRANDOM, URANDOM, BRANDOM, and PRANDOM. (These commands are described in Chapters 3 and 5.) NOPRINT applies to all commands which follow it. If you want to "turn off" NOPRINT, use the command PRINT.

PRINT

The command PRINT with no column numbers following it restores the automatic printing which may have been suppressed by NOPRINT. PRINT applies to all commands which follow it. To "turn off" PRINT, use the NOPRINT command.

APPENDIX 1b
More About Minitab

Let us look at what Minitab does with the following program:

```
SET THE FOLLOWING DATA INTO C1
1 2 3 4 5
SET INTO C2
10  11  12.0
AVERAGE C1, PUT IN C4
SUBTRACT C4 FROM C1 PUT IN C5
PRINT C1 C2 C4 C5
PRINT C4
STOP
```

Here is what the worksheet will contain at the end of this program:

Col. 1	Col. 2	Col. 3	Col. 4	Col. 5	
1	10		3	−2	
2	11		3	−1	
3	12		3	0	
4			3	1	
5			3	2	
			3		
			3		
			.		
			.		
			.		
			.		
			.		
			3		

Exhibit 1.3 shows part of the output from this program. Note that although column c4 contains 200 numbers, only 5 are printed out. Col-

EXHIBIT 1.3

**Minitab Output Showing Printing of
"Artificially Long" Constant Columns**

```
-- AVERAGE C1, PUT IN C4
   AVERAGE = 3.0000
-- SUBTRACT C4 FROM C1, PUT IN C5
-- PRINT C1 C2 C4 C5
   COLUMN      C1        C2        C4        C5
   COUNT        5         3       200         5
ROW
   1           1.       10.        3.       -2.
   2           2.       11.        3.       -1.
   3           3.       12.        3.        0.
   4           4.                  3.        1.
   5           5.                  3.        2.
-- PRINT C4
   COLUMN C4
   COUNT 200
        3.
```

umn C4 is called "artificially long" since the average was put in every row of C4. Usually you would not want all the rows of an "artificially long" column printed out, so Minitab prints out this column only as far as the longest "normal length" column which is printed out with it. If no "normal length" columns are printed out with an "artificially long" column, only its first row is printed. See, for example, the results of the command PRINT C4 in Exhibit 1.3.

Now let us see what happens if numbers are put in a column which already contains some numbers. Consider, for example, the program:

```
SET INTO C1
1  2  3  4  5
MULTIPLY C1 BY C1, PUT INTO C2
SET INTO C1
10,11,12
PRINT C1 C2
STOP
```

At the end of this program, this is what the worksheet will contain:

C1	C2	
10	1	
11	4	
12	9	
	16	
	25	

Note that before the numbers 10, 11, and 12 are put into c1, the entire column is erased automatically.

General Rule

Any time a column is reused, it is first completely erased. Reusing columns that are no longer needed is sometimes useful when you're doing a large problem.

2

Descriptive Statistics

In this chapter we show how Minitab can be used to help do simple descriptive statistics. One thing to bear in mind is that not every step of every problem could or should be done by the computer. Some combination of hand and computer work is frequently the most efficient method. Generally, for very large data sets we will want to do more of the work on the computer than we will for small data sets. However, we will often use small data sets in order to illustrate methods which are really most appropriate and useful when working with large data sets. Also bear in mind that good statistical work is rarely done all in one step. Usually it is necessary to make one pass on the computer or by hand, and then study these results for a while before making a second pass.

2.1 Histograms

HISTOGRAM OF DATA IN COLUMN **C**

Prints out a histogram of the data in the column. Minitab chooses intervals (classes) with "nicely" rounded midpoints, then prints the midpoint of each interval, the number of observations in the interval, and a graph.

Observations falling on a boundary are put in the upper (higher values) interval. If you want to specify your own intervals rather than have Minitab choose them, use

HISTOGRAM OF **C**, FIRST MIDPOINT AT **K**, USE INTERVALS OF

WIDTH **K**

Example

HISTOGRAM OF C6, FIRST MIDPOINT AT 0.0, WIDTH OF 2

We can use the command HISTOGRAM to study the OTIS scores obtained in the **Cartoon** experiment. (See page 270 for a complete description of this experiment.) Nine variables were measured on 179 people. The OTIS score is variable 5. One way to get a histogram of the OTIS scores is given in the following program:

```
READ DATA INTO C1-C9
    1    0    0    1  107    4    4   -9   -9
    2    0    0    2  106    9    9    6    5
    .    .    .    .    .    .    .    .    .

    .    .    .    .    .    .    .    .    .

    .    .    .    .    .    .    .    .    .
  179    1    2    4  103    4    3    2    1
HISTOGRAM OF C5
STOP
```

This is the **Cartoon** data from pages 272-276

Output from the HISTOGRAM command is given in Exhibit 2.1. Here Minitab chose intervals of width 5 with a starting midpoint of 80. The first interval goes from 77.5 to 82.5, the second interval from 82.5 to 87.5, etc. Notice that the OTIS scores have a fairly symmetrical shape, with a peak in the middle at about 105, and that about half of the scores fell in the middle three intervals. The lowest score was about 80 and the highest about 135.

EXHIBIT 2.1

Histogram of OTIS Scores Obtained in the Cartoon Experiment

```
-- HISTOGRAM OF C5
   MIDDLE OF        NUMBER OF
   INTERVAL         OBSERVATIONS
      80.              6    ******
      85.             13    *************
      90.             12    ************
      95.             14    **************
     100.             20    ********************
     105.             26    **************************
     110.             23    ***********************
     115.             21    *********************
     120.             14    **************
     125.             15    ***************
     130.             12    ************
     135.              3    ***
```

Exercises

2-1   (a) Write and run a Minitab program to get a histogram for the following data:
           21, 43, 92, 86, 81, 85, 45, 60, 64, 71, 89, 78, 79, 43, 79.

      (b) What are the boundaries for each of the intervals (the class boundaries)? In what interval (class) did the number 86 fall? The number 45?

2-2   (a) Get histograms of the OTIS scores from the **Cartoon** experiment using the following scales:

           (1) First midpoint at 78, interval width of 1.
           (2) First midpoint at 78, interval width of 2.
           (3) First midpoint at 80, interval width of 10.
           (4) First midpoint at 70, interval width of 20.
           (5) First midpoint at 70, interval width of 30.

Compare these 5 histograms as well as the one in Exhibit 2.1. Do some histograms give a better picture of the data than others? Are some of the histograms more useful for certain purposes? Explain.

(b) In part (a), we changed the interval width. Suppose we keep the interval width constant, and change just the starting midpoint. Compare the following histograms:

(1) First midpoint at 77, interval width of 5.
(2) First midpoint at 79, interval width of 5.

2-3 (a) Do a histogram of the scores on the "cartoon test" given immediately after presentation in the **Cartoon** experiment.

(b) Do a histogram of the scores on the "realistic test" given immediately after presentation.

(c) Compare the two histograms. Do the scores seem to differ in any significant way? If so, what would be the practical importance of such a difference?

2-4 Let's take a look at the **Cancer** data (page 289) and see what we can learn by comparing histograms. Compare the ages of the four groups of patients (page 293) by making four histograms, one for each group of patients. You may want to make sure they all have the same scales. Do some groups seem older or younger by and large? Do some seem to have more variation in the ages? How else might they differ? In particular, compare the true positives with the false positives. Would knowing a person's age help you decide whether he really had cancer or not? (Remember to always give the practical interpretation of your results.)

2.2 Mean, Median, Quartiles, Percentiles, Range and Midrange

The *mean, sample mean,* or *average* (these words all mean the same thing) of a set of numbers can be obtained by using the AVERAGE command discussed in Section 1.3 (page 10).

To obtain the *median* of a set of data you can use the MEDIAN command. (The median of a set of data is the value that falls in the middle when the data are put in order. If there is an even number of observations, the two middle values are averaged.)

MEDIAN OF THE DATA IN COLUMN C

Finds and prints the median.

MEDIAN OF COL C, PUT MEDIAN IN C

Finds, prints, and stores the median in the worksheet.

The best way to have Minitab help you find the *quartiles* or *percentiles* of a set of data is to have it put the data in order and print them out, then do the rest by hand.

ORDER THE NUMBERS IN C, PUT REARRANGED NUMBERS IN C

Puts the numbers in increasing order. (Note: They are not printed out automatically.)

Example

ORDER C3, PUT IN C8

Col. 3	Col. 8
1.5	−2.0
−2.0 →	1.5
3.8	1.7
1.7	3.8

(Note: The contents of c3 have not been changed.)

Finding the *range* or *midrange* of a large set of numbers can be done by having Minitab locate the maximum and minimum observations in the column. The range is then easily found by hand as the maximum minus the minimum, while the midrange is the average of the two extremes.

MINIMUM OF COLUMN **C**

MAXIMUM OF COLUMN **C**

Finds the smallest (minimum) or largest (maximum) value in the column and prints out the answer.

MINIMUM OF **C,** PUT MINIMUM INTO **C**

MAXIMUM OF **C,** PUT MAXIMUM INTO **C**

Finds, prints, and stores the smallest or largest value.

Exercises

2-5   Suppose that the final exam scores for one section of a statistics course were as follows: 97, 80, 31, 100, 91, 86, 72, 68, 74, 19, 98, 82, 85, 88, 93, 78, 79.

   (a)   Find the sample mean and median by hand, and check your results by using Minitab.

(b) Use Minitab to make a histogram of the observations.

(c) What does this picture tell you about why there is a difference between the sample mean and sample median?

2-6   If your data are symmetric (the left half of a histogram looks like a reflection of the right half) then the sample mean and median will be approximately equal.

(a) Get a histogram of the 57 men's heights in the **Pulse** data (page 285). Does the histogram appear symmetric? Find the sample mean and median. Are they close?

(b) Repeat part (a) using weight instead of height.

2-7   Suppose a man buys gas for his car once each week. He keeps a record of how much he bought and the price per gallon. His record for last winter is given below.

Week	1	2	3	4	5	6	7	8	9	10	11	12	13
Amount (gallons)	10	12	8	5	8	12	6	6	11	12	6	13	5
Price	54.9	54.9	52.9	56.9	54.9	54.9	56.9	57.9	54.9	55.9	55.9	52.9	55.

(a) How many gallons of gas, on the average, did he buy each week?

(b) How much, on the average, did he spend for gas each week?

(c) How much, on the average, did he pay per gallon? (Be careful with this one.)

(d) If he budgets $5.50 a week for gas, did he ever go over his budget on any given week?

(e) How much money did he spend for all the gas he bought last winter?

2-8   Find the quartiles for the OTIS scores obtained in the **Cartoon** experiment (page 270).

2-9   Find the quartiles for the AKP values in group B of the **Cancer** data (page 289).

2.3 Sample Standard Deviation and Variance

STANDARD DEVIATION OF COL **C**

Calculates and prints the sample standard deviation using the usual formula

$$s = \sqrt{\frac{\Sigma(x - \bar{x})^2}{(n - 1)}}$$

STANDARD DEVIATION OF **C**, STORE IN **C**

Calculates, prints, and stores the standard deviation.

If the data are in column C5, the standard deviation can be found by the instruction

STANDARD DEVIATION OF COL C5.

If one wanted to find the variance too, this could be readily accomplished by the instructions

STANDARD DEVIATION OF C5, PUT IN C12
MULTIPLY C12 by C12, PUT IN C13
PRINT C13.

Exercises

2-10   (a) For the data in Exercise 2-1, find the sample standard deviation using Minitab, but without using the STANDARD DEVIATION command. (You will have to use several commands, such as SUBTRACT, AVERAGE, and SQRT, and put them together in a little program. Try to imitate the steps that you follow when calculating a standard deviation by hand.)

(b) Use Minitab's STANDARD DEVIATION command to check your answer to part (a).

2-11 Consider the following data:

6, 12, 16, 8, 4, 18, 14, −3, 8, 4, −3, 4, 8, 14, 13, 8, 13, 10, 21, −2, 9, 3, 10, 16, 15.

(a) Make a histogram of the data. Find the sample mean, $\bar{x}$, and the standard deviation, s. On the axis of the histogram, show how many observations fell between $\bar{x} - s$ and $\bar{x} + s$, and how many fell between $\bar{x} - 2s$ and $\bar{x} + 2s$. (Often the answers will be about 68% and 95% respectively.)

(b) Use Minitab to add 6.0 to all the observations above, and find $\bar{x}$ and s. How do the results compare to those for part (a)?

(c) Multiply all the observations by 6.0. Now what happens to $\bar{x}$ and s?

2-12 Consider the following data:

.08, .19, −.05, .11, .17, .16, .20, .15, −.16, .12, .11, −.03, .18, .12, .19, .20, .17, .10, .10, .10, .29, .10, .04, .30, .11, .15, .25, −.07, −.01, −.12.

Do parts (a), (b), and (c) as in Exercise 2-11.

2-13 (a) Men and women certainly have different average heights—but are the standard deviations of their heights different? Use the heights of the 57 men and 35 women who participated in the **Pulse** experiment (page 285). Calculate the two sample standard deviations. Do they differ much?

(b) Do men's weights seem to be more variable than women's? Compare the standard deviation of the men's weights in the **Pulse** experiment with those of the women's.

(c) Make and compare the histogram for women's weights with the histogram for men's weights. Do the two variations seem different?

2-14 Write a Minitab program to put the data given in Exercise 2-11 in order. Print out the ordered data. Use your output to find (a) the median, (b) the range, (c) the first and third quartiles, and (d) the midrange. (e) Use the output to help you draw (by hand) a histogram of the data.

2-15 The standard deviation is one way to measure how spread out a set of data is. Another measure of spread is "the mean absolute deviation from the mean." If you have n observations, then the

$$\text{mean absolute deviation from mean} = \Sigma\,|x - \bar{x}|/n.$$

Notice this is just the average of how far the observations are from the mean of the data. Write a Minitab program to calculate the mean absolute deviation for the data given in Exercise 2-11. You will need to use the ABSOLUTE command, which is described on page 324.

2-16   See if any of the laboratory values from the **Cancer** data (page 289) can improve the usefulness of the band-test for cancer.

(a) First consider AKP (variable 5). For each of the 4 groups, calculate the mean and standard deviation of AKP, and get a histogram. Use the following scale for all 4 histograms: first midpoint at 0.0, width of 3.0.

   (1) Are there any observations of AKP that seem to be unusually high or low, in comparison with the rest of the data? Such observations, called outliers, should always be carefully checked for possible errors.

   (2) Suppose someone tests positive using this band test for cancer. Do you think it would be useful, for determining whether he has cancer or not, to measure his AKP level?

   (3) Suppose someone tests negative using the band test. Does it appear that his AKP level could help decide whether he has cancer or not?

   (4) Compare the means, standard deviations, and histograms for the 4 groups. Do you see anything else of interest?

(b) Repeat part (a) using P (variable 6). For the 4 histograms, use the scale with first midpoint at 0.0, width of 0.5.

(c) Repeat part (a) using LDH (variable 7). For the 4 histograms, use the scale with first midpoint at 0.0, width of 10.0.

2.4 Selecting Parts of a Data Set

Use of The CHOOSE Command

In Section 2.1, we looked at a histogram of the OTIS scores for all 179 participants in the **Cartoon** experiment. Here we'll compare the 89 participants who saw black and white slides to the 90 participants who saw color slides. Our first problem is to separate the full data set into these two parts. This can be done in several different ways depending on what form you have the data in. For example, if you have the data punched on cards, you might just separate the cards by hand. Here we will use Minitab's CHOOSE command.

CHOOSE ROWS WITH THE NUMBER **K** IN **C**, CORRESPONDING

ROWS OF **C**, ..., **C**, PUT INTO **C, C**, ..., **C**

Example

CHOOSE ROWS WITH 1 IN C2, CORR. ROWS OF C3 AND C4, PUT IN C12-C14

Col. 2	Col. 3	Col. 4	Col. 12	Col. 13	Col. 14
1	98.3	5	1	98.3	5
1	101.2	3	1	101.2	3
2	100.5	8	1	99.3	6
1	99.3	6	1	100.1	6
2	98.6	7			
2	98.9	6			
1	100.1	6			

Here the full data set is in columns c2-c4, and we want just those observations with a 1 in c2 (perhaps 1 stands for women and 2 for men). CHOOSE takes the 4 rows with a 1 in c2 and the corresponding 4 rows of c3 and c4 and puts them into c12, c13, and c14, respectively. c2-c4 are not changed. Note that the column we are using as a basis for our choosing (column 2 in the example) must also be stored.

(*More about* CHOOSE *is given on page 49.*)

In the **Cartoon** data (page 270), variable 2 gives the "color" of the slides (0 = black and white, 1 = color). We used the following program to analyze these two groups:

```
READ DATA INTO C1-C9
    1   0   0   1  107   4   4  -9  -9
    2   0   0   2  106   9   9   6   5
    .   .   .   .   .    .   .   .   .

    .   .   .   .   .    .   .   .   .

    .   .   .   .   .    .   .   .   .
  179   1   2   4  103   4   3   2   1
NOTE FIRST ANALYZE OTIS SCORES FOR THOSE WHO SAW BLACK AND WHITE
CHOOSE ROWS WITH 0 IN C2, CORR. ROWS OF C5, PUT INTO C12, C15
HISTOGRAM OF C15, FIRST MID. 80, INTERVAL WIDTH OF 5
AVERAGE OF C15
MEDIAN OF C15
STANDARD DEVIATION OF C15
MAXIMUM OF C15
MINIMUM OF C15
NOTE NOW ANALYZE OTIS SCORES FOR THOSE WHO SAW COLOR SLIDES
CHOOSE ROWS WITH 1 IN C2, CORR. ROWS OF C5, PUT INTO C12, C15
HISTOGRAM OF C15, FIRST MID. AT 80, INTERVAL WIDTH OF 5
AVERAGE OF C15
MEDIAN OF C15
STANDARD DEVIATION OF C15
MAXIMUM OF C15
MINIMUM OF C15
STOP
```

Since we wanted to compare the two histograms, we wanted them to be on the same scale. To guarantee this, we specified the scales in the two HISTOGRAM commands.

Use of The OMIT Command

Suppose we want to calculate the mean of the OTIS scores for all the participants in the **Cartoon** experiment who took the delayed cartoon test. To do this we must omit those participants who failed to take this test, and average those remaining.

OMIT ROWS WITH THE NUMBER **K** IN **C**, CORR. ROWS OF

C,...,C, PUT REMAINING ROWS INTO **C,...,C**

Example

OMIT ROWS WITH 0 IN C4, CORR. ROWS C1-C3, PUT INTO C14, C11-C13

Col. 1	Col. 2	Col. 3	Col. 4		Col. 11	Col. 12	Col. 13	Col. 14
1	64	21	0		0	60	24	103
0	60	24	103		1	63	16	115
1	63	16	115	⟶	0	62	28	111
1	68	30	0		1	65	31	120
0	62	28	111					
1	65	31	120					

Here the full data set is in C1-C4, and we want to omit those with a 0 in C4. (Perhaps they failed to respond to question 4.) OMIT removes the two rows with a 0 in C4 and the corresponding two rows of C1-C3. The remaining four rows of C4 are put into C14, and the corresponding four rows of C1-C3 are put into C11-C13. C1-C4 are not changed.

(*More about* OMIT *is on page 50.*)

In the **Cartoon** experiment, the "delayed realistic score" is variable 8. Those who did not take the test were given a missing data code of -9. The following program omits those participants who have -9 for variable 8 and averages the OTIS scores of the others:

```
READ DATA INTO C1-C9
    1    0    0    1   107    4    4   -9   -9
    2    0    0    2   106    9    9    6    5
```

```
  .      .      .      .      .      .      .      .      .
  .      .      .      .      .      .      .      .      .
  .      .      .      .      .      .      .      .      .
 179     1      2      4    103      4      3      2      1
OMIT ROWS WITH −9 IN C8, PUT REMAINING ROWS IN C18
AVERAGE C18
STOP
```

Exercises

2-17   Run the program on page 38 and compare the OTIS scores for those who saw black and white slides with those who saw color slides. Do these two groups seem to be almost the same? What are the differences?

2-18   Consider the data for the 179 participants in the **Cartoon** experiment (page 270).

   (a)   Do a histogram and compute the mean, median, and standard deviation of variable 4. Which of these answers can you interpret meaningfully?

   (b)   Do a histogram and compute the mean, median, and standard deviation of variable 7. Are there any problems in interpreting these answers?

   (c)   Do a histogram and compute the mean, median, and standard deviation of variable 9. Are there any problems in interpreting these answers meaningfully?

2-19   For group D of the **Cancer** data (page 289), get separate histograms for the ages of the males and females. Also compute their means, medians, and standard deviations. Do you notice any differences between the ages of the males and females among this group of false positives? What are the practical consequences of any differences?

2.5 Scatterplots

The descriptive statistics discussed so far in this chapter have concerned only one variable at a time. Often we will be interested in the relationships between two or more variables, such as the relationship between height and weight, between smoking and lung cancer, or between college board scores and college grades. One very useful way to describe the relationship between two variables is to make a scatterplot. As an example, suppose we had the following heights and weights of 10 people:

Person	Height (in.)	Weight (lb.)
1	68	150
2	70	159
3	64	110
4	74	180
5	71	165
6	69	170
7	67	125
8	66	140
9	71	175
10	70	160

With a small set of data like this, it is usually easiest to do the plot by hand. But, if you had more data, say the heights and weights of 100 people, it would probably be faster to have the computer do the plot for you. This can be done in Minitab by using the PLOT command.

PLOT COLUMN C VS. COLUMN C

Gives a scatter plot of the data given in the two columns. Ordinarily, each point is plotted with the symbol *, but when more than one point falls on the same plotting position, a count of the number of points falling there is given. When more than 9 points fall on the same plotting position, the symbol + is given. Scales for both axes are chosen automatically. The first named column is the vertical axis, the second named column is the horizontal axis.

(More about PLOT is given on page 52.)

The following program plots weight versus height:

```
READ HEIGHT INTO C1, WEIGHT INTO C2
68   150
70   159
64   110
74   180
71   16
69   170
67   125
66   140
71   175
70   160
PLOT WEIGHT IN C2 VS. HEIGHT IN C1
STOP
```

The resulting plot is shown in Exhibit 2.2. Note that two people were 70 inches tall and weighed approximately 160 pounds, so a "2" is printed on the graph to indicate that two values fell there.

Another Example

Exhibit 2.3 shows a plot of some data from the **Cartoon** experiment (page 270). We read the whole set of data into c_1-c_9. Then we used the command PLOT c_6 VS c_5 to get a plot of the "immediate cartoon" scores against the OTIS scores.

Several interesting facts can be observed from this plot. First, people with higher OTIS scores tend to get higher cartoon scores, as you might expect. Note also, that the highest cartoon score possible is 9, so that a person with very high ability can't really demonstrate the full extent of his knowledge. The best he can do is get a 9. In this plot, the scores of people who had OTIS scores below 100 show no evidence that they were held down to the maximum score. But, the scores of people with OTIS scores over 100 do show the effect of this limitation. This effect is sometimes called *truncation* and results in some loss of information in the data. If the experiment were to be done over again, it would be better to develop a slightly longer or harder test so that everyone would have a chance to demonstrate his full ability.

EXHIBIT 2.2

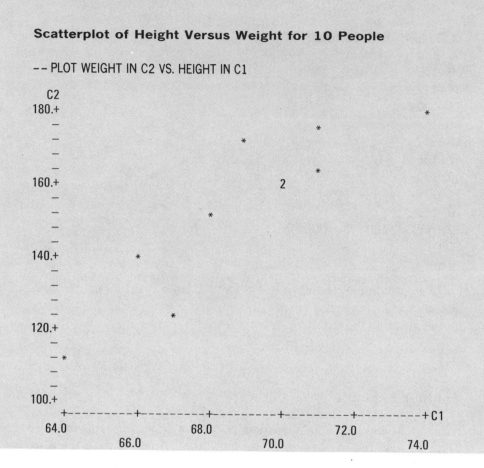

Scatterplot of Height Versus Weight for 10 People

```
-- PLOT WEIGHT IN C2 VS. HEIGHT IN C1

    C2
  180.+                                                            *
     -
     -                                      *
     -                           *
     -
  160.+                                 2
     -
     -                 *
     -
     -
  140.+        *
     -
     -
     -
     -           *
  120.+
     -
     - *
     -
     -
  100.+
       +---------+---------+---------+---------+---------+C1
      64.0      68.0      72.0
           66.0      70.0      74.0
```

Exercises

2-20   Consider the **Trees** data (page 278).

   (a) Plot volume versus diameter. Is the plot what you might expect?

   (b) Plot volume versus height. Compare this plot to the one in part (a).
        Does volume seem to depend more strongly on height or diameter?

   (c) Plot height versus diameter. Do tall trees tend to be wider?

EXHIBIT 2.3

Plot of "Immediate Cartoon" Scores Against OTIS Scores for Cartoon Experiment

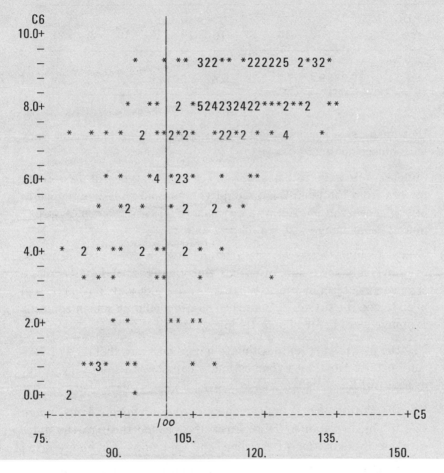

2-21   Consider the **Cartoon** experiment (page 270).

    (a) Plot "immediate realistic" score versus "immediate cartoon" score. Try to interpret the results.

    (b) Plot OTIS scores versus "education" and try to interpret the results.

2-22   When a magnifying glass is used to view an object, there is a simple
relationship between the apparent size of the object as seen through the
lens (image size) and the distance the object is from the lens (object
distance). Here are some data obtained by a student in an introductory
physics class.

Object Distance (cm)	12	13	14	15	16	17	18	19	20	21	22
Image Size (cm)	12.0	9.4	7.2	6.2	5.2	4.5	4.0	3.6	3.2	3.0	2.7

(a)   Plot image size versus object distance. How does image size vary
with object distance?

(b)   Suppose you were to place the object at a distance of 12.5 centimeters from the lens. What would you estimate the image size to
be? Suppose you place it at a distance of 23 centimeters. Approximately what image size would you expect?

(c)   Now, let's investigate the relationship between these two variables.
It's obviously some sort of curve? But what curve? Plot 1/(image
size) versus object distance. What does your plot look like? (You will
need to use the DIVIDE command to create a column which contains
1/(image size) before doing the plot.)

(d)   Use the plot in part (c) to estimate image size at a distance of 12.5
centimeters. How does your estimate compare to the one you got
in part (b)?

(e)   Use the plot in part (c) to develop an equation which relates image
size to object distance. (Hint: First draw a line through the data,
estimate the equation of this line, and then solve for image size.)

2-23   During the winter months, you have probably noticed that on days when
the wind is blowing it seems particularly cold. The explanation lies in
the fact that wind creates a slight lowering of atmospheric pressure on
exposed flesh thereby enhancing evaporation, which has a cooling effect.
Thus the effective temperature (how cold it seems to you) depends on
two factors: thermometer temperature and wind speed. The following
table was prepared by the U. S. Army. It gives the effective temperature
corresponding to a given thermometer temperature and wind speed.

Wind Chill Index

		Thermometer		Temperature		(degrees F)	
		30	20	10	0	−10	−20
	5	27	16	6	−5	−15	−26
	10	16	4	−9	−21	−33	−46
Wind	15	9	−5	−18	−36	−45	−58
Speed	20	4	−10	−25	−39	−53	−67
(m.p.h.)	25	0	−15	−29	−44	−59	−74
	30	−2	−18	−33	−48	−63	−79

There is an error in this table. Can you find it? Plotting the data will help.

(a) For each thermometer temperature, make a plot of effective temperature versus wind speed. That is, plot each column of the table versus the numbers 5, 10, 15, 20, 25, 30. You will need 6 plots.

(b) For each wind speed, make a plot of the effective temperature versus thermometer temperature. That is, plot each row of the table versus the numbers 30, 20, 10, 0, −10, −20. To do this, you will need to put the data into the computer again, so that 30, 20, 10, 0, −10, −20 is in one column, 27, 16, 6, −5, −15, −26 is in another column, and so on.

2.6 More About Plotting Data

Exhibit 2.4 gives the winning times for three Olympic races. A quick look tells us that the winners have gotten faster over the years. Suppose we want to compare the "progress" made in the different races. We could plot these winning times, but since the races are of different lengths, probably the average speeds are easier to compare. So let's plot speed versus year for each of the three races. We'll put all three plots on the same set of axes, to make comparisons easier. This can be done using the MPLOT command.

> **MPLOT C** VS **C,** AND **C** VS **C,...,** AND **C** VS **C**

> Produces several plots all on the same axes. The first pair of columns
> are plotted using the symbol A, the second pair with the symbol B, and
> so on. If several points fall on the same spot, a count is given.

The following program plots the track speeds:

```
READ YEAR INTO C1, WINNING TIMES INTO C2-C4
1900        10.8        22.2        49.4
1904        11          21.6        49.2
  .           .           .           .

  .           .           .           .

  .           .           .           .
1972        10.1        20.0        44.7
DIVIDE 100 BY C2, PUT SPEEDS INTO C12
DIVIDE 200 BY C3, PUT SPEEDS INTO C13
DIVIDE 400 BY C4, PUT SPEEDS INTO C14
MPLOT C12 VS C1, C13 VS C1, C14 VS C1
STOP
```

The resulting plot is in Exhibit 2.5. The letter A identifies the winning
speeds for the 100-meter races, B identifies those for the 200, and C for
the 400. Occasionally, two speeds fall on the same position and the
number 2 is plotted. By looking at this plot we can get a very good idea
of what happened. On the average, all three races had increased speeds
over the years. One thing we might not have realized, before seeing this
plot, is that the 100-meter and 200-meter races are run at about the same
speed. Some years the 100-meter was faster and some years the 200-
meter was faster. The 400-meter race however has always been run at
a much slower pace. We can also spot a number of very "good" years,
where progress was made in all three races—in 1924, 1932, 1960, and
1968. We can also see that essentially no progress was made in the three
Olympics following World War II. Creative plotting can reveal a lot that
is not apparent in a simple table of numbers.

Using letters to identify the different races was helpful to us in
learning about the winning speeds in Olympic races. Another command,
LPLOT, produces *letter plots* when the data are stored in the computer
in a different way.

EXHIBIT 2.4

Winning Times in Men's Olympic Track Races

Year	100-Meter Race	200-Meter Race	400-Meter Race
1900	10.8	22.2	49.4
1904	11.0	21.6	49.2
1908	10.8	22.4	50.0
1912	10.8	21.7	48.2
1920	10.8	22.0	49.6
1924	10.6	21.6	47.6
1928	10.8	21.8	47.8
1932	10.3	21.2	46.2
1936	10.3	20.7	46.5
1948	10.3	21.1	46.2
1952	10.4	20.7	45.9
1956	10.5	20.6	46.7
1960	10.2	20.5	44.9
1964	10.0	20.3	45.1
1968	9.9	19.8	43.8
1972	10.1	20.0	44.7

LPLOT **C** VS **C,** USING LETTERS AS CODED IN **C**

Produces a plot where different groups are plotted using different symbols.

Example

Suppose we have data for 50 people and c1 contains the person's height, c2 his weight, and c3 a sex code with 1 = male and 2 = female. Then,

LPLOT HEIGHT IN C1 VS WEIGHT IN C2, SEX CODED IN C3

produces a plot of height versus weight in which all points corresponding to men are plotted using the letter A, and all points corresponding to women are plotted using the letter B. In general, the letters used for different numerical codes are as follows:

```
... −2  −1   0   1   2   3 ...  24  25  26  27  28 ...
...  X   Y   Z   A   B   C ...   X   Y   Z   A   B ...
```

If several points fall on the same spot, a count is given.

EXHIBIT 2.5

Winning Speeds in Olympic Races for Various Years
(A = 100-m race B = 200-m race C = 400-m race)

-- MPLOT C12 VS C1, C13 VS C1, C14 VS C1

```
    C12
10.50+
    -
    -
    -
    -
10.00+                                              2
    -                                          A     B
    -                                          B     A
    -                                     2
    -                    A 2        A B B
    -                               A
 9.50+                            B     A
    -
    -              A     B
    - A B A A    A B A
    -       B           B
    -   A         B                        C
 9.00+ B
    -     B                          C C   C
    -
    -            C         C C
    -          C              C
 8.50+
    -        C C
    -      C
    -
    - C C       C
 8.00+    C
    +---------+---------+---------+---------+---------+C1
    1900.         1940.         1980.
         1920.         1960.         2000.
```

APPENDIX 2a.
More on Editing and Manipulating Data

(Continued from page 36.)

The following is a second form of the CHOOSE command:

CHOOSE ROWS WITH VALUES FROM **K** TO **K** IN **C**, CORR.

ROWS OF **C,...,C**, PUT INTO **C,...,C**

Example

CHOOSE 1 TO 4 IN C2, CORR. ROWS C5, C8, PUT IN C10, C20, C21

Col. 2	*Col. 5*	*Col. 8*	*Col. 10*	*Col. 20*	*Col. 21*
1	10	1.2	1	10	1.2
8	18	1.8	2	16	2.0
2	16	2.0	2	20	2.4
7	14	2.3	4	10	1.1
2	20	2.4	2	11	1.8
5	13	3.6			
4	10	1.1			
2	11	1.8			
8	12	2.0			

(Continued from page 38.)

The following is a second form of the OMIT command:

OMIT ROWS WITH VALUES FROM **K** TO **K** IN **C,** CORR. ROWS

OF **C,...,C,** PUT REMAINING ROWS INTO **C,...,C**

Example

OMIT 5 TO 8 IN C2, CORR. ROWS C5, C8, PUT IN C10, C20, C21

Col. 2	*Col. 5*	*Col. 8*		*Col. 10*	*Col. 20*	*Col. 21*
1	10	1.2		1	10	1.2
8	18	1.8		2	16	2.0
2	16	2.0	$\longrightarrow$	2	20	2.4
7	14	2.3		4	10	1.1
2	20	2.4		2	11	1.8
5	13	3.6				
4	10	1.1				
2	11	1.8				
8	12	2.0				

JOIN E TO THE BOTTOM OF **E,** PUT INTO **C**

Allows you to join columns and numbers together.

Example

JOIN C2 TO C3, PUT INTO C10

Col. 2	Col. 3	Col. 10
2	1	1
3	1	1
6	4	4
8	⟶	2
7		3
		6
		8
		7

JOIN E TO E TO E TO ... TO E, PUT INTO C

You can join several columns and constants together in one command.

Example

JOIN C1 TO 5.2 TO 3.8 TO C2 TO C3, PUT IN C5

Col. 1	Col. 2	Col. 3	Col. 5
1	10	101	101
2	14	105	105
3			10
		⟶	14
			3.8
			5.2
			1
			2
			3

> **PICK** OUT ROWS **K** TO **K** OF C, PUT INTO **C**

Example

PICK ROWS 3 TO 6 OF C2, PUT INTO C5

Col. 2	*Col. 5*
10	13
20	16
13 $\longrightarrow$	9
16	16
9	
16	
8	

(The first value of K must be less than or equal to the second value of K.)

APPENDIX 2b.
More on Plotting Data

(Continued from page 40.)

You can specify your own scales in a plot by using the following form of the PLOT command.

> **PLOT C** FROM **K** TO **K** VS. **C** FROM **K** TO **K**

Example

PLOT C1 FROM 0 TO 10 VS. C2 FROM 101 TO 102

The horizontal axis will run from 0 to 10, and the vertical axis will run from 101 to 102. Any observation outside these ranges will not be plotted.

There are several reasons to specify scales on a plot. First, you may wish to compare two plots. If you specify the same scales in both plots, you are sure the two plots will both be done on the same scale. Second, you may want to look more closely at one portion of your data. For example, suppose you want to do the plot in Exhibit 2.3 for only those with OTIS scores over 100. You could use the command

PLOT C6 FROM 0 TO 10 VS. C5 FROM 100 TO 150

The observations outside this specified range would not be plotted, but those inside this range would be shown in greater detail.

The following command allows you to control the size of your plots. You can make them larger to gain better resolution, or you can make them smaller to save printing time and paper.

WIDTH OF PLOTS = K SPACES

Allows you to make plots wider or narrower. The width may be from 20 to 100 spaces. Minitab adjusts the height automatically to match the width you've specified. K should be a multiple of 10. WIDTH applies to all plotting commands that follow (PLOT, LPLOT, MPLOT), until a new WIDTH command is specified.

Example

WIDTH OF PLOTS 40 SPACES
PLOT C2 VS. C1

The resulting plot will be 40 (actually 41) spaces wide.

WIDTH OF PLOTS K SPACES, HEIGHT K SPACES

Allows you to specify both the width and height of plots. The height may be from 10 to 200 spaces high.

Example

WIDTH OF PLOTS 30 SPACES, HEIGHT 200 SPACES
PLOT C2 VS. C1
LPLOT C3 VS. C1, USING SYMBOLS IN C8

Both plots will be very tall and narrow.

3

Simulation

A good way to learn about statistics is to plan an experiment or survey, carry it out, and then analyze the results. Unfortunately even the very simplest experiment, like rolling a pair of dice 50 times, is time consuming. So instead of actually performing the experiment, we can have the computer simulate the results of the experiment.

Simulation also plays a role in the development of statistical theory. Many problems are just too difficult or too complex to solve using the usual techniques in mathematics. For such problems simulation may provide the best way of obtaining answers.

3.1 Rolling Dice

Suppose you roll a die 12 times. You would expect each of the six faces to appear about the same number of times. This does not mean, of course, that in 12 rolls you will get each face exactly twice. In fact, there is a fairly good chance that at least one of the faces will not turn up at all in the 12 rolls.

You might find it interesting to actually do this experiment by rolling a die 12 times to see if all faces appear. Of course, doing the experiment just once doesn't say much about what the chances really are. You could do it again, and again, keeping a tally of how many experiments have all six faces showing and how many have one or more faces missing. After a while you should get a good idea of what the chances are.

To simulate this experiment using the computer you could use the *integer random* data simulator, IRANDOM.

IRANDOM CHOOSE **K** INTEGERS BETWEEN **K** AND **K**, PUT IN **C**

IRANDOM chooses K integers and stores them in the worksheet. There is an equal chance of choosing each integer and each is chosen independently. The results are printed out automatically (unless the NOPRINT command has been used). The numbers are chosen with replacement, so the same number can appear over and over again.

The commands below simulate the experiment 30 times.

	IRANDOM 12 INTEGERS BETWEEN 1 AND 6, PUT IN C1
	IRANDOM 12, 1, 6, C1
There are a	IRANDOM 12, 1, 6, C1
total of 30	IRANDOM 12, 1, 6, C1
IRANDOM	. .
commands	. .
	. .
	IRANDOM 12, 1, 6, C1

A part of the output is shown in Exhibit 3.1. Overall there were 11 experiments in which all six faces turned up and 19 in which one or more faces were missing. So you could estimate the chances as being 11/30 = 0.37 that all six faces will turn up.

You could also try to solve this problem mathematically using the basic laws of probability, but it is very difficult. (The correct answer turns out to be 0.44.) With simulation you can get answers to such difficult problems even when you can't solve them mathematically. There is a disadvantage, however. The simulation answer is only approximate, while the theoretical answer is exact. Of course, if you simulate the experiment many times, your answer will probably be very close to the theoretical answer.

EXHIBIT 3.1

The First Part of the Output from Simulating 30 Die Rolling Experiments

(A ✓ means one or more faces are missing.)

```
-- IRANDOM 12 INTEGERS BETWEEN 1 AND 6, PUT IN C1
 ✓   12 RANDOM INTEGERS BETWEEN    1 AND    6
     1.   6.   2.   2.   4.   1.   2.   3.
     4.   4.   4.   6.
-- IRANDOM 12, 1, 6, C1
 ✓   12 RANDOM INTEGERS BETWEEN    1 AND    6
     1.   2.   6.   1.   5.   3.   3.   5.
     1.   1.   6.   1.
-- IRANDOM 12, 1, 6, C1
     12 RANDOM INTEGERS BETWEEN    1 AND    6
     2.   5.   2.   3.   1.   4.   6.   5.
     5.   3.   4.   3.
-- IRANDOM 12, 1, 6, C1
 ✓   12 RANDOM INTEGERS BETWEEN    1 AND    6
     2.   3.   6.   5.   5.   5.   6.   3.
     3.   5.   5.   4.
-- IRANDOM 12, 1, 6, C1
 ✓   12 RANDOM INTEGERS BETWEEN    1 AND    6
     3.   1.   2.   1.   6.   1.   3.   3.
     1.   4.   6.   1.
-- IRANDOM 12, 1, 6, C1
 ✓   12 RANDOM INTEGERS BETWEEN    1 AND    6
     4.   3.   6.   6.   1.   1.   4.   5.
     4.   6.   3.   5.
-- IRANDOM 12, 1, 6, C1
 ✓   12 RANDOM INTEGERS BETWEEN    1 AND    6
     1.   1.   5.   5.   5.   2.   6.   1.
     2.   4.   2.   2.
```

Exercises

3-1 (a) An "experiment" consists of rolling a die 8 times. Estimate the probability that all six faces turn up by simulating the experiment 30 times.

(b) How do you think the (theoretical) probability of all six faces turning up in 8 rolls compares with the probability of all six faces turning up in 12 rolls? (Larger? Smaller?) How does your estimate for the 8 rolls compare with the 0.37 we got for 12 rolls?

3-2 Suppose there are 30 people at a party. Do you think it's very likely that at least two of the 30 people have the same birthday? Try estimating this probability by a simulation. To simplify things ignore leap years (thus, assume all years have 365 days) and assume all days of the year are equally likely to be birthdays. Use IRANDOM and simulate 30 birthdays. Then put the 30 numbers in order and print them out. (Ordering helps find duplicates.) Repeat all of this 9 more times. (Use the NOPRINT command first if you don't want the unordered observations printed.) Now, what do you think the chances are?

3.2 Bernoulli Trials and Coin Tossing

There are many cases where outcomes can be classified into two categories: a coin either falls heads or tails; a patient either responds to treatment or he doesn't; our team either wins or it doesn't; a person either smokes or he doesn't; the next child born in the hospital is either a boy or a girl; and so on. When the relative chances of the two possible outcomes remain the same from trial to trial, independent of the outcome of all previous trials, we say that we have *Bernoulli Trials*.

We can simulate the outcome of a series of Bernoulli trials using the BTRIALS command.

> BTRIALS **K** RANDOM TRIALS WITH P = **K**, PUT INTO **C**

Simulates the result of K Bernoulli trials. One outcome is coded as a 0 by the computer and the other as a 1. The probability of a 1 on any given trial is p. The results are stored and automatically printed out (unless the NOPRINT command has been used).

Example

Suppose we had a loaded coin with the probability of a head being 0.6 and a tail being 0.4. We could simulate flipping this coin 10 times with the following command:

BTRIALS 10 TRIALS WITH P = 0.6, PUT IN C3

The output is in Exhibit 3.2. Here we happened to get exactly 6 heads in 10 tosses, which agrees perfectly with the 60% successes we would get in the long run if we kept flipping this "coin" indefinitely. Usually, we won't be so lucky.

Other aspects of Bernoulli trials, including a discussion of the BRANDOM command for generating binomial data, are discussed in Chapter 5.

Exercises

3-3   Suppose a basketball team wins a game, on the average, 55% of the time. Suppose we make the simplifying assumptions that there is a 55% chance of winning each game, and that these odds are not influenced by what the team has done so far. Then we can simulate a "season" for the team using BTRIALS. Suppose a season contains 30 games. Simulate one season.

(a) Did the team have a winning season (won more games than it lost)?

(b) How long was the team's longest winning streak? How long was its longest losing streak?

(c) Simulate four more seasons and answer the questions in (a) and (b) for each season.

3-4   Suppose someone gives you a coin which is loaded, so that heads comes up more often than tails. You want to know exactly how loaded the coin is. To estimate the probability of a head (p), you could toss the coin, say, 100 times.

(a) How could you simulate this, assuming that p is really 0.6? Will your estimate be exactly equal to the true value?

(b) Suppose you asked 5 friends to estimate the probability of a head by having each toss the coin 100 times. Will their estimates all be equal to the true value? Will they all get the same estimate? How can you simulate the results for all 5 friends?

(c) Perform the simulation for you and your 5 friends. How much do the 6 estimates vary?

EXHIBIT 3.2

Results from Simulating 10 Tosses of a Loaded Coin, with 1 = Head and 0 = Tail

```
-- BTRIALS 10 TRIALS WITH P = 0.6, PUT IN C3
   10 BERNOULLI TRIALS WITH P = 0.6000
      0.   1.   0.   1.   0.   0.   1.   1.   1.   1.
   SUMMARY
   VALUE    FREQUENCY
     0          4
     1          6
```

3.3 Sampling Normal Populations

Usually, when we do statistics in the real world we have to make inferences from a relatively small sample about the properties of a large population. For example, the national public opinion polls conducted by

George Gallup, Fred Harris, and others take a sample of about 1500 adults and, based on these results, try to predict what 100,000,000 adults are thinking. Many people find it difficult to believe that these pollsters can survey such a small percentage of the population of U. S. adults, and accurately predict what the population as a whole is thinking.

In this section we will see how the computer can be used to demonstrate how much the results from small samples can be expected to depart from what we would learn if we could look at the whole population. Here, in these simulations, we will be able to specify the population, then repeatedly take samples from this population. After we get each sample, we can pretend we are statisticians who know nothing about the population. Then we can try to make predictions about the entire population and see how well we do.

One very common "distribution" for characteristics of populations, and the one we will use in this section, is the *normal distribution* (also called the bell-shaped curve). A histogram for the entire population would look like this:

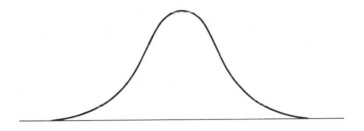

Many things in nature, like people's heights or weights, sizes of automobile pistons made on an assembly line, and errors of measurement, tend to fall into an approximately normal distribution.

As an example, suppose we simulate measuring heights of people. More specifically, suppose we want to find out how much the average height of a sample of 10 college-age females varies from sample to sample. Indications are that the average height of all college-age females is about 64 inches and that about two-thirds of them fall within about 3 inches of this average (i.e., between 61 and 67 inches). This information is enough to allow us to do a simulation using the *normal random* data simulator NRANDOM.

NRANDOM **K** OBSERVATIONS WITH MU = **K**, SIGMA = **K**, PUT

INTO **C**

Simulates a random sample from a normal population with mean mu (μ) and standard deviation sigma (σ). The results are stored in the indicated column. They are also printed out automatically (unless the command NOPRINT has been used).

Mu (or μ) is the average of all of the observations in the population and sigma (or σ) is how far you need to go above and below the average to catch about two-thirds of the observations in the population. Thus, in our simulation, mu will be 64 inches and sigma will be about 3 inches.

We want to simulate selecting 10 people at random from this population and look at what happens to the average of their heights. To do this we can use the following two instructions:

```
NRANDOM 10 OBSN, MU = 64, SIGMA = 3, PUT IN C5
AVERAGE THE OBSERVATIONS IN C5.
```

This gives us one sample of 10 female heights and their average.

Now suppose we want to see what would happen if this were done 20 times. We might do this to study how much the sample average varies from experiment to experiment. We could just repeat the two instructions 20 times. The program would look like this:

```
NOPRINT (WE DON'T WANT INDIVIDUAL OBS. PRINTED)
NRANDOM 10 OBSN, MU = 64, SIGMA = 3, PUT IN C5
AVERAGE THE OBSERVATIONS IN C5
NRANDOM 10  64  3  C5
AVERAGE THE OBSERVATIONS IN C5


      .
      .
      .


NRANDOM 10  64  3  C5
AVERAGE C5
```

(If you are using a keypunch to do these problems, perhaps you have discovered by now that it is very easy to make multiple copies of the same instruction by duplicating the card.)

Part of the output is in Exhibit 3.3. Exhibit 3.4 contains a (hand drawn) histogram of the 20 averages. Notice how the averages cluster around 64, with just about all of them within 1 or 2 inches of 64. Averages just don't vary too much. This seems to indicate that if we want to estimate the average height of all college-age women, and we take a sample of 10 women and calculate the average height, that sample average is not likely to be too far off from the true average—probably within 1 inch of the true value. Here we've been able to get a fairly good estimate of the average height for a very large population, with only 10 observations. Beginning in the next chapter, we'll see how we can be more

EXHIBIT 3.3

Averages of Observations from a Normal Population

```
-- NOPRINT (WE DON'T WANT INDIVIDUAL OBS. PRINTED)
-- NRANDOM 10 OBSN, MU = 64, SIGMA = 3, PUT IN C5
-- AVERAGE THE OBSERVATIONS IN C5
   AVERAGE -      63.803
-- NRANDOM 10 OBSN, MU = 64, SIGMA = 3, PUT IN C5
-- AVERAGE THE OBSERVATIONS IN C5
   AVERAGE =      63.580
-- NRANDOM 10 OBSN, MU = 64, SIGMA = 3, PUT IN C5
-- AVERAGE THE OBSERVATIONS IN C5
   AVERAGE =      65.984
-- NRANDOM 10 OBSN, MU = 64, SIGMA = 3, PUT IN C5
-- AVERAGE THE OBSERVATIONS IN C5
   AVERAGE =      64.075
-- NRANDOM 10 OBSN, MU = 64, SIGMA = 3, PUT IN C5
-- AVERAGE THE OBSERVATIONS IN C5
   AVERAGE =      64.471
```

EXHIBIT 3.4

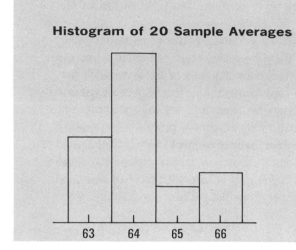

Histogram of 20 Sample Averages

precise in our statement of how close our estimate is likely to be to the true value.

Exercises

3-5 (a) Simulate the experiment of finding the average height for a random sample of college-age females, but use a sample size of 25 instead of 10. Simulate 20 samples and construct a histogram of the averages.

(b) How does your histogram compare to the one in Exhibit 3.4? What does this say about the relationship between sample averages and sample size?

3-6 (a) Simulate choosing 10 college-age females at random. Instead of finding the average height, find the maximum height (the height of the tallest woman in the sample of 10). Simulate this 20 times, and construct a histogram of the maximums. (Note Minitab has a command MAXIMUM.)

(b) Repeat part (a), but now use a sample size of 50 instead of 10.

(c) Compare the results of parts (a) and (b). How do maximums seem to behave?

3.4 Sampling Without Replacement

Suppose there are 14 people in a group and their heights are 67, 64, 61, 71, 60, 70, 66, 64, 66, 70, 71, 74, 66, and 67 inches. The median of these 14 values is 66.5 inches. If someone were to choose individuals at random from this group, the following questions might be asked:

(a) If one person is chosen from this small group, what are the chances that he will be exactly the same height as the median? What are the chances that he will be taller than the median? Shorter than the median?

(b) If two people are chosen, what are the chances they will both be taller than the median? That they will both be shorter? That the median will be somewhere between their heights, or the same height as one or both of them?

    Perhaps you can figure out the answers to these questions theoretically. Alternatively, you could estimate the chances by putting the 15 heights on slips of paper, repeatedly mixing and drawing slips, and keeping track of the results. Or you could use Minitab's SAMPLE command.

SAMPLE K OBSERVATIONS FROM C, PUT INTO C

Takes a random sample of size K from the numbers that have previously been stored in the first column, and stores the sample in the second column. It also prints out the sample (unless the NOPRINT command has been used). Sampling is done *without* replacement.

(*A more general form of* SAMPLE *is described on page 81.*)

    The following commands will help you get estimates of the answers to the questions in part (b):

SET HEIGHTS IN COL C3
67, 64, 61, 71, 60, 70, 66, 64, 66, 70, 71, 74, 66, 67
SAMPLE 2 OBSERVATIONS FROM COL C3, PUT IN C6
SAMPLE 2 C3 C6
SAMPLE 2 C3 C6

    .

    .

    .

SAMPLE 2 C3 C6

This program was run with a total of 30 samples. Part of the output is shown in Exhibit 3.5. In the 30 samples, there were 5 samples in which both of the observations drawn were taller than the median, 10 samples in which they were both shorter than the median, and 15 where they bracketed the median. Thus we could roughly estimate the chances of these three events as, $5/30 = 0.167$, $10/30 = 0.333$, and $15/30 = 0.500$ respectively.

Exercise

3-7   A hat contains 10 slips of paper numbered 1 to 10.

    (a) Suppose you draw 5 slips *without* replacement. How would you simulate this using Minitab?

    (b) Suppose you draw 5 slips *with* replacement. How would you simulate this using Minitab?

3.5 Other Discrete Distributions

Drawing samples (with replacement) from virtually any discrete distribution can be simulated with the DRANDOM command.

DRANDOM K OBSERVATIONS, USING VALUES IN **C**, PROB. IN **C**,

PUT IN **C**

Simulates drawing a sequence of independent observations according to the probabilities given. The results are always stored. They are also printed automatically (unless the command NOPRINT has been used). Sampling is done *with* replacement, so the same number can appear over and over again.

EXHIBIT 3.5

The First 5 Samples from the Simulation of Drawing 2 People at Random

```
-- SET HEIGHTS IN COL C3
   COLUMN  C3
   COUNT    14
    67.   64.   61.    71. ...
-- SAMPLE 2 OBSERVATIONS FROM COL C3, PUT IN C6
     2 ROWS SELECTED OUT OF    14
   THE ROWS SELECTED FROM COLUMN C3    CONTAIN:
    74.0000   64.0000
-- SAMPLE 2 C3 C6
     2 ROWS SELECTED OUT OF    14
   THE ROWS SELECTED FROM COLUMN C3    CONTAIN:
    67.0000   66.0000
-- SAMPLE 2 C3 C6
     2 ROWS SELECTED OUT OF    14
   THE ROWS SELECTED FROM COLUMN C3    CONTAIN:
    71.0000   61.0000
-- SAMPLE 2 C3 C6
     2 ROWS SELECTED OUT OF    14
   THE ROWS SELECTED FROM COLUMN C3    CONTAIN:
    71.0000   67.0000
-- SAMPLE 2 C3 C6
     2 ROWS SELECTED OUT OF    14
   THE ROWS SELECTED FROM COLUMN C3    CONTAIN:
    66.0000   64.0000
```

For example, suppose we want to simulate drawing 50 observations from a population which gives the values +1 and −1, each with probability 1/4, and the value 0 with probability 1/2. We could use the following program:

```
READ VALUES IN C1, PROB IN C2
−1    .25
 1    .25
 0    .50
DRANDOM 50 OBS., VALUES IN C1, PROB IN C2, PUT OBS. IN C3
STOP
```

3.6 Two Examples

In this section, two detailed examples are given which demonstrate some results that you may find surprising. These examples also demonstrate how simulation can be used to get answers to questions where the theoretical calculations are difficult.

Example 1: Losing Streaks

Gamblers, sports fans, and investors in the stock market all claim there are times when they have a "streak of good luck" and times when they have a "streak of bad luck." In this example, simulation will be used to show that their "luck" may be nothing more than chance fluctuations. Consider the following simple gambling game. You and your opponent each bet a dollar. Then you toss a fair coin. If it comes up tails, you win one dollar. If it comes up heads, you lose one dollar. Would you expect to be ahead for a short while, then behind for a short while, then ahead again, and so on? Or would you expect to be ahead for a long time (in a streak of good luck) and then behind for a long time (in a streak of bad luck)?

The following program simulates this game for 100 plays:

```
READ C1 C2
−1    .5
 1    .5
DRANDOM 100 OBS., VALUES IN C1, PROB. IN C2, PUT IN C3
PARSUM C3, PUT PARTIAL SUMS IN C4
```

```
GENERATE 100 INTEGERS INTO C5
WIDTH 100 HEIGHT 20 FOR PLOT
PLOT C4 VS. C5
STOP
```

In this program, a sequence of one hundred random +1's and −1's was simulated to indicate for each toss whether you won or lost. They were put in c3. Then the command PARSUM calculated total winnings or losses after each toss.

PARSUM OF **C**, PUT PARTIAL SUMS INTO **C**

Example

PARSUM C1 PUT IN C2

$c1$	$c2$
1	1
3	4
−2	2
4	6
−8	−2
0	−2

The first number in c2 is the first number in c1, the second number in c2 is the sum of the first two numbers in c1, the third number in c2 is the sum of the first three numbers in c1, the fourth number in c2 is the sum of the first four numbers in c1, and so on.

When the simulation was run, the first five entries in c1 were −1, 1, −1, −1, 1. This means you lost on the first, third, and fourth tosses, and won on the second and fifth tosses. So after one play you were behind by $1, after two plays you were even, after three plays, behind $1, after

EXHIBIT 3.6

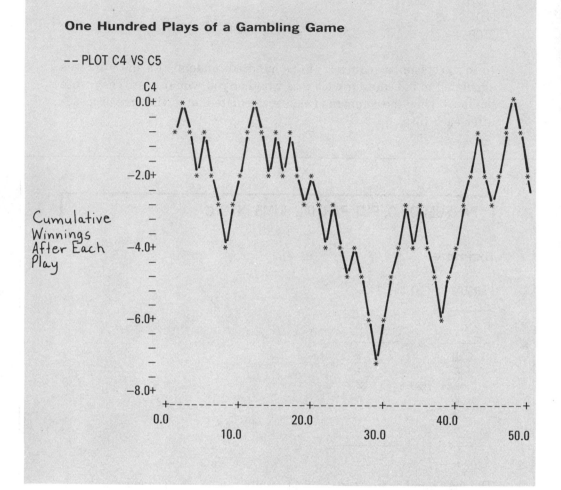

One Hundred Plays of a Gambling Game

-- PLOT C4 VS C5

four, behind $2, and after five plays, behind $1. These cumulative "win-nings," —1, 0, —1, —2, -1, and so on, are in c2. You could just print out c2 and see how long you were ahead and behind, but it's more interesting to plot the results. The last three commands plot your cumulative "win-nings" as the game progresses. This plot is shown in Exhibit 3.6. (See page 53 for a description of the WIDTH command.) It's quite vivid from the plot that you had a very long streak of bad luck. As a matter of fact, this sort of pattern of being ahead or behind for a long time is quite typical. You might try running the program a few times yourself and see what sort of "luck" you have. You will probably spend most of the

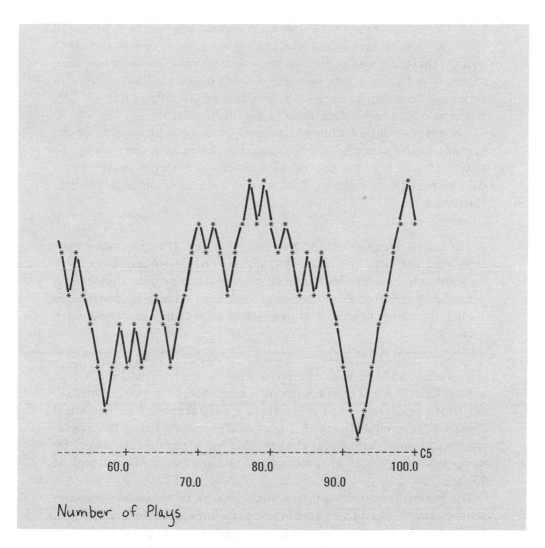

Number of Plays

time in a long streak of being ahead or in a long streak of being behind. So it may not be "luck" after all that gives gamblers their streaks. It may be just the laws of chance.

Example 2: Having Babies

Some people have suggested that the new more effective methods of birth control will eventually lead to a change in the ratio of men to women in our society. For example, it has been observed that large families tend to have more girls while small families tend to have more boys. One could argue that better birth control will lead to fewer large families. This, in turn, would lead to a higher ratio of men to women in society. One could also argue that many couples value having a boy more highly than having a girl; so many couples might use birth control to terminate their family once they have one or possibly two boys. This might also lead to a higher ratio of men to women.

Are either of these arguments correct? Or, in general, could the widespread practice of birth control change the sex ratio in our society? To study this problem, we will choose a simplified model to describe how couples might have children. Then we will use the computer to simulate the model.

The model: Suppose each couple has 2 children. If by then they have at least one boy, they stop. But, if they don't have any boys, they continue to have children until they have a boy or until they have a total of 8 children. Then they stop. Let's also assume that with each birth the chance of having a boy is 1/2 and the chance of having a girl is 1/2.

This model builds in both a preference for having boys, and an attempt to limit family size. It is, of course, over simplified, as are all mathematical models of the real world. Nevertheless, such simplified mathematical models have frequently been found useful in predicting the consequences of some behavioral change. We will simulate this model by using a combination of computer output and handwork. We will look at 75 families.

The easiest way to begin this simulation is to simulate a random sequence of 8 0's and 1's. A 1 will stand for a boy and a 0 for a girl. Then, if either of the first 2 numbers is a 1 (i.e., a boy), the couple stops having children and their family consists of just these 2 children. Otherwise, we continue down the list of random 0's and 1's until we get a 1, or until we use up all 8 numbers. We then count how many boys and girls that family had. Then we simulate another 8 random numbers to get a second family, and so on. We continue this until we get 75 families. Then we look at the ratio of boys to girls in this little "society."

You might try this simulation just to see what happens. To save paper and some work, we will do the same simulation, but use a slightly more sophisticated method. Notice that if we were to use the simple method we described above, we would have to simulate 75 separate families each with potentially 8 children. This would require using the command

BTRIALS 8 TRIALS WITH P = .5, PUT IN C3

75 times. Since most couples in our simulation will stop having children after only 2 or 3, many of the random numbers simulated by this program will be wasted.

The more "sophisticated" procedure we will use says, let's just generate one long string of random 0's and 1's, then split it up into families as we proceed through the list. After all, we are assuming that the chances of having a boy or girl on the next birth do not depend on how many children are already in the family or what sexes they are.

Look at Exhibit 3.7. This long list of 200 0's and 1's was simulated by the single instruction

BTRIALS 200 TRIALS, P = .5, PUT IN C1

This single command will replace all 75 of the instructions in the "simple" method. (By being a little clever, we saved ourselves a lot of work.) In this example, the first family had a boy, then a girl, then stopped. The second family had 2 boys, then stopped. It was not until we got to the fifth family that we found a couple who had to have more than 2 children to have their first boy. We kept on going down the list until we had 75 families altogether.

The results for this "society" of 75 families were as follows:

Children in Family	2B	1B 1G	1B 2G	1B 3G	1B 4G	1B 5G	1B 6G	1B 7G	8G
Number of Families	19	38	8	4	4	1	1	0	0

First notice that in our 75 families, there are 93 girls, and 94 boys. So the sex ratio has apparently not been affected in our hypothetical model. Society would still be about half male and half female, even if people worked this hard at having a boy. Also, notice that the larger families have more girls, while the smaller families have more boys. In fact, in the $19 + 38 = 57$ families which have just 2 children there are 76 boys among the 114 children, or $76/114 = 67\%$ boys. Whereas in the 18 families which have more than 2 children, there are 18 boys among the 73 children or only $18/73 = 25\%$ boys. These results indicate that our model may not be too far from reality, since as we observed initially, large families tend in reality to have a higher percentage of girls.

EXHIBIT 3.7

Simulation of 200 Children, with 1 = Boy, 0 = Girl; Separate Families Are Circled by Hand

`-- BTRIALS 200 TRIALS, P = .5, PUT IN C1`
`   200 BERNOULLI TRIALS WITH P = 0.5000`

1.	0.	1.	0.	0.	1.	0.	1.	1.	1.
0.	0.	1.	0.	0.	1.	1.	1.	1.	1.
0.	0.	1.	0.	0.	1.	1.	0.	0.	1.
1.	1.	1.	1.	0.	0.	1.	1.	0.	1.
1.	1.	0.	0.	0.	0.	0.	1.	1.	0.
1.	0.	1.	1.	1.	0.	0.	0.	1.	0.
1.	1.	1.	1.	1.	1.	0.	1.	1.	0.
1.	1.	1.	1.	0.	0.	1.	1.	1.	0.
0.	0.	1.	0.	1.	1.	1.	0.	0.	0.
0.	1.	0.	0.	0.	0.	1.	1.	1.	0.
1.	1.	0.	1.	0.	1.	1.	0.	1.	0.
1.	1.	0.	0.	0.	0.	0.	1.	1.	0.
1.	0.	1.	1.	0.	1.	0.	0.	0.	0.
0.	0.	1.	1.	0.	0.	0.	1.	1.	1.
1.	1.	1.	1.	0.	0.	0.	1.	1.	0.
1.	0.	0.	1.	0.	0.	0.	1.	0.	1.
0.	1.	1.	0.	1.	0.	0.	0.	1.	0.
1.	0.	0.	0.	0.	0.	1.	0.	1.	1.
0.	0.	0.	0.	1.	1.	0.	1.	1.	1.
0.	1.	1.	1.	0.	0.	1.	0.	1.	0.

```
SUMMARY
VALUE   FREQUENCY
  0        98
  1       102
```

There are other interesting features of these results that you could note. For example, since boys tend to be in smaller families than girls, a girl will have to look pretty hard if she wants to find a boy from a large family to marry. Similarly, when couples marry, the wife is likely to come from a large family. If children from large families tend to have different values, women will have different values in this society, not because of inherent sexual differences, but because of their childhood environment. You can also note that the most common type of family is one boy and one girl; the average family size is 2.5 children; 76% of the families have only 2 children.

You might try imagining a different model of how couples have children. For example, suppose each couple continues to have children until they have at least one boy and one girl, then they stop. If you try simulating various models, one thing you will observe is that although different models change the composition of families, they will *never* change the sex ratio of society. The only way that this can be changed is by changing the probability that a given *birth* results in a boy or girl.

Exercises

3-8   Run the program for the Losing Streaks Example (page 68) and see what kind of luck you have. (Note, if you have a printer that is too narrow to handle plots as wide as 100, simulate the game for just 50 plays, or as wide as the printer will handle.)

3-9   Run the Losing Streaks program, but with slightly different odds. Assume the coin is loaded so that the probability of tails is 0.6. How did you do this time? How did the plot change?

3-10   Refer to the output in Exhibit 3.7. In what percentage of the 75 families, is the oldest child a boy? In what percentage is the youngest child a boy? Why are these two percentages so different? Is it just random fluctuation?

3-11   Simulate the model for having children, mentioned in the last paragraph of Section 3.6, until you have 50 families.

(a)   What is the average family size? What is the most common size?

(b)   How many boys and girls are there in the 50 families?

(c)   Suppose we look only at larger families (3 or more children). What proportion of the children in these families are boys?

3.7 Some More About Simulation

Suppose we want to simulate the experiment of rolling a pair of dice 100 times. We could use the following very lengthy program, which has a total of 100 IRANDOM commands:

```
IRANDOM 2 INTEGERS BETWEEN 1 AND 6 PUT IN C1
IRANDOM  2  1  6  C1

     .       .         .

     .       .         .

     .       .         .

IRANDOM  2  1  6  C1
STOP
```

Or, we can use a simple trick which gives the following much shorter program:

```
IRANDOM 100 INTEGERS BETWEEN 1 AND 6 PUT IN C1
IRANDOM 100 INTEGERS BETWEEN 1 AND 6 PUT IN C2
STOP
```

Here, we switched things around. In C1, we put all 100 outcomes from rolling the first die in the pair. And, in C2 we put all 100 outcomes from rolling the second die in the pair. When we were finished, the first row of the worksheet contained the first outcome from rolling the pair of dice, the second contained the second outcome, and so on.

We could use this "row-wise" technique to simulate 20 experiments of sampling 10 female heights, instead of the "column-wise" technique used in Section 3.3. The following program simulates the 20 samples, calculates the $\bar{x}$'s, and gives a histogram of the $\bar{x}$'s:

```
NOPRINT
NRANDOM 20 OBSN, MU = 64, SIGMA = 3, PUT IN C1
NRANDOM 20              64          3          C2

     .                   .          .          .

     .                   .          .          .

     .                   .          .          .

NRANDOM 20              64          3          C10
ADD C1-C10, PUT SUM IN C11
DIVIDE C11 BY 10 PUT IN C12 (XBARS)
```

HISTOGRAM OF C12
STOP

We have made use of a more general form of the ADD command.

ADD E TO **E** ... TO **E**, PUT SUM INTO **C**

MULTIPLY **E** BY **E** ... BY **E**, PUT PRODUCT INTO **C**

Allows you to do several additions (or multiplications) at one time.

Examples

ADD 5 TO C1 TO C3, PUT INTO C5
MULTIPLY C10-C12, PUT INTO C1

Thus, there are two basic ways to have Minitab simulate data—you can put each sample in a column, or you can put each sample in a row. Which method should you use? If the number of experiments you want to simulate exceeds the sample size, then "row-wise" simulation will probably be easier, whereas if the number of experiments is less than the sample size, "column-wise" simulation will probably be easier. However, the easier method will also depend on what you want to do with the simulated data. For example, notice that when we used the "row-wise" technique for female heights, we were able to use Minitab to get a histogram of the $\bar{x}$'s. With the "column-wise" technique, we'd have to do the histogram by hand or read the simulated $\bar{x}$'s back into the computer.

Exercises

3-12   Consider the experiment of tossing a coin 5 times and recording the number of heads. Simulate this experiment 100 times, using the BTRIALS command and the techniques of this section. If you let 1 represent a head, then adding the 5 columns will give you the number of heads in 5 tosses. Get a histogram of the 100 observations of the number of heads. How often did all 5 tosses come up heads? Tails?

3-13   (a) Simulate 100 times the experiment of rolling a pair of dice and finding the sum of the two numbers. Use the technique discussed in this section. (Use NOPRINT to reduce unnecessary output.) Get a histogram of the sum.

       (b) How often did the largest sum $(6 + 6 = 12)$ come up in the 100 simulations? How often did the smallest sum $(1 + 1 = 2)$ come up?

       (c) Repeat parts (a) and (b), but roll 3 dice instead of 2.

3.8 Number of Times to Simulate an Experiment

As we have already mentioned, simulation can be a useful tool for estimating probabilities which cannot be calculated theoretically. An obvious question is, How many times should an experiment be simulated to give a good estimate? Certainly, the more times an experiment is simulated, the better the estimate, but the higher the cost. As computers become faster and less expensive, researchers tend to simulate more and more repetitions. Right now, as a rough guideline, simulating an experiment 20 to 200 times can be used to get a rough preliminary guess. More repetitions, say 500 to 5000, are usually needed to provide reasonable estimates of probabilities. Higher numbers of repetitions, say 10,000 or more, are used only where very high accuracy is required. In these cases, very careful checking of the properties of the random data generator should be done as well.

We might mention that Exercise 5-12 (page 101) illustrates how you can use some of your knowledge of statistics to tell how accurate the results of a simulation will be.

Some Advanced Exercises

3-14   *The Law of Large Numbers.*   Suppose you toss a fair coin 10 times and calculate (number of heads)/10. This number will probably be close to 1/2. Suppose you continue to toss the coin until you have a total of 20 tosses and calculate (number of heads)/20. This ratio will probably be even closer to 1/2. In general, the more tosses, the closer to 1/2 the ratio of (number of heads in n tosses)/n is likely to be. This phenomenon is called the *law of large numbers*. The following simulation makes it more vivid.

The program below simulates tossing a coin 50 times. After each toss, it calculates the ratio (number of heads so far)/(number of tosses so far). These ratios are then plotted.

```
BTRIALS 50 OBS., P=.5, PUT INTO C1 (FIFTY TOSSES)
GENERATE FIRST 50 INTEGERS INTO C3
PARSUM C1, PUT INTO C2
DIVIDE C2 BY C3, PUT INTO C4 (SUCCESSIVE RATIOS)
PLOT RATIOS IN C4 VS NO. OF TOSSES IN C3
PRINT C1-C4
STOP
```

(a) Run the program.

(b) How many heads were there in the first 10 tosses? In the first 20 tosses?

(c) To make the plot clearer, you might connect the dots. What seems to be happening to the ratios as the number of tosses gets larger?

3-15 (a) Repeat the simulation in Exercise 3-14, but now use a coin that is loaded so that the probability of a head is 0.2, and a tail is 0.8.

(b) Compare the plot to the plot in Exercise 3-14. What difference do you see? What happens to the ratios as the number of tosses gets larger?

3-16 Simulation can be used to estimate the value of π. Consider the diagram below.

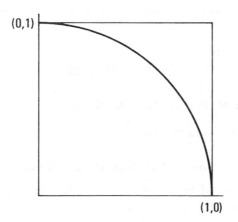

$$\frac{\text{area of quarter circle}}{\text{area of square}} = \frac{\pi r^2 / 4}{1^2} = \frac{\pi}{4}$$

If we can estimate the ratio of the two areas, we can get an estimate of π. Simulation can be used to estimate this ratio. First simulate 200 uniform (from 0 to 1) observations into c1, and another 200 uniform observations into c2 (see URANDOM, page 82). Then we have 200 pairs, call them (x,y), which can be viewed as points in the plane. These points are distributed uniformly over the square. So, the ratio

$$\frac{\text{number of points in the quarter circle}}{\text{number of points in the square}}$$

is an estimate of the ratio of the two areas.

Finish writing a Minitab program to estimate π. (Hint: A point is in the quarter circle if and only if $x^2 + y^2 - 1 < 0$. Use the SIGNS command (described on page 240) to get a count of the number of negative values.)

3-17 Suppose U_1 and U_2 are two independent random variables, each having a uniform (0,1) distribution (see URANDOM, page 82). Answer these questions for each of the following random variables: (1) Guess what its density function looks like. (2) Simulate 200 observations of the random variable and get a histogram. Does the picture agree with your guess? (3) Can you derive the exact density, using mathematics? In some cases, this may be difficult.

(a) $Z = 2U_1$ (b) $Z = U_1^2$
(c) $Z = \min(U_1, U_2)$ (d) $Z = U_1 + U_2$
(e) $Z = U_1 U_2$

APPENDIX 3a.
Simulating Other Distributions

Binomial and Poisson Distributions

These will be described in Chapter 5.

Sampling from Several Columns at Once

An extended form of the SAMPLE command allows you to sample the same rows from several columns.

(Continued from page 65.)

SAMPLE K ROWS FROM C, C,...,C, PUT INTO C, C,...,C

Samples rows without replacement from several columns at once (the same rows from each column). The numbers sampled in the first column are printed out (unless the NOPRINT command is in effect).

As an example, suppose we have the heights, weights, IQ scores, grade-point averages, and residence areas for several hundred students stored in columns C1, C2, C3, C4, and C5 respectively. Then we can use SAMPLE to choose a random sample of these students and store their five characteristics in some other columns. The following instruction would choose a random sample of 10 students:

```
SAMPLE 10 ROWS FROM C1-C5, PUT INTO C11-C15
```

The heights, weights, and so on of these 10 students would be put into columns C11, C12, C13, C14, and C15, and further analysis could be done on these values.

The Hypergeometric Distribution

The SAMPLE command may be used to simulate observations from the hypergeometric distribution. For example, suppose we want to simulate drawing a sample of size 3, without replacement, from an urn containing 2 red and 6 white balls. We can code the 2 colors using a 1 for red and a 0 for white and use the following program:

```
SET INTO C1
1  1  0  0  0  0  0  0
SAMPLE 3 OBS. FROM C1, PUT IN C2
SUM C2
```

Notice that because of the way we coded red and white, the command SUM C2 gives a count of the number of red balls in our sample. If we want to simulate what would happen if we drew a number of such samples, the last two commands could be repeated as many times as desired.

Uniform Distribution

> **URAN**DOM, GENERATE **K** UNIFORM OBSERVATIONS, PUT IN **C**
>
> Simulates observations that have an equal chance of falling anywhere between 0 and 1. The results are also printed (unless the command NOPRINT is in effect).

Some Other Distributions

In the examples that follow, we give a program that can be used to simulate 100 observations from each population.

Exponential Distribution with density $f(x) = \lambda e^{-\lambda x}$, $x > 0$.

We will do the simulation for $\lambda = 2.1$.

```
NOPRINT (WE DON'T WANT UNIFORMS PRINTED)
URANDOM 100 OBS, PUT IN C1
LOGE OF C1, PUT IN C2
DIVIDE C2 BY −2.1, PUT IN C3 (EXPONENTIAL DATA)
PRINT C3 (IF YOU WANT RESULTS PRINTED)
```

Cauchy Distribution with density function $f(x) = 1/[\pi(1 + x)^2]$.

We use the fact that the quotient of two independent normal ($\mu = 0$, $\sigma = 1$) random variables has a Cauchy distribution.

```
NOPRINT (WE DON'T WANT NORMAL DATA PRINTED)
NRANDOM 100 OBS MU = 0.0, SIGMA = 1.0, PUT IN C1
```

NRANDOM 100 OBS MU = 0.0, SIGMA = 1.0, PUT IN C2
DIVIDE C1 BY C2, PUT IN C3 (CAUCHY DATA)
PRINT C3 (IF YOU WANT RESULTS PRINTED)

Chi-Square Distribution with 1 degree of freedom.

NOPRINT
NRANDOM 100 OBS, MU = 0.0, SIGMA = 1.0, PUT IN C1
MULTIPLY C1 BY C1, PUT IN C2 (CHI-SQUARE DATA)
PRINT C3 (IF YOU WANT RESULTS PRINTED)

Chi-Square Distribution with 2 degrees of freedom.

Simulate samples from the exponential distribution with $\lambda = 0.5$.

Chi-Square Distribution with higher degrees of freedom.

These can be simulated by just adding up chi-squares with 2 and 1 degrees of freedom.

APPENDIX 3b.
The BASE Command

Minitab does not actually do an experiment to simulate "random" data. Rather it uses a mathematical function which creates a long list of numbers that appear to be random. The list always stays the same, so it is important to be able to begin each use of this list at a different, haphazardly chosen, starting point. Accomplishing this will differ from place to place. Many institutions will do this automatically by using the clock in the computer to give each run a different starting point.

At other institutions, it may be necessary to use the BASE command to get different starting points.

| **BASE** FOR RANDOM NUMBER GENERATORS = **K** |

K should be a positive integer, which will tell the random number generator where to start in its list of random numbers. Numbers between 1
and 1000000 are recommended. Ordinarily, it is sufficient to use the BASE
command just once at the beginning of any program that simulates
random data. After this, the computer will proceed down the long list
automatically. Note, K cannot contain any commas.

Occasionally you may want to simulate the same set of "random"
numbers over and over again. In this case, simply use the same base
each time you run the program. For example, if every student in a class
used the same base, then they would all get identical sets of "random"
data.

4

An Introduction to Statistical Inference

Whenever we try to make statements about an entire population, based on a sample of observations from that population, we are doing *inference*. Statistical inference enables us to make such statements, and control the probability of being wrong. For example, we might look at the voting patterns of a few people, then project the winner of a national election. Our projection might be right or it might be wrong. Sound statistical procedures will help us be right most of the time.

In this chapter, we will show how simulation can be used to get a feel for what statistical inference is all about.

4.1 Informal Hypothesis Tests

You and a "friend" often play a gambling game which involves tossing a coin—tails you win, heads your opponent wins. Recently you've noticed that your opponent seems to be winning a lot. In particular, he often has what seems to be a long stretch of winning every game. You're beginning to suspect that he slips in a loaded coin for a part of each session. So you decide to keep track of the next gambling session. You get the following results:

H T T H H H H H T H

Again, your opponent had a long stretch of winning: 5 heads in a row here. Should you accuse him of cheating? Is it reasonable to expect to get as many as 5 heads in a row, when you toss a fair coin 10 times? Perhaps you should find the odds of this happening, just by chance.

Let's try playing the game ourselves, using a fair coin. Then we'll see how often our opponent is so "lucky." If a stretch of winning 5 or more in a row occurs frequently, we'll just have to accept it as part of the game. *But* if it occurs very infrequently, then...

Instead of actually tossing a coin 10 times, we can use the BTRIALS command to do our tossing for us. The command,

BTRIALS 10 TOSSES, P = 0.5, PUT IN C1

simulates one gambling session. Let's use $0 = H$, $1 = T$. The first time we did this we got,

0 0 0 1 1 0 1 1 1 1

Here our opponent's winning streak was only 3 games. But we must look at many more sessions before we can draw any strong conclusions. We simulated a total of 40 sessions, each with 10 games, and got the following results:

Length of Opponent's Longest Stretch of Wins	10	9	8	7	6	5	4	3	2	1	0
Number of Sessions in Which This Occurred	0	0	1	0	4	1	9	12	9	4	0
Percentage of Sessions	0	0	2.5	0	10.0	2.5	22.5	30.0	22.5	10.0	0
Cumulative Percentage	0	0	2.5	2.5	12.5	15.0	37.5	67.5	90.0	100	100

In one session "our opponent" had a stretch of 8 wins in a row. In 4 more sessions, he had 6 wins in a row. In fact, this imaginary opponent had streaks of 5 or more 15% of the time. So our suspicion has not been confirmed. Based on this evidence, we really can't accuse our opponent of cheating. It's just not that unlikely to get 5 wins in a row by chance alone. Does this prove our opponent is not cheating? Certainly not. We just don't have enough evidence to go out on a limb and say he is. If we want to have a chance of confirming our suspicion, we are going to have to plan a much more powerful test.

4.2 Simple Confidence Intervals

When a safety expert announces that 16% of all the vehicles on the highways would fail a safety inspection, he probably doesn't mean that exactly 16.0000% would fail. He probably means that something in the "ball park" of 16% will fail. The size of his "ball park" tells us a lot. Does he mean that about 16% will fail, but maybe as few as 5% or as many as 18%? Or does he mean, as few as 15.99% or perhaps as many as 16.01%? Our interpretation of his original statement will depend on how much uncertainty there is in his estimate.

An Example: Hemoglobin Levels

Suppose you had chosen three people at random from some population, and had recorded their hemoglobin levels as 17.1, 15.2, and 14.3. The median of these three gives us an estimate of the median of all of the hemoglobin levels in the population. Since our estimate is based on such a small sample—only three people—it's a pretty poor estimate. It might be way above the population median, or way below. It would be nice to have an interval that would tell us how far off it might be.

A very simple and useful procedure is to take the region from the smallest observation, 14.3, to the largest observation, 17.1, as our interval. Using intervals like this—from the smallest to the largest observation in a sample of size 3—gives us a 75% chance of catching the population median. Why? Because the only way an interval can miss is if all three of the observations are below the population median, or if all three are above the median. The probability that all three observations are below the median is

(probability that first is below) ×
(probability that second is below) ×
(probability that third is below) = 1/2 × 1/2 × 1/2 = 1/8.

Similarly, the probability that all three are above the population median is 1/8. So the chances of missing the population median are 1/8 +

EXHIBIT 4.1

10 Simulated Samples of Size 3 of Hemoglobin Level

-- NRANDOM 3 OBSN, MU = 15, SIGMA = 2, PUT IN C1
  3 NORMAL OBS. WITH MU = 15.0000 AND SIGMA = 2.0000
  13.8528   12.1008   15.8644
-- NRANDOM 3 OBSN, MU = 15, SIGMA = 2, PUT IN C1
  3 NORMAL OBS. WITH MU = 15.0000 AND SIGMA = 2.0000
  18.7796   12.1482   16.7888
-- NRANDOM 3 OBSN, MU = 15, SIGMA = 2, PUT IN C1
  3 NORMAL OBS. WITH MU = 15.0000 AND SIGMA = 2.0000
  13.2640   16.4814   14.6702
-- NRANDOM 3 OBSN, MU = 15, SIGMA = 2, PUT IN C1
  3 NORMAL OBS. WITH MU = 15.0000 AND SIGMA = 2.0000
  14.7333   13.9734   14.1944
-- NRANDOM 3 OBSN, MU = 15, SIGMA = 2, PUT IN C1
  3 NORMAL OBS. WITH MU = 15.0000 AND SIGMA = 2.0000
  20.1786   16.5378   12.9396
-- NRANDOM 3 OBSN, MU = 15, SIGMA = 2, PUT IN C1
  3 NORMAL OBS. WITH MU = 15.0000 AND SIGMA = 2.0000
  11.7098   15.8083   15.1807
-- NRANDOM 3 OBSN, MU = 15, SIGMA = 2, PUT IN C1
  3 NORMAL OBS. WITH MU = 15.0000 AND SIGMA = 2.0000
  15.4851   11.1936   17.0689
-- NRANDOM 3 OBSN, MU = 15, SIGMA = 2, PUT IN C1
  3 NORMAL OBS. WITH MU = 15.0000 AND SIGMA = 2.0000
  14.0156   15.3070   19.1867
-- NRANDOM 3 OBSN, MU = 15, SIGMA = 2, PUT IN C1
  3 NORMAL OBS. WITH MU = 15.0000 AND SIGMA = 2.0000
  15.8452   20.7709   14.4776
-- NRANDOM 3 OBSN, MU = 15, SIGMA = 2, PUT IN C1
   3 NORMAL OBS. WITH MU = 15.0000 AND SIGMA = 2.0000
  14.6053   14.3970   17.5503

$1/8 = 2/8 = 1/4$. Our chances of *catching* the population median are thus $1 - 1/4$, or 75%.

Let's do a simulation where we know the population median and see how this procedure works. We'll draw three observations at random from a population and pretend we don't know the population median. Then we'll bet it's somewhere between the smallest and largest of the three. On the average, we should win about 75% of the time.

The population of all hemoglobin levels has an approximately normal or bell-shaped distribution with a mean of 15.0 grams per hundred milliliters and a standard deviation of 2.0 grams per hundred milliliters. Therefore we'll use NRANDOM (see Section 3.3) to simulate our observations. Normal populations are symmetric, and in any symmetric population the mean and median are equal. So the median of this population is also 15.0.

The instruction below, repeated a number of times, will simulate the samples we need. The rest we'll do by hand.

NRANDOM 3 OBSN MU = 15.0, SIGMA = 2.0.

The results of 10 samples are shown in Exhibit 4.1. In the first sample the three observations were 13.9, 12.1, and 15.9. So our interval went from 12.1 to 15.9. That time we were lucky. Our interval did catch the population median. The next interval went from 12.1 to 16.8, and was also a lucky one.

Exhibit 4.2 shows all 10 intervals plotted with the population median drawn in. Overall, we were lucky 9 times (caught the median), and unlucky 1 time (missed the median). So we were right 90% of the time. In the long run we'd be right about 75% of the time. Of course, in a real application, we'd probably never know if our interval covered the median or not, but we could still bet that it covered with the confidence that we'd win 75% of the time.

Exercises

4-1   Suppose you had a sample of 5 hemoglobin levels instead of just 3. To estimate the median, you again formed the interval from the smallest to the largest. Simulate 10 such intervals and plot them as we did in Exhibit 4.2. How does using the procedure with a sample of size 5 compare to using it with a sample of size 3? Are the intervals wider or narrower, on the average? Do you seem to catch the median more often?

4-2   Using the same reasoning as in the text, figure out the probability of catching the median with a sample of size 5. How does this answer agree with the results of the simulation in Exercise 4-1?

EXHIBIT 4.2

10 Simulated Intervals

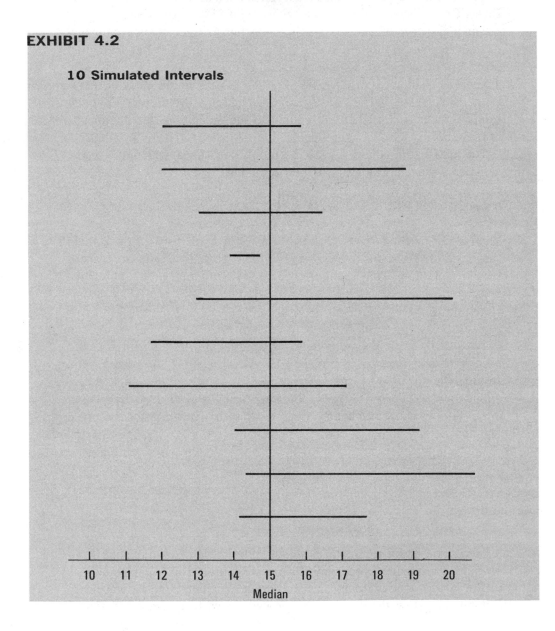

5

Binomial and Poisson Distributions

5.1 The Binomial Distribution

Suppose you bought 4 light bulbs. The manufacturer claims that 85% of all their bulbs will last at least 700 hours. What are the chances that all 4 of your bulbs will last over 700 hours? That 3 will last 700 hours, but 1 will fail before that?

Consider another situation. You just went into a class in ancient Chinese literature. You haven't even learned the alphabet yet, but they've given you a pop quiz. You'll have to guess on every question. It's a multiple choice test, with each of the 20 questions having three possible answers. What are the chances you'll get 10 or more questions right?

Questions like these can sometimes be answered with the help of the *binomial distribution.*

The following five conditions must be met before the binomial distribution applies:

(a) There must be a fixed number of trials or events (e.g., 20 questions to be answered).

(b) The outcome of each trial can be classified in one of two ways, usually called "success" and "failure" (e.g., a bulb lasts 700 hours, or it doesn't).

(c) We are interested in counting the number of successes.

(d) The probability of a success is the same for all trials.

(e) The trials are independent. That is, a success on one trial does not change the probability there will be a success on another trial.

   If these conditions are met (or nearly so), Minitab's BINOMIAL PROBABILITIES command can help with computations.

BINOMIAL PROBABILITIES FOR N = **K**; AND P = **K**

Prints out a table of binomial probabilities. The standard formula is used:

$$f(x) = \binom{n}{x} p^x q^{n-x}, \text{ where } q = 1 - p.$$

Both the individual probabilities and the cumulative probabilities are printed out.

BINOMIAL PROBABILITIES FOR N = **K** AND P = **K**, PUT INTO **C**

If you specify a column as the third argument in the BINOMIAL command, then Minitab stores the probabilities in that column, as well as printing out a table.

   For example, to compute the probabilities for the multiple choice exam, you could use

BINOMIAL PROBABILITIES, N = 20, P = 0.333333.

The output from this command is given in Exhibit 5.1. We see, for example, that the probability of 10 successes is 0.0543 and the probability of 10 or fewer successes is .9624. To find the probability of more than 10 successes, all we need to do is subtract .9624 from 1, getting .0376.

   We could also get a plot of these binomial probabilities by using the following program:

GENERATE THE INTEGERS FROM 0 TO 20 INTO C1
BINOMIAL PROB. FOR N = 20, P = 0.333333, PUT IN C2
PLOT C2 VS. C1
STOP

The plot is in Exhibit 5.2.

EXHIBIT 5.1

Binomial Probabilities

```
-- BINOMIAL PROBABILITIES FOR N = 20, P = 0.33333333
   BINOMIAL PROBABILITIES FOR N = 20 AND P = 0.333333
```

K	P(X = K)	P(X LESS OR = K)
0	0.0003	0.0003
1	0.0030	0.0033
2	0.0143	0.0176
3	0.0429	0.0604
4	0.0911	0.1515
5	0.1457	0.2972
6	0.1821	0.4793
7	0.1821	0.6615
8	0.1480	0.8095
9	0.0987	0.9081
10	0.0543	0.9624
11	0.0247	0.9870
12	0.0092	0.9963
13	0.0028	0.9991
14	0.0007	0.9998

Exercises

5-1   (a) For the light bulbs example write a program to compute the probabilities of various numbers of bulbs lasting longer than 700 hours.

(b) If you bought all 4 bulbs in one box, which condition(s) for the binomial distribution is (are) most likely to be violated? Why?

EXHIBIT 5.2

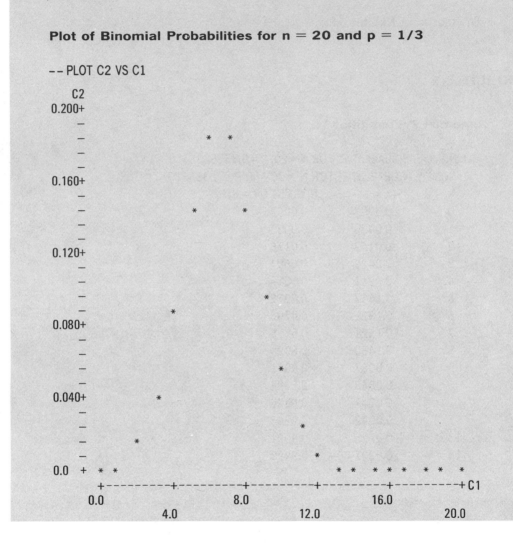

Plot of Binomial Probabilities for n = 20 and p = 1/3

```
-- PLOT C2 VS C1
     C2
 0.200+
      -
      -                        *   *
      -
      -
 0.160+
      -
      -                    *           *
      -
      -
 0.120+
      -
      -
      -                                   *
      -                 *
 0.080+
      -
      -
      -                                     *
 0.040+
      -             *
      -
      -         *
      -                                        *
 0.0  +  *  *                          * *   * * *   * *   *
         +---------+---------+---------+---------+---------+ C1
        0.0                 8.0                16.0
                 4.0                12.0                 20.0
```

5-2   Sixteen mice are sent down a maze. From previous experience, it is believed that the probability that a mouse turns right is 0.38.

(a) What is the probability that exactly 7 of these 16 mice turn right?

(b) That 8 or fewer turn right?

(c) That more than 8 turn right?

(d) That 8 or more turn right?

5-3   This exercise has you compute and plot some binomial probabilities so you'll have a better idea what they look like.

(a) First, let's fix n at 8 and vary p. Use p = 0.01, 0.1, 0.2, 0.5, 0.8, and 0.9. For each value of p, compute the binomial probabilities and get a plot like the one in Exhibit 5.2.

     (i) How does the shape of the plot change as p increases?

     (ii) Compare the 2 plots where p = .1 and p = .9. Do you see any relationship? What about the 2 plots where p = .2 and p = .8?

(b) Next, let's fix p at 0.2 and vary n. Use n = 2, 5, 10, 20, and 40. For each value of n, compute the binomial probabilities and get a plot as in part (a). How does the plot change as n increases? How about the spread? The shape? Does the "middle" move when n increases?

5-4   Two instruments are used to measure the amount of pollution in Lake Erie. They sit side by side but they never agree exactly. Sometimes instrument A gets a higher reading than B, and sometimes it's the other way around. If the instruments are identical, then each one has a 50-50 chance of giving the bigger reading on any given occasion.

(a) What are the chances that one instrument will give the higher reading 15 or more times out of 20?

(b) What would you think if you measured the water quality 20 times with each instrument and A was bigger 15 times out of 20? What are some of the possible causes of such an event?

5-5   *Acceptance Sampling.* When a company buys a big lot of materials, they usually won't check every single item to see if it's satisfactory. Instead, they try to pick a random sample of items, then check these and if they don't find many defective items, they go ahead and accept the whole lot. In this problem we'll look at the kind of risk they run when they do this. Often the risk isn't very much, and inspecting a few items is much cheaper than inspecting the whole lot. (Also, some types of testing destroy the items. We certainly wouldn't want to test every item in that case!)

Suppose the inspection plan consists of looking at 10 items chosen at random from a large shipment, then accepting the entire shipment if there are 0 or 1 defective items, and rejecting the shipment if there are 2 or more defective items.

(a) If in the entire shipment 10% of the items are defective, what is the probability the shipment will be accepted?

(b) Compute the probability of acceptance if the shipment has 1% defective; 5% defective; 10%; 20%; 30%; 50%; 80% defective. Then sketch a plot of the probability of acceptance versus the percent defective.

(c) About what percent defective leads to a 50-50 chance of acceptance?

(d) Repeat part (b) but use a different plan where 20 items are checked and the lot is accepted if only 0, 1, or 2 are found defective, and rejected otherwise.

(e) Sketch both graphs [from (b) and (d)] on the same plot. Discuss the advantages and disadvantages of the two different plans.

5-6   Suppose X is a binomial random variable with n = 16 and p = 0.75.

(a) Write a Minitab program to calculate the mean of X using the formula $\mu = \Sigma \, x \, P(X = x)$. Does the answer agree with the answer you get when you use the formula $\mu = np$?

(b) Write a Minitab program to calculate the variance of X using the formula $\sigma^2 = \Sigma (x - \mu)^2 \, P(X = x)$. Use the value of μ from part (a). Does the answer agree with the formula $\sigma^2 = npq$?

5-7   In the **Pulse** experiment (page 285), students were asked to toss a coin. If the coin came up heads they were asked to run in place. Tails meant they did not run in place. Do you think all students who got a head ran in place? Compare the data with the output from the appropriate BINOMIAL PROBABILITIES command.

5.2 Simulating Binomial Data

In Section 3.2 (page 58) we showed how the BTRIALS command could be used to simulate binomial experiments. To simulate flipping a balanced coin 10 times, we could use the command

BTRIALS 10 TRIALS WITH P = 0.5, PUT IN C1.

Then we could count up how many "successes" we get (e.g., how many heads). That would correspond to one binomial experiment. If we want to simulate 25 such experiments, we could repeat the BTRIALS command 25 times, each time counting up how many successes we got. But suppose we were interested only in the number of successes in each experiment—not in what order they came in, or anything else. Then it would be easier to use the BRANDOM command.

BRANDOM K BINOMIAL EXPERIMENTS WITH N = **K,** P = **K,** PUT

IN **C**

Simulates a random sample from the binomial distribution

$$f(x) - \binom{n}{x} p^x \, q^{n-x}, \; q = 1-p.$$

The value of n must be less than or equal to 100. The results are stored in the indicated column. They are also printed out automatically (unless the command NOPRINT has been used). In addition, Minitab always prints out a summary which contains the number of experiments with 0 successes, the number with 1 success, the number with 2 successes, and so on.

The output from the instruction

BRANDOM 25 EXPERIMENTS, N = 10, P = .5, PUT IN C1

is given in Exhibit 5.3. There we can see that the first experiment resulted in 6 successes (heads), the second in 5 successes, and so on. There were no experiments in which all 10 coins came up heads (10 successes) and none in which all 10 came up tails (0 successes). There were 3 cases out of 25 in which there were either 9 heads or 9 tails.

Exercises

5-8   An experiment consists of flipping 6 fair coins and recording the number of heads.

EXHIBIT 5.3

Results of 25 Binomial Experiments

(Note: Histogram is Hand Drawn)

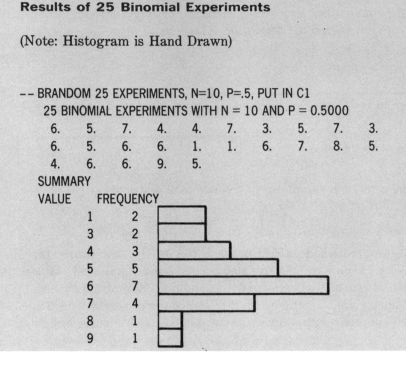

```
-- BRANDOM 25 EXPERIMENTS, N=10, P=.5, PUT IN C1
   25 BINOMIAL EXPERIMENTS WITH N = 10 AND P = 0.5000
      6.    5.    7.    4.    4.    7.    3.    5.    7.    3.
      6.    5.    6.    6.    1.    1.    6.    7.    8.    5.
      4.    6.    6.    9.    5.
   SUMMARY
   VALUE      FREQUENCY
       1          2
       3          2
       4          3
       5          5
       6          7
       7          4
       8          1
       9          1
```

(a) Simulate this experiment 100 times. Sketch a histogram of your results (as in Exhibit 5.3).

(b) How often did all 6 coins come up heads? How often would you expect this event to occur in the 100 simulations?

(c) How often did you get more heads than tails? How often would you expect this event to occur in the 100 simulations?

(d) Does your histogram look symmetric (more or less)? Would you expect it to?

5-9   An experiment consists of flipping a "loaded" coin 20 times, where the coin is loaded so that the probability of a head is 0.9.

(a) Simulate this experiment 100 times. Convert the frequency table into a relative frequency table. Compare the relative frequencies with the exact probabilities from the BINOMIAL PROBABILITIES command.

(b) Repeat part (a), but simulate the experiment 1000 times. How do the relative frequencies compare to the true probabilities?

5.3 Normal Approximation to the Binomial

For many combinations of n and p the binomial distribution can be well approximated by a normal distribution with the same mean and standard deviation. That is, with mean np and standard deviation $= \sqrt{np(1-p)}$. The program below lets us look at three binomial distributions. All have p $= 1/2$, and n varies from 3 to 7 to 15. The last 2 plots are in Exhibit 5.4.

```
BINOMIAL PROB. FOR N = 3, P = .5, PUT IN C1
GENERATE INTEGERS FROM 0 TO 3, PUT IN C2
PLOT C1 VS. C2
BINOMIAL PROB. FOR N = 7, P = .5, PUT IN C1
GENERATE INTEGERS FROM 0 TO 7, PUT IN C2
PLOT C1 VS. C2
BINOMIAL PROB. FOR N = 15, P = .5, PUT IN C1
GENERATE INTEGERS FROM 0 TO 15, PUT IN C2
PLOT C1 VS. C2
STOP
```

We converted the plots, by hand, to histograms. Look at the general shape of the 2 distributions. Both are somewhat similar in shape to the normal curve. The distribution corresponding to n $= 15$ is closer. If we were to plot the distribution for p $= 1/2$ and n $= 30$, it would look even more like a normal distribution. In general, for any fixed value of p, the larger n is, the closer the distribution is to a normal. Here we used p $= 0.5$. In the exercises, we'll look at other values of p.

EXHIBIT 5.4

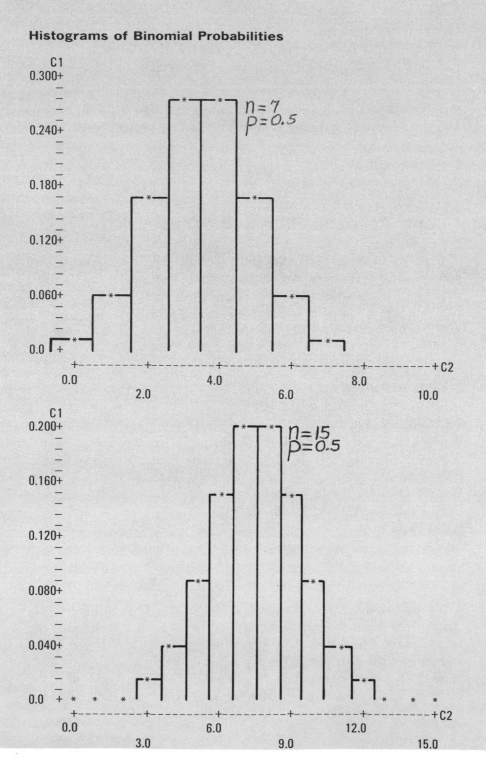

Histograms of Binomial Probabilities

Exercises

5-10 (a) Get plots, as in Exhibit 5.4, but use p = 0.4 instead of p = 0.5. Use n = 3, 7, 15, and 30. Convert these four plots to histograms and compare their shape to the shape of the normal curve.

(b) Repeat part (a) using p = 0.2.

(c) What can you say about the normal approximation to the binomial? For what values of n and p does it seem to work best?

5-11 Suppose X is a binomial random variable with p = 0.8 and n = 25. Use Minitab to calculate each of the probabilities below exactly. Also use a normal table to approximate the probabilities. Compare the answers.
(a) $P(X \leq 21)$
(b) $P(X \leq 23)$
(c) $P(X \geq 24)$
(d) $P(X = 24)$

5-12 In Section 3.1 we used simulation to estimate the probability that all six faces turn up when you roll a die 12 times. Estimating this probability (let's call it p) by simulation is just like estimating p by doing an experiment. So all you know about calculating a confidence interval for probabilities (or proportions) can be used in simulation. Use the data from the simulation in Section 3.1 (page 55) to construct a 95% confidence interval for p.

5.4 The Poisson Distribution

A famous statistician once called the Poisson distribution "the distribution to read newspapers by." He did this because so many times we read facts like "crime increases 25% in year," or "543 fatalities expected this weekend." Such figures can frequently be predicted with the Poisson distribution.

The Poisson distribution arises when we count the number of occurrences of an event that happens relatively infrequently, given the number of times it could happen. For example, the number of automobile accidents that will occur in Centre County, Pennsylvania, next weekend could be very large. Any motorist in the area might have an accident. But the chance that any given motorist will have an accident is very small, so the actual number of accidents probably won't be too large.

When the Poisson distribution holds, all we need to know to compute the probability of any number of accidents (or other events) is the average. For example, if we know that there are, on the average, 6 accidents per weekend, then we can compute the probability there will be, say, 10 or more accidents next weekend. The POISSON PROBABILITIES command can help with the calculations.

POISSON PROBABILITIES FOR MEAN = K

Prints out a table of Poisson probabilities. The standard formula is used:

$$f(x) = \frac{e^{-\mu}\mu^x}{x!}, \; x = 0,1,2,...$$

where μ is the mean, and e is 2.718... (the base of "natural" logarithms). Both the individual probabilities and the cumulative probabilities are printed out. Minitab prints out f(0), f(1), f(2), up until f(x) is essentially equal to 0.0.

The mean μ must be less than or equal to 100.

The command

POISSON PROB. FOR MU = 6

gave us the output in Exhibit 5.5. From this we see, for example, that the probability of no accidents next weekend is 0.0025; the probability of 6 or fewer is 0.6063; and the probability of having 10 or more accidents is $1 - 0.9161 = 0.0839$. What's the probability of having 20 accidents? This value isn't in the table. Minitab prints the probabilities only as far as 18. From there on they are all essentially zero.

Suppose the sheriff decides to crack down on speeders and that next weekend there are only 3 accidents. We can imagine a headline: "Sher-

EXHIBIT 5.5

Probabilities for a Poisson Distribution

```
-- POISSON PROB. FOR MU = 6
   POISSON PROBABILITIES FOR MEAN = 6.000
```

K	P(X = K)	P(X LESS OR = K)
0	0.0025	0.0025
1	0.0149	0.0174
2	0.0446	0.0620
3	0.0892	0.1512
4	0.1339	0.2851
5	0.1606	0.4457
6	0.1606	0.6063
7	0.1377	0.7440
8	0.1033	0.8472
9	0.0688	0.9161
10	0.0413	0.9574
11	0.0225	0.9799
12	0.0113	0.9912
13	0.0052	0.9964
14	0.0022	0.9986
15	0.0009	0.9995
16	0.0003	0.9998
17	0.0001	0.9999
18	0.0000	1.0000

iff's crackdown on speeders leads to 50% reduction in accidents." What do you think? Suppose we find the probability of 3 or fewer accidents for $\mu = 6$. It's 0.1512. That is, there is over a 15% chance of a 50% or better reduction in accidents even if his crackdown has no effect whatsoever.

Simulating Poisson Data

Minitab has a command to simulate Poisson random numbers.

> **PRANDOM K OBSERVATIONS WITH MU = K, PUT IN C**
>
> Simulates random sample from the Poisson distribution
>
> $$f(x) = e^{-\mu} \mu^x /x! , x = 0,1,2,...$$
>
> The results are stored in the indicated column. They are also printed out (unless the command NOPRINT has been used).

Exercises

5-13 Our favorite typist makes an average of only one error every two pages, or 0.5 errors per page.

(a) What is the probability our typist will make no errors on the next page?

(b) 1 error?

(c) Less than 2 errors?

(d) 1 or more errors?

(e) Sketch a histogram of this distribution.

5-14 In high energy physics, the rate at which some particles are emitted has a Poisson distribution. If, on the average, 15 particles are emitted per second,

(a) What is the probability that exactly 15 will be emitted in the next second?

(b) That 15 or fewer will be emitted?

(c) That 15 or more will be emitted?

(d) Find a number such that, approximately 95% of the time, fewer than that number of particles will be emitted.

(e) Sketch a histogram of this distribution.

5-15 If you have a binomial distribution with a large value of n and a small value of p, its probabilities can be closely approximated by a Poisson distribution with mean equal to np.

(a) Use n = 30 and p = 0.01 and compute the corresponding binomial and Poisson probabilities. Do they seem to be pretty close?

(b) Sketch both histograms on the same plot. Do they agree pretty well everywhere?

(c) Repeat (a) but use n = 30 and p = 0.5. How good is the approximation now?

(d) Sketch both histograms from part (c) on the same plot. How well do they agree?

5-16 In the fall of 1971 testimony was presented before the Atomic Energy Commission that the nuclear reactor used in teaching at Penn State University was causing increased infant mortality in the surrounding town, State College, Pa. This reactor had been installed in 1965. The following data for State College were presented as part of the testimony. In addition, data for Lebanon, Pa., a city of similar size and rural character were presented.

	State College, Pa.			Lebanon, Pa.		
Year	Live Births	Infant Deaths	Infant Deaths per 1000 Births	Live Births	Infant Deaths	Infant Deaths per 1000 Births
1962	369	4	10.8	666	16	24.0
1963	403	4	9.9	646	15	23.2
1964	365	5	13.7	668	9	13.5
1965	365	6	16.4	582	10	17.2
1966	327	4	12.2	538	8	14.9
1967	385	6	15.6	501	8	16.0
1968	405	10	24.7	439	5	11.4
1969	441	6	13.6	434	3	6.9
1970	452	8	17.7	500	8	16.0

One of us (Brian Joiner) was asked to examine the evidence in detail and find out whether there was cause for concern or not. A wide variety of statistical procedures were used but one important discussion centered on whether there had been an abnormal peak in infant mortality in State College in 1968.

(a) Suppose we assume that infant deaths follow a Poisson distribution. Over the 9 year period presented in the testimony, there were 53 deaths in State College. On the average, this is $53/9 = 5.9$ per year. Simulate 9 observations from a Poisson distribution with $\mu = 5.9$. Repeat this simulation 10 times. Are peaks such as the one in State College in 1968 unusual?

(b) One of the strongest critics of Penn State's reactor drew the following conclusions from the data:

> Following the end of atmospheric testing by the U.S., U.S.S.R., and Britain in 1962, infant mortality declined steadily for Lebanon, while it rose sharply for State College. Using 1962 as a reference equal to 100, State College rose to $24.7/10.8 = 229$ by 1968 while Lebanon declined to $11.4/24.0 = 48$. Furthermore, not only is there an anomalous rise above the 1962 levels in State College after 1963, but there are two clear peaks of infant mortality rates in 1965 and 1968. Especially the high peak in 1968 has no parallel in Lebanon.

Do you think the data support his conclusions that Penn State's reactor has led to a significant rise in infant mortality? What criticism of his argument can you make?

6

The Normal Distribution

6.1 Normal Populations

Many populations in nature have an approximately normal distribution. These populations have a histogram which looks about like this:

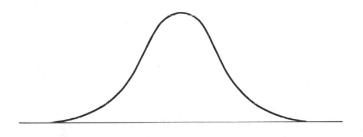

Suppose we take a random sample from a normal population. The histogram of the sample will look somewhat like the histogram of the population (not exactly, of course, because we will not have all of the population, but only a small part of it). A random sample usually has properties that are similar to the properties of the whole population. This includes the general shape of the histogram, the average, the standard deviation, and so on. The larger the sample size, the greater the similarity between the sample and the population.

In Chapter 2 (page 28) we made a histogram of the OTIS scores from the **Cartoon** experiment (page 270). This gave us a histogram of a sample. Do you think this sample might have come from a normal population?

To get some idea about what histograms of samples from a normal distribution look like, we did a small simulation. Exhibit 6.1 gives four histograms. Each is for a random sample of size 100 from a normal distribution. The following pair of instructions was used to make each histogram:

EXHIBIT 6.1

Histograms of 4 Samples from a Normal Population

MIDDLE OF INTERVAL	NUMBER OF OBSERVATIONS	
−2.5	1	*
−2.0	3	***
−1.5	8	********
−1.0	12	************
−0.5	18	******************
0.0	19	*******************
0.5	13	*************
1.0	12	************
1.5	4	****
2.0	5	*****
2.5	3	***
3.0	2	**

MIDDLE OF INTERVAL	NUMBER OF OBSERVATIONS	
−2.5	3	***
−2.0	6	******
−1.5	7	*******
−1.0	4	****
−0.5	17	*****************
0.0	17	*****************
0.5	20	********************
1.0	15	***************
1.5	10	**********
2.0	0	
2.5	1	*

NRANDOM 100 OBSN, MU = 0, SIGMA = 1, PUT IN C1
HISTOGRAM OF DATA IN C1

These histograms show that not all histograms of normal samples look
very "normal," even for samples as large as 100 observations.

EXHIBIT 6.1 (Cont'd)

MIDDLE OF INTERVAL	NUMBER OF OBSERVATIONS	
−3.0	1	*
−2.5	1	*
−2.0	3	***
−1.5	6	******
−1.0	12	************
−0.5	20	********************
0.0	19	*******************
0.5	21	*********************
1.0	12	************
1.5	2	**
2.0	3	***

MIDDLE OF INTERVAL	NUMBER OF OBSERVATIONS	
−4.0	1	*
−3.5	0	
−3.0	0	
−2.5	1	*
−2.0	2	**
−1.5	7	*******
−1.0	18	******************
−0.5	13	*************
0.0	20	********************
0.5	18	******************
1.0	12	************
1.5	5	*****
2.0	2	**
2.5	1	*

Exercises

6-1   Simulate 10 histograms to compare with the histogram of OTIS scores. What values of n, μ and σ might you use? Make sure all histograms (including the one of OTIS scores) are on the same scale, so you can make comparisons easily. Do you think the OTIS scores might have come from a normal population?

6-2   (a) Make a histogram for the SAT math scores for the first set of data in the **Grades** example (page 279). Do you think these scores might have been a random sample from a normal distribution? Why or why not?

(b) Make histograms for each of the other 3 sets of data in the **Grades** example. Compare all 4 histograms. How much do they vary in shape? Do they all look bell-shaped? Do they all look like they might have been random samples from a normal population? Do they look like they might all have come from the *same* population?

6-3   In samples from the normal distribution, about 68% of the observations should fall between $\bar{x} - s$ and $\bar{x} + s$. About 95% should fall between $\bar{x} - 2s$ and $\bar{x} + 2s$. Simulate a random sample of size 100 from a normal distribution. What percentages do you find in these two regions (you choose μ and σ)?

6-4   Repeat Exercise 6-3 using real data. For example, use the OTIS scores from the **Cartoon** data (page 270) or the SAT scores from sample A of the **Grades** data (page 279).

6-5   In general, the "95% rule" mentioned in Exercise 6-3 does not depend too much on the assumption of a normal distribution. (The "68% rule" is sensitive to non-normality.) To illustrate this, look at the Cancer data (page 289). Make a histogram of the glucose measurements for group B. Do you think glucose has a nomal distribution? What percentage of the observations fall between $\bar{x} - 2s$ and $\bar{x} + 2s$?

Advanced Exercises

6-6   Write a program to calculate and print out a table of the normal density function, $\phi(x)$, for x going from -3 to 3 in steps of 0.1.

$$\phi(x) = \frac{1}{\sqrt{2\pi}} \, e^{-x^2/2}, \text{ and } \frac{1}{\sqrt{2\pi}} = 0.3989423$$

Use the advanced form of the GENERATE command (described on page 319) to put the x-values into a column, and the EXPONENTIAL command (described on page 324) to calculate e^x. Plot the values of $\phi(x)$ versus x.

6-7   Most integrals involving the normal curve cannot be evaluated using standard calculus methods. Instead, techniques from numerical analysis are used to get approximate answers. One simple example of this is described below.

(a) Suppose, we want to evaluate

$$\frac{1}{\sqrt{2\pi}} \int_0^1 e^{-x^2/2} \, dx,$$

that is, the area under the standard normal curve from 0 to 1. Divide the interval from 0 to 1 into 10 equal intervals. Then approximate the area under the normal curve by rectangles, as shown in the illustration. If we add up the areas of these 10 rectangles, we get an approximate value for the integral. Write a Minitab program to do this. The program for Exercise 6-6 will help here. Compare this approximate answer to the answer from a table of the normal distribution. How close is this approximation?

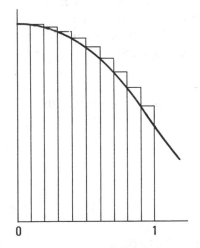

(b) Repeat the approximation technique from part (a), but divide the interval from 0 to 1 into 100 equal intervals. How much better is the approximation?

6-8   (a)   The heights of women are approximately normal with $\mu = 64$ and
             $\sigma = 3$. The heights of men are approximately normal with $\mu = 69$
             and $\sigma = 3$. Suppose you took a sample of 200 people, 100 men and
             100 women, and drew a histogram of the 200 heights. Do you think
             it would look normal? Should it look normal? Use Minitab to simu-
             late this experiment. Simulate 100 men's heights and put them in
             c1. Simulate 100 women's heights and put them in c2. Then JOIN
             c1 TO c2 and put the combined sample into c3. Then get a histogram
             of the data. Does it look normal?

       (b)   Part (a) is an example of a mixture of two populations. Let's try a
             slightly more extreme example. Take a sample of 200 observa-
             tions—100 of them from a normal population with $\mu = 5$ and
             $\sigma = 1$, and the other 100 from a normal population with $\mu = 10$ and
             $\sigma = 1$. Get a histogram of the 200 observations. Does this histogram
             seem to indicate that there might be 2 populations mixed together
             in the sample?

6.2 How Sample Means Vary—Normal Populations

In Section 3.3, we simulated sampling heights of college-age women. We
will repeat that simulation, using the techniques of Section 3.7, to further study the properties of sample means. The following program simulates 100 experiments of drawing a random sample of n = 10 heights
and finding the sample mean, $\bar{x}$:

```
NOPRINT
NRANDOM 100 OBSN. MU = 64, SIGMA = 3, PUT INTO C1
NRAN      100            64          3          C2
NRAN      100            64          3          C3

   .        .            .           .          .

   .        .            .           .          .

   .        .            .           .          .

NRAN      100            64          3          C10
ADD C1-C10, PUT SUMS INTO C11
DIVIDE C11 BY 10, PUT INTO C12 (XBARS)
AVERAGE C12
STANDARD DEVIATION OF C12
HISTOGRAM OF XBARS IN C12, FIRST MIDPT 55, WIDTH .5
STOP
```

Part of the output is in Exhibit 6.2. Keep in mind that in real life you usually have just *one* sample—not 100. That one sample would give just one x̄—not 100 of them. We did this simulation to get 100 x̄'s so we could study how x̄ varies from sample to sample. The histogram in Exhibit 6.2 shows that the 100 x̄'s did vary—but not much. All of them are between 61.25 and 66.25, and well over half are between 63 and 65.

On the histogram of the 100 x̄'s, we sketched a histogram of the population of individual heights. This underlying population is normal, so its histogram is bell-shaped. What about the histogram of the x̄'s? It seems to be pretty much bell-shaped too. If we simulated many more x̄'s, the histogram would be even closer to bell-shaped. This illustrates the important fact that if the underlying population is normal, the distribution of the x̄'s will also be normal.

Also notice that the average of the 100 x̄'s is 64.002 which is very close to 64, the average of the population of individual observations. Even if we take samples from non-normal distributions, it will always be true that the mean of the population of x̄'s will be equal to the mean of the population of individual observations. In symbols, we write

$$\mu_{\bar{x}} = \mu_x$$

The distribution of x̄'s does differ from that of the individual observations in one important respect—it is much less spread out. And, in fact, for random samples of size n from any population,

$$\sigma_{\bar{x}} = \frac{\sigma_x}{\sqrt{n}}.$$

In our simulation, $\sigma_x = 3$ and $\sqrt{n} = \sqrt{10} = 3.16$, so $\sigma_{\bar{x}} = 3/3.16 = 0.95$. This value, 0.95, is the standard deviation for the population of all x̄'s. The standard deviation of our collection of 100 x̄'s is 0.93582, which is fairly close.

Exercise

6-9 (a) Run the program used in Section 6.2, but use n = 2, instead of n = 10. Discuss the output.

(b) Run this program using n = 1, then n = 6, then n = 16. Compare all 5 outputs (n = 1, 2, 6, 10, 16). You might make sure all histograms are on the same scale. How does the distribution of x̄ change as n increases?

EXHIBIT 6.2

One Hundred Means of Samples of Size 10 from a Normal Population with Mean 64 and Standard Deviation 3

```
-- AVERAGE C12
   AVERAGE =     64.002
-- STANDARD DEVIATION OF C12
   ST. DEV. =    0.93582
-- HISTOGRAM OF XBARS IN C12, FIRST MIDPT 59, WIDTH .5
   MIDDLE OF      NUMBER OF
   INTERVAL       OBSERVATIONS
     59.0          0
     59.5          0
     60.0          0
     60.5          0
     61.0          0
     61.5          2        **
     62.0          1        *
     62.5          3        ***
     63.0         13        **************
     63.5         21        *********************
     64.0         24        ************************
     64.5         14        **************
     65.0         14        **************
     65.5          5        *****
     66.0          3        ***
```

population of individual heights

6.3 Sample Means—Non-Normal Populations

In the preceding section, we simulated drawing samples of n = 10 observations from a normal population. Here we will draw samples from a population which is very different from normal—the population of the numbers which come up when you roll a die. This population has just 6 values (1,2,3,4,5,6), and all are equally likely. As in Section 6.2, we'll take a sample of 10 observations and calculate $\bar{x}$. The program below does this 100 times and gets a histogram of the 100 $\bar{x}$'s. It also finds the mean and standard deviation of the 100 $\bar{x}$'s.

```
NOPRINT
IRANDOM 100 OBS. BETWEEN 1 AND 6, PUT INTO C1
IRAN      100                1    6           C2
IRAN      100                1    6           C3

 .         .                 .    .           .

 .         .                 .    .           .

 .         .                 .    .           .

IRAN     ·100                1    6           C10
ADD C1 C10, PUT SUM INTO C11
DIVIDE C11 BY 10, PUT INTO C12 (XBARS)
AVERAGE C12
STANDARD DEVIATION C12
HISTOGRAM OF C12
STOP
```

Look at the histogram in Exhibit 6.3. The $\bar{x}$'s have an approximately normal distribution even though we sampled from a clearly non-normal population. In general, if samples are taken from a population with virtually any shape, the means of the samples will have an approximately normal distribution. The approximation becomes better as the sample size, n, increases. (This rather amazing property is proven mathematically in the *Central Limit Theorem*, which is discussed in advanced statistics courses.)

Exercise

6-10 (a) Run the program used in Section 6.3, but use n = 2 instead of n = 10. Compare your output with that in Exhibit 6.3.

 (b) Run this program using n = 1, then n = 6, then n = 16. Compare all 5 outputs (n = 1, 2, 6, 10, 16). You might make sure all histograms are on the same scale. How does the distribution of $\bar{x}$ change as n increases?

EXHIBIT 6.3

Histogram of 100 Sample Means from a Non-Normal Population

```
-- AVERAGE C12
   AVERAGE =    3.5250
-- STANDARD DEVIATION C12
   ST. DEV.=    0.53510
-- HISTOGRAM OF C12
   MIDDLE OF      NUMBER OF
   INTERVAL       OBSERVATIONS
       2.2          2     **
       2.4          1     *
       2.6          4     ****
       2.8          3     ***
       3.0          7     *******
       3.2         13     *************
       3.4         14     **************
       3.6         10     **********
       3.8         18     ******************
       4.0         10     **********
       4.2         12     ************
       4.4          5     *****
       4.6          0
       4.8          0
       5.0          1     *
```

6.4 Probability Plots

If we want to decide whether a sample of data might have come from a normal population, we could look at a histogram of the sample. We did this in Section 6.1 with the OTIS scores. A second way is to plot the data on a special kind of graph paper, called "normal probability" paper. This plot, called a *normal probability plot*, will be approximately a straight line if the data came from a normal population. If the plot curves substantially, then very likely the data did not come from a normal population.

Minitab can be used to make a normal probability plot. If c1 contains a set of data, use the two commands

```
NSCORES OF C1 PUT IN C2
PLOT C1 VS C2
```

NSCORES OF C PUT IN C

Calculates the normal scores of a set of data.

Example

NSCORES OF C1 PUT IN C2

Col. 1	Col. 2
1.1	−.20
1.9	1.28
.8 ⟶	−1.28
1.3	.64
1.2	.20
.9	.64

Loosely speaking, the normal scores can be defined as follows: The number −1.28, in c2 is the smallest value you would get, on the average, if you took samples of size $n = 6$ from a standard normal population (with $\mu = 0$, $\sigma = 1$). This number is placed next to the smallest value in c1. The number −.64, in c2, is the second smallest value you would expect to get in a sample of size 6 from a standard normal. It is placed next to the second smallest value in c1. This is continued for all 6 values in c1. (More precisely, the i-th smallest normal score is the $(i - 3/8)/(n + 1/4)$ percent point of the standard normal distribution.)

Exhibit 6.4 gives a probability plot of the OTIS scores from the **Cartoon** experiment (page 270). Again we are faced with the problem of

EXHIBIT 6.4

Normal Probability Plot of OTIS Scores From the Cartoon Experiment

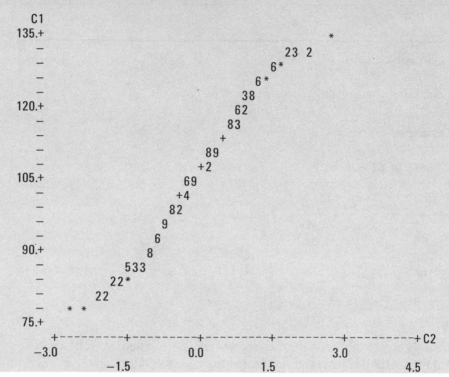

```
-- PLOT DATA IN C1 VS NORMAL SCORES IN C2

   C1
 135.+                                                    *
   -                                          23 2
   -                                     6 *
   -                                  6 *
   -                                 38
 120.+                               62
   -                               83
   -                             +
   -                          89
   -                          +2
 105.+                       69
   -                       +4
   -                      82
   -                    9
   -                  6
  90.+               8
   -              533
   -            22*
   -          22
   -     *  *
  75.+
     +---------+---------+---------+---------+---------+ C2
    -3.0               0.0               3.0
          -1.5              1.5               4.5
```

judging a picture. Does this plot look straight? There is certainly some curvature. But is it curved enough to doubt the normality of the OTIS scores? Good judgment of graphs comes from experience. Most people find it easier to learn how to judge probability plots than histograms.

Exercises

6-11   (a) Simulate 100 observations from a normal population with $\mu = 0$, $\sigma = 1$. Get a histogram and a probability plot.

    (b) Repeat part (a) until you have 5 histograms and 5 probability plots. How do the histograms and plots compare?

6-12   Simulate 5 probability plots to compare with the OTIS scores. (Choose appropriate values for μ, σ, and n.) Compare these with the probability plot of OTIS scores. Does there seem to be any strong evidence that the OTIS scores did not come from a normal population?

6-13   Get a probability plot for the SAT math scores for the first set of data from the **Grades** example. Compare this with the histogram you got in Exercise 6-2. What is your opinion of the normality of SAT math scores now?

7

One Sample Confidence Intervals and Tests for Population Means

Minitab can be used to obtain confidence intervals for population means, or do hypothesis tests for population means. In this chapter, we will look at one population at a time. In the next chapter, we'll compare two populations.

All procedures discussed in this chapter, and indeed in this whole book, for making inferences about populations require that our sample be drawn at *random* from the population. In practice, we rarely have random samples, so most of our inferences must be made with some degree of caution.

The techniques in this chapter all require one more condition if they are to be *exactly* valid. They require that the population from which our sample is drawn have a *normal distribution*. This would seem to rule out most applications of these techniques since no real population is ever *exactly* normal. But, in fact, it does not. Student's t procedures, discussed in this chapter, are very useful even when the population is not normal because they are *robust* to the shape of the population. Loosely speaking, this means that they really don't care much about the shape of the population. If we use these procedures to construct a 95% confidence interval for a population mean when the population is not normal, the real confidence might not be exactly 95%. It might be 94% or 97%. But it won't be very far off. It won't be as far off as, say, 50%. We'll be closer than that, no matter what shape the population has. This is what we mean when we say that Student's t procedures are *robust* with respect to the shape of the population. We should mention that even though these procedures usually work well for non-normal populations, some of the methods in Chapter 12 are more powerful for many non-normal populations.

Suppose our sample is not drawn at *random* from the population. Then our confidence may be way off. It may be only 50%, or even only 10%. Student's t procedures, and all the other procedures of basic statistics, are *not robust* to non-random sampling. The moral is, when collecting data, strive for a random sample. And, when interpreting results, keep a wary eye for the effect of non-random sampling.

7.1 Confidence Interval for μ: σ Known

Suppose we want to estimate the mean μ of a population. We would take a sample, calculate $\bar{x}$, and use this as a point estimate of μ. But how close to μ is $\bar{x}$ likely to be? This is where a confidence interval can help. A 95% confidence interval is an interval, calculated from the sample, which will cover the unknown mean, μ, 95% of the time. The value 95% is called the confidence level of the interval. Of course, we can calculate an interval with any specific confidence (e.g., 99% or 90% or 80%).

Suppose we happen to know the standard deviation of the population. Then we could use the ZINTERVAL command to find a confidence interval for the population mean.

ZINTERVAL K PERCENT CONFIDENCE, SIGMA = K, DATA IN **C**

Calculates the usual, normal theory, two-sided confidence interval for the population mean, μ.

$$\bar{x} - z^*(\sigma/\sqrt{n}) \text{ to } \bar{x} + z^*(\sigma/\sqrt{n})$$

Here σ is the known value of the population standard deviation, x is the mean of the sample, n is the number of observations in the sample, and z^* is a value from the table of the normal distribution. For example, for 95% confidence, $z^* = 1.96$.

This command prints out the sample mean, the sample standard deviation, and the confidence interval.

As an example, suppose we want to find a 95% confidence interval for μ based on a sample of 8 observations: 4.9, 4.7, 5.1, 5.4, 4.7, 5.2, 4.8, 5.1. If we knew that $\sigma = 0.2$ then we could use the following program:

```
SET DATA INTO C1
4.9, 4.7, 5.1, 5.4, 4.7, 5.2, 4.8, 5.1
ZINTERVAL 95 PERCENT CONFIDENCE, SIGMA = 0.2, DATA IN C1
STOP
```

The ZINTERVAL command gave the following results:

```
-- ZINTERVAL 95 PERCENT CONFIDENCE, SIGMA = 0.2, DATA IN C1
   C1    N = 8    MEAN = 4.9875    ST.DEV. = 0.253
   THE ASSUMED SIGMA = 0.2000
   A 95.00 PERCENT C.I. FOR MU IS ( 4.8487, 5.1263)
```

The 95% confidence interval goes from 4.8487 to 5.1263. This set of data happens to be one we generated ourselves using the procedures in Chapter 3, so we know $\mu = 5$. Since 5 is inside our confidence interval, we had a successful interval. We know that in the long run 95% of our intervals will be successful and 5% will be failures. Here we got one of the lucky ones.

Exercise

7-1   An experiment consists of choosing $n = 9$ men at random and measuring their heights. Assume that the heights of men are normal, with $\mu = 69$ inches and $\sigma = 3$ inches. Simulate the results of this experiment with the NRANDOM command. Then find a 90% confidence interval for μ, using the command ZINTERVAL. Repeat this for a total of twenty samples.

(a) Plot the twenty 90% confidence intervals on a common axis, as in Exhibit 4.2.

(b) How many of the intervals contain μ?

(c) Would you expect all twenty of the intervals to contain μ? Explain.

(d) Do all the intervals have the same width? Why or why not?

(e) Suppose you took 95% intervals instead of 90%. Would they be narrower or wider?

(f) How many of your intervals contain 72? 70? 69?

(g) Suppose you took samples of size n = 100 instead of n = 9. Would you expect more or fewer intervals to cover 72? 70? 69? What about the width of the intervals for n = 100? Would they be longer or shorter than for n = 9?

(h) Suppose you calculated twenty 90% confidence intervals for *real* data. About how many would you expect to contain the true μ? Could you tell which?

7.2 Confidence Interval for μ: σ Not Known

Usually we don't know the standard deviation of the population and must estimate it from the data at hand. Then we can use Student's t confidence interval procedure and the TINTERVAL command.

TINTERVAL WITH K PERCENT CONFIDENCE FOR DATA IN C

Calculates the usual two-sided t confidence interval for the population mean, μ.

$$\bar{x} - t^*(s/\sqrt{n}) \text{ to } \bar{x} + t^*(s/\sqrt{n})$$

Here $\bar{x}$ is the sample mean, s is the sample standard deviation, n is the sample size, and t^* is the value found in a table of the Student's t distribution with (n − 1) degrees of freedom.

The sample mean, standard deviation, and confidence interval are printed out.

As an example, suppose we want to find a 90% confidence interval based on the random sample: 4.9, 4.7, 5.1, 5.4, 4.7, 5.2, 4.8, 5.1. We could use the following program:

```
SET INTO C2
4.9, 4.7, 5.1, 5.4, 4.7, 5.2, 4.8, 5.1
TINTERVAL WITH 90 PERCENT CONFIDENCE, DATA IN C2
STOP
```

The TINTERVAL command gave the following results:

```
-- TINTERVAL WITH 90 PERCENT CONFIDENCE, DATA IN C2
   C2    N =  8     MEAN =   4.9875      ST.DEV. =   0.253
   A 90.00 PERCENT C.I. FOR MU IS (    4.8179,     5.1571)
```

Based upon this output we might say, "We estimate the mean to be about 4.99, and we are 90% confident that it is somewhere between 4.82 and 5.16."

Exercises

7-2   (a) Get a histogram for the SAT verbal scores in sample B of the **Grades** data (page 279). Calculate $\bar{x}$ and get a 95% confidence interval for μ = mean score.

     (b) Also get a 90% and a 99% confidence interval for mean SAT verbal scores. How do they compare with the 95% confidence interval in part (a)? Do they have the same centers? Do they have the same widths?

7-3   Repeat the simulation of Exercise 7-1. But now assume σ is unknown and use the TINTERVAL command. Get a total of twenty confidence intervals.

     (a) How many of the twenty intervals contain μ?

     (b) Would you *expect* all of the intervals to contain μ? Explain.

     (c) Do all of the intervals have the same width?

     (d) Compare the t intervals of this exercise to the z intervals of Exercise 7-1. On the average, which kind of interval seems to be wider?

(e) Plot the twenty t intervals on a common axis, as in Exhibit 4.2.

(f) Suppose you calculated 95% t intervals instead of 90%. Would they be narrower or wider?

(g) How many of your intervals contain 72? 70? 69?

(h) Suppose you took samples of size n = 100 instead of n = 9. Would you expect more or fewer intervals to cover 72? 70? 69? What about the size of the intervals for n = 100? Would they be longer or shorter than those for n = 9?

(i) Suppose you calculated twenty 90% t intervals for *real* data. About how many would you expect to contain the true μ? Could you tell which?

7-4   For the **Integration** data (page 287) construct a 95% confidence interval for the mean of each group.

(a) Sketch these 4 confidence intervals, side by side, on a piece of paper.

(b) Does it seem likely that the population mean is the same for the 4 groups?

(c) What is the practical significance of your answer to part (b)?

7.3 Test of Hypothesis for μ: σ Known

Suppose a machine is set to roll aluminum into 0.0400-inch thick sheets. You suspect the machine is misadjusted. So you take 15 measurements of sheet thickness and get

.0397   .0393   .0402   .0409   .0393   .0404   .0396   .0404
.0399   .0399   .0397   .0398   .0413   .0404   .0395

This sample has a mean of 0.0398, which is below the desired mean of $\mu = 0.0400$. Is this discrepancy just due to random fluctuation or does it indicate the machine is misadjusted? To answer this, we must have some idea of how much the thickness usually varies from sheet to sheet. Suppose we happen to know that the standard deviation of sheet thickness is $\sigma = 0.0005$. Then we can use Minitab's zTEST command to test the null hypothesis that the machine is probably adjusted, H_0: $\mu = 0.0400$, versus the alternative hypothesis that the machine is misadjusted, H_1: $\mu \neq 0.0400$.

ZTEST OF POPULATION MU = K, WHERE SIGMA = K, DATA

IN C

Tests the null hypothesis $H_0: \mu = K$ against the alternative hypothesis $H_1: \mu \neq K$, where μ is the population mean. This command calculates the usual, normal theory test statistic

$$z = \frac{\bar{x} - K}{\sigma / \sqrt{n}}$$

Here x is the sample mean, n is the size of the sample, σ is the known population standard deviation, and K is the hypothesized value of the population mean.

The sample mean, sample standard deviation, value of z, and the significance level are all printed out. A two-sided test is done. (Another form of this command, explained in Section 7.6 (page 132) does one-sided tests.)

The following program does the test for the machine data:

```
SET DATA INTO C1
.0397   .0393   .0402   .0409   .0393   .0404   .0396   .0404
.0399   .0399   .0397   .0398   .0413   .0404   .0395
ZTEST MU = 0.0400, SIGMA = 0.0005, DATA IN C1
STOP
```

The ZTEST command gave the following results:

```
-- ZTEST MU = 0.0400, SIGMA = 0.0005, DATA IN C1
   C1      N = 15      MEAN = 0.040020      ST.DEV. = 0.000576
   TEST OF MU =   0.0400 VS. MU N.E. 0.0400
```

```
THE ASSUMED SIGMA =    0.0005
Z = 0.155
THE TEST IS SIGNIFICANT AT 0.8769
CANNOT REJECT AT ALPHA = 0.05
```

The output says we cannot reject the null hypothesis at $\alpha = 0.05$. This means that we must expect a value of $\bar{x}$ this far from the mean at least 5% of the time even if the machine is properly adjusted. Thus, the discrepancy between $\bar{x}$ and μ is not extreme enough to give us strong evidence that the machine is misadjusted.

7.4 Test of Hypothesis for μ: σ Not Known

We usually do not know σ, and must estimate it from the data at hand. In this case we can use the TTEST command.

TTEST OF POPULATION MU = K, DATA IN C

Tests the null hypothesis $H_0: \mu = K$ against the alternative hypothesis $H_1: \mu \neq K$.

This command calculates the usual Student's t-test statistic

$$t = \frac{\bar{x} - K}{s / \sqrt{n}}.$$

Here $\bar{x}$ is the sample mean, s is the sample standard deviation, n is the size of the sample, and K is the hypothesized value of the population mean.

The sample mean, standard deviation, the value of t, and the significance level are printed out. A two-sided test is done. (Another version of this command, described in Section 7.6 (page 132) does one-sided tests.)

Suppose we once again test whether or not the aluminum sheet machine mentioned in the previous section is correctly adjusted. But this time let's not assume we know the value of σ. Then the following program can be used:

```
SET DATA INTO C1
.0397  .0393  .0402  .0409  .0393  .0404  .0396  .0404
.0399  .0399  .0397  .0398  .0413  .0404  .0395
TTEST OF MU = 0.0400, DATA IN C1
STOP
```

The TTEST command gave the following output:

```
-- TTEST OF MU = 0.0400, DATA IN C1
   C1    N =  15    MEAN =  0.040020    ST.DEV. =0.000576
   TEST OF MU =   0.0400 VS. MU N.E.   0.0400
   T = 0.134
   THE TEST IS SIGNIFICANT AT 0.8949
   CANNOT REJECT AT ALPHA = 0.05
```

Again, we find no statistically significant evidence that the rolling machine is out of adjustment. The hypothesized value of μ, 0.0400, is not rejected.

Exercise

7-5   Do a test to see if there is evidence that the pre-professionals who participated in the **Cartoon** experiment (page 270) have OTIS scores which differ significantly from the national norm of 100. First get a histogram of the data. What do you think? Then do the appropriate test, using $\alpha = 0.05$.

7.5 An Example

Suppose that over the last 5 years, students attending a university have had an average SAT verbal score of 615. Suppose we want to compare this year's freshman class with the students of the preceding 5 years. A sample of 50 students was drawn at random (we'll use sample A of the **Grades** data from page 279). The following program was run to do some calculations for an analysis:

```
READ VERBAL SAT SCORES INTO C1
```

(data from page 280)

```
HISTOGRAM OF C1
TINTERVAL 90 PERCENT CONFIDENCE INTERVAL FOR DATA IN C1
TINTERVAL 95 PERCENT, C1
TTEST MU = 615, ON DATA IN C1
STOP
```

We can see from the output in Exhibit 7.1, that the sample from this year's class has a mean verbal score of 596.26 which is 18.7 points lower than the average for the preceeding 5 years. Is it *significantly* different? Well, the 90% confidence interval for μ, the unknown mean for all of this year's freshmen, does not contain 615. So we are 90% "confident" that μ is not 615. If we perform a t-test for H_0: $\mu = 615$ versus H_1: $\mu \neq 615$ using $\alpha = .10$, we will reject the null hypothesis. Actually, we really don't need to perform the test since we've calculated the corresponding confidence interval. We reject the null hypothesis exactly when the corresponding confidence interval does not cover the hypothesized mean. So, for this sample, we can say $\mu \neq 615$, if $\alpha = 0.10$. Suppose we repeat this procedure with a 95% confidence interval and do the corresponding $\alpha = 0.05$ test. The 95% confidence interval on the output does cover 615. Thus, we cannot reject H_0, if we use $\alpha = 0.05$.

So we can reject if $\alpha = 0.10$, and we cannot reject if $\alpha = 0.05$. What about $\alpha = 0.06$, or $\alpha = 0.07$? Just where is the dividing line between where we can reject and cannot reject? This dividing line is called the *attained significance level* or the *p value*, and is part of the output from the TTEST command. In Exhibit 7.1, we see that the attained significance is 0.0788. Thus we can reject if we use an $\alpha > .0788$, but we cannot reject if we use an $\alpha < .0788$. Equivalently, if the null hypothesis is true, we will observe a result this extreme or more extreme only 0.0788 (about 8%) of the time.

EXHIBIT 7.1

SAT Verbal Scores

```
-- HISTOGRAM OF C1
   MIDDLE OF       NUMBER OF
   INTERVAL        OBSERVATIONS
      400.         1    *
      450.         1    *
      500.         7    *******
      550.         9    *********
      600.        15    ***************
      650.        10    **********
      700.         5    *****
      750.         2    **
-- TINTERVAL 90 PERCENT CONFIDENCE FOR DATA IN C1
   C1    N =  50     MEAN =   596.26     ST.DEV. =   73.8
   A 90.00   PERCENT C.I. FOR MU IS (   578.7512,   613.7681)
-- TINTERVAL 95 PERCENT, C1
   C1    N =  50     MEAN =   596.26     ST.DEV. =   73.8
   A 95.00   PERCENT C.I. FOR MU IS (   575.2732,   617.2461)
-- TTEST MU =  615, ON DATA IN C1
   C1    N =  50     MEAN =   596.26     ST.DEV. =   73.8
   TEST OF MU =   615.0000 VS. MU N.E.   615.0000
   T =  -1.795
   THE TEST IS SIGNIFICANT AT   0.0788
   CANNOT REJECT AT ALPHA = 0.05
```

Exercises

7-6   (a)   Get a 95% confidence interval for the mean SAT math scores, using
           sample A from the **Grades** data (page 279).

      (b)   Get 3 more 95% confidence intervals, one for each of the other 3 sets
           of data (samples B, C, and D).

(c) How do these 4 confidence intervals compare? Do they all have the same width? The same center? Do they overlap some common value?

7-7   Imagine choosing n = 16 women at random and measuring their heights. Assume that the heights of women are normal, with $\mu = 64$ inches and $\sigma = 3$ inches. Simulate a sample of 16 heights with the NRANDOM command. Then test the null hypothesis H_0: $\mu = 64$ versus the alternative that H_1: $\mu \neq 64$, using $\alpha = 0.10$. Assume σ is unknown. Repeat this for a total of 20 tests.

(a) In how many tests did you fail to reject H_0? That is, how many times did you make the "correct decision"?

(b) How many times did you make an "incorrect decision" (that is, reject H_0)? On the average, how many times out of 20 would you expect to make the wrong decision?

(c) What is the attained significance level of each test? Are they all the same?

(d) Suppose you used $\alpha = 0.05$ instead of $\alpha = 0.10$. Does this change any of your decisions to reject or not? Should it?

7-8   As in Exercise 7-7, simulate choosing 16 women at random, measuring their heights, and testing H_0: $\mu = 64$ versus H_1: $\mu \neq 64$, but this time assume that the population really has a mean of $\mu = 63$, instead of 64. Thus, use the command NRANDOM with $\mu = 63$ and $\sigma = 3$ to simulate the samples. Use $\alpha = 0.10$ and assume σ is unknown. Repeat this for a total of 20 tests.

(a) In how many tests did you reject H_0? That is, how many times did you make the "correct decision"? How many times did you make an "incorrect decision"?

(b) What we are investigating here is what's called the *power of a test*, that is, how well the test procedure does in detecting that your null hypothesis is wrong, when indeed it is wrong. Repeat the above simulation, but now assume the true population mean is $\mu = 62$ (still use $\sigma = 3$ and the same null hypothesis). How often did you make the correct decision (reject) in these 20 tests? On the average, would you expect to do better if the true mean were 62 or if the true mean were 63?

7-9   In Exercise 2-16 (page 35) we started an investigation of whether 3 laboratory variables, AKP, P, and LDH, could be used to improve the usefulness of the band-test for cancer. Now use confidence intervals to help your investigation.

(a) Get a 95% confidence interval for the mean value of AKP, for each of the 4 groups in the **Cancer** study (page 289). Compare these 4 intervals. (Try graphing them side by side.) Do they all overlap some common value? Where are the biggest differences? Do the confidence intervals tell you anything new? Does the analysis in Exercise 2-16 tell you anything you cannot learn from the confidence intervals?

(b) Repeat part (a), using P.

(c) Repeat part (a), using LDH.

7.6 One-Sided Tests

To do one-sided tests we can use the more general form of the ZTEST and TTEST commands.

(Continued from pages 126 and 127.)

ZTEST OF MU $=$ **K** VS. THE ALTERNATE $=$ **K**, SIGMA $=$ **K**, ON

DATA IN **C**

TTEST OF MU $=$ **K** VS. THE ALTERNATE $=$ **K**, ON DATA IN **C**

We can specify the alternative hypothesis using the following codes:

$$\text{alternate} = -1 \text{ means } \mu < \text{hypothesized value}$$
$$\text{alternate} = 0 \text{ means } \mu \neq \text{hypothesized value}$$
$$\text{alternate} = +1 \text{ means } \mu > \text{hypothesized value}$$

(Note: using alternate $= 0$ is equivalent to the commands on pages 126 and 127.)

Example

Suppose we want to test the hypothesis $\mu = 5.3$ versus the alternative hypothesis $\mu > 5.3$. If we don't know σ, and if the data are in c1, then we can use the command

TTEST MU = 5.3, ALTERNATIVE +1, ON DATA IN C1

8

Comparing Two Means: Confidence Intervals and Tests

Often we are interested in the question, "How different are the means of these two populations?" This chapter shows how Minitab can be used to answer this question in the most common situations.

The remarks in Chapter 7 concerning normal populations apply here. That is, while these methods are "exact" only if the populations have normal distributions, they still work quite well for most populations. However, the "nonparametric" methods of Chapter 12 are more powerful for many non-normal populations.

The methods of this chapter do require random samples, as do most statistical methods.

8.1 Differences Between Two Means: Paired Data

In 1971, data were collected at a medical center in Pennsylvania concerning the blood cholesterol levels of heart-attack patients. Twenty-eight heart-attack patients had their cholesterol levels measured 2 days after the attack, 4 days after, and 14 days after. In addition, the cholesterol levels were recorded for a control group of 30 people who had not had a heart attack. Part of these data were given in Section 1.1 and the full set is given in Exhibit 8.1.

Here we will analyze only the first two columns of data from this table. (Further analyses, given in the exercises, will involve the other two columns of data.)

How did cholesterol level change between the second and fourth days

EXHIBIT 8.1

Blood Cholesterol Levels After Heart Attacks
(Note: —1 indicates a missing value.)

	Experimental Group		*Control Group*
2 Days After	*4 Days After*	*14 Days After*	
270	218	256	196
236	234	—1	232
210	214	242	200
142	116	—1	242
280	200	—1	206
272	276	256	178
160	146	142	184
220	182	216	198
226	238	248	160
242	288	—1	182
186	190	168	182
266	236	236	198
206	244	—1	182
318	258	200	238
294	240	264	198
282	294	—1	188
234	220	264	166
224	200	—1	204
276	220	188	182
282	186	182	178
360	352	294	212
310	202	214	164
280	218	—1	230
278	248	198	186
288	278	—1	162
288	248	256	182
244	270	280	218
236	242	204	170
			200
			176

following the heart attack? This is an example of *paired data*—each value in the sample for 2 days after a heart attack is paired with one particular value in the sample for 4 days after an attack. We are interested in estimating how much *difference* there is between the mean of the population of all cholesterol levels 2 days after a heart attack, μ_1, and the mean of the population of all cholesterol levels 4 days after an attack, μ_2. Put another way, we are interested in the average amount of *change* in the cholesterol levels, $(\mu_2 - \mu_1)$.

Confidence Interval

To get a confidence interval for the difference $(\mu_2 - \mu_1)$, we look at the difference in each individual's cholesterol level. The mean of these differences gives us a point estimate of $(\mu_2 - \mu_1)$. To get some idea of the uncertainty in this estimate, we compute a t confidence interval for $(\mu_2 - \mu_1)$. In Minitab, we can use a program like the following:

```
READ TWO-DAY INTO C1, FOUR-DAY INTO C2
270  218
236  234

 .    .

 .    .

 .    .

236  242
SUBTRACT C1 FROM C2, PUT DIFFERENCES INTO C3
TINTERVAL 95 PERCENT CONFIDENCE, DIFFERENCES IN C3
STOP
```

This program produced the following results:

```
-- TINTERVAL 95 PERCENT CONFIDENCE, DIFFERENCES IN C3
   C3     N =   28     MEAN =   -23.286     ST.DEV. =   38.3
   A 95.00 PERCENT C.I. FOR MU IS: (  -38.1320,  -8.4394)
```

The output tells us that, based on these 28 changes, our best estimate of the average change in cholesterol level is -23.286. The minus sign tells us that the average change was negative, so cholesterol level decreased on the average. The rest of the output tells us that we can be 95% confident that the average change is between -38.1320 and -8.4394. Thus, we can be 95% confident that cholesterol level decreased by at least 8.4394, but by no more than 38.1320.

Paired t-Test

To do a paired t-test with Minitab, just do a t-test on the differences. For example, to test H_0: $\mu_2 = \mu_1$, or equivalently, H_0: $(\mu_2 - \mu_1) = 0$, for the cholesterol data, we could use the following program:

```
READ TWO-DAY INTO C1, FOUR-DAY INTO C2
244  270
270  218
 .    .

 .    .

 .    .
236  242
SUBTRACT C1 FROM C2, PUT DIFFERENCES INTO C3
TTEST MU = 0, FOR DIFFERENCES IN C3
STOP
```

This program produced the following output:

```
-- TTEST MU = 0, ON DIFFERENCES IN C3
   C3   N =  28     MEAN =  -23.286     ST.DEV. =   38.3
   TEST OF MU =   0.0     VS. MU N.E.   0.0
   T = -3.219
   THE TEST IS SIGNIFICANT AT 0.0033
```

We see, as before, that the estimate of the mean change is -23.286. Based on these 28 changes, there is statistically significant evidence, at the 0.05 level, that there was a change in cholesterol level. The attained level of significance is 0.0033. Thus, we could reject the null hypothesis that $(\mu_2 - \mu_1) = 0$, if we had used $\alpha = 0.05$, or $\alpha = 0.01$, or any value of α down to 0.0033.

Exercises

8-1   (a) We just saw that the cholesterol level of heart-attack patients de-
           creases by about 23 units between the second and fourth day after
           a heart attack. Estimate how much change there is between the
           fourth and fourteenth day following the attack. Notice there are
           some missing observations in the data. You will have to omit those
           patients for which we don't have a reading for 14 days after an
           attack.

      (b) What effect might the missing data have on your answer to part (a)?
           Do you think the patients who have a missing value for 14 days after

a heart attack might differ from the rest of the patients? Do the data show any evidence of this?

8-2   (a)   How does pulse rate change with exercise? Compare the pulse rate before and after exercise for the 35 students in the experimental (i.e., those who ran) group of the **Pulse** experiment (page 285).

(b)   Also compare the "first pulse rate" with the "second pulse rate" for the 57 students in the control (i.e., those who didn't run) group of the **Pulse** experiment. Is there any significant change here?

8.2 Difference Between Two Means: Independent Samples (Unpaired Data)

Is the average pulse rate for males (μ_1) different from the average pulse rate for females (μ_2)? And if so, by how much? We'll use the data for the 57 men and 35 women who participated in the **Pulse** experiment (page 285) to help answer this question. Let's use the "first pulse rate" data, since this was taken before anyone exercised.

Here we have two independent samples: one of 57 males and the other of 35 females. There is no pairing between the two samples. The first male is not associated with any particular female, nor is the second, and so on. (These data might be considered paired if, for example, we had male-female pairs who were brother and sister.)

Population Variances Assumed Equal

If we can reasonably assume that the two populations have approximately the same variance, then we can use the POOLED command.

> **POOL**ED T FIRST SAMPLE IN **C** AND SECOND SAMPLE IN **C**
>
> Let μ_1 be the mean of the first population, and μ_2 the mean of the second. The two populations are assumed to have equal variances. This command does two things:

(a) It finds a two-sided 95% confidence interval for $(\mu_2 - \mu_1)$.

(b) It tests $H_0:\mu_1 = \mu_2$ versus $H_1:\mu_1 \neq \mu_2$.

Both (a) and (b) use the following pooled estimate for the common variance of the two populations:

$$s_p^2 = \frac{(n_1 - 1)s_1^2 + (n_2 - 1)s_2^2}{n_1 + n_2 - 2}$$

The confidence interval in (a) goes from

$$(\bar{x}_1 - \bar{x}_2) - t^* s_p \sqrt{\frac{1}{n_1} + \frac{1}{n_2}} \quad \text{to}$$

$$(\bar{x}_1 - \bar{x}_2) + t^* s_p \sqrt{\frac{1}{n_1} + \frac{1}{n_2}},$$

where t^* is the value from a t-table, corresponding to 95% confidence and $n_1 + n_2 - 2$ degrees of freedom. The test statistic for (b) is

$$t = \frac{(\bar{x}_1 - \bar{x}_2)}{s_p \sqrt{\frac{1}{n_1} + \frac{1}{n_2}}}.$$

Here $\bar{x}_1$ is the sample mean of the first column, $\bar{x}_2$ is the sample mean of the second column, s_1 and s_2 are the sample standard deviations of the two columns, and n_1 and n_2 are the two sample sizes. Minitab prints out n_1, n_2, $\bar{x}_1$, $\bar{x}_2$, s_1, s_2, degrees of freedom, the test statistic, the attained significance level, and the confidence interval.

In the **Pulse** example, the assumption of equal variances seems pretty reasonable. We used the following program on the **Pulse** data to produce the output in Exhibit 8.2:

```
SET MALES INTO C1
(data for males)
```

SET FEMALES INTO C2
(data for females)
POOLED T FOR MALES IN C1, FEMALES IN C2
STOP

The POOLED command does both a confidence interval and a test. The value of the test statistic t is −2.825, which, as the output indicates, is significant at the 0.05 level. That is, there is statistically significant evidence, using $\alpha = .05$, that the average pulse rate is different for males and females. (We note that our assumption of equal variances still seems reasonable, since the two standard deviations, 9.95 for the males and 11.6 for the females, are reasonably close.)

Population Variances Not Assumed Equal

If you use the POOLED command when it's not appropriate—that is, when the variances of the two populations are not equal—you could be seriously mislead. For example, you might falsely claim to have evidence that the two populations differ when they really do not. Of course, you always have a chance of making such an error (called a Type I error) whenever you do a statistical test. In fact, this is exactly what α measures. When you do a test at $\alpha = .05$ you are supposed to have a 5% chance of claiming there is a difference when in actuality there isn't any. But

EXHIBIT 8.2

Pooled t-Test to Compare Male and Female Pulse Rates

```
-- POOLED T FOR MALES IN C1, FEMALES IN C2
   C1   N =  57   MEAN =  70.421   ST.DEV. =  9.95
   C2   N =  35   MEAN =  76.857   ST.DEV. =  11.6
   DEGREES OF FREEDOM = 90
   A 95.00 PERCENT C.I. FOR MU1-MU2 IS: ( −10.9633,  −1.9089)
   TEST OF MU1 = MU2 VS. MU1 N.E. MU2
   T = −2.825
   THE TEST IS SIGNIFICANT AT 0.0058
```

if you use the POOLED command when the population variances are not equal, your chances of a Type I error may be very different from 5%. How different depends on how unequal the variances are, the sample sizes, etc.

Minitab has a second command to compare two independent samples—a command that does not require the population variances to be equal.

TWOSAMPLE T FIRST SAMPLE IN C, SECOND SAMPLE IN C

Let μ_1 be the mean of the first population, and μ_2 the mean of the second population. This command does two things:

(a) It finds a two-sided 95% confidence interval for $(\mu_2 - \mu_1)$.

(b) It does a t-test of H_0: $\mu_1 = \mu_2$ versus H_1: $\mu_1 \neq \mu_2$.

Both (a) and (b) use a method, which does not require that the variances of the two populations be identical.

The confidence interval in (a) goes from

$$(\bar{x}_1 - \bar{x}_2) - t^* \sqrt{\frac{s_1^2}{n_1} + \frac{s_2^2}{n_2}} \quad \text{to}$$

$$(\bar{x}_1 - \bar{x}_2) + t^* \sqrt{\frac{s_1^2}{n_1} + \frac{s_2^2}{n_2}},$$

where t^* is the value from a t-table corresponding to 95% confidence and degrees of freedom given below. The test statistic for (b) is

$$t = \frac{(\bar{x}_1 - \bar{x}_2)}{\sqrt{\frac{s_1^2}{n_1} + \frac{s_2^2}{n_2}}}.$$

Here $\bar{x}_1$ is the sample mean of the first column, $\bar{x}_2$ is the sample mean of the second column, s_1 and s_2 are the sample standard deviations of the two columns, and n_1 and n_2 are the two sample sizes.

The degrees of freedom is based on the following approximation:

$$d.f. = \frac{[(s_1^2/n_1) + (s_2^2/n_2)]^2}{\dfrac{(s_1^2/n_1)^2}{(n_1 - 1)} + \dfrac{(s_2^2/n_2)^2}{(n_2 - 1)}}.$$

Minitab prints out n_1, n_2, $\bar{x}_1$, $\bar{x}_2$, s_1, s_2, degrees of freedom, the test statistic, the attained significance, and the confidence interval.

When we used the TWOSAMPLE command to compare the pulse rate data for males and females, we got the output in Exhibit 8.3. This output is very similar to the output from the POOLED command. The confidence interval is just slightly wider and the test just slightly less significant.

If you use TWOSAMPLE when you could have used POOLED (i.e., when the variances are equal), then, on the average, your analysis will be slightly conservative. That is, you will get a slightly larger confidence interval and you'll be slightly less likely to reject a true null hypothesis. This conservatism essentially disappears with moderately large sample sizes (say, if both n_1 and n_2 are greater than 30). So, in most cases—especially for large sample sizes—it's better to use the TWOSAMPLE command rather than the POOLED command. If the variances are equal, you've lost little and if they're unequal, you may have gained a lot.

Exercises Involving Both Paired and Unpaired Data

8-3   We just saw that men and women have different pulse rates on the average, so perhaps we should study the change in pulse rate, due to exercise, separately for men and women in the **Pulse** experiment (page 285).

(a) Compare the "first pulse rate" data with the "second pulse rate" data for the 24 men in the experimental group.

(b) Compare the "first pulse rate" data with the "second pulse rate" data for the 11 women in the experimental group.

EXHIBIT 8.3

Twosample t-Test to Compare Male and Female Pulse Rates

```
-- TWOSAMPLE T FOR MALES IN C1, FEMALES IN C2
   C1    N =  57    MEAN =  70.421    ST.DEV. =  9.95
   C2    N =  35    MEAN =  76.857    ST.DEV. =  11.6
   APPROX. DEGREES OF FREEDOM = 64
   A 95.00 PERCENT C.I. FOR MU1-MU2 IS: (  -11.1689,   -1.7032)
   TEST OF MU1 = MU2 VS. MU1 N.E. MU2
   T = -2.722
   THE TEST IS SIGNIFICANT AT 0.0085
```

8-4   Let's look at how cholesterol level changes when you have a heart attack? (Data on page 135.)

    (a)   Compare the cholesterol level for 2 days after an attack with the cholesterol level for people in the control group. Is cholesterol level substantially changed right after a heart attack?

    (b)   What happens after two weeks have passed? Has cholesterol level returned to normal? (Is there a significant difference between the control group and the group for 14 days after?)

8-5   (a)   For the **Integration** data (page 287) do a test of the null hypothesis that the attitude of white children is the same, on the average, whether the school is integrated or not.

    (b)   Do the same test for the black children.

    (c)   Compare the results of (a) and (b).

8-6   Physicists are constantly trying to obtain more accurate values of the fundamental physical constants, such as the mean distance from the earth to the sun and the force exerted on us by gravity. These are very difficult measurements and require the utmost ingenuity and care. Here are results obtained in a Canadian experiment to measure the force of gravity. The first group of 32 measurements was made in August, the second group in December of the following year. (Note: The force of gravity measured in centimeters per second squared could be obtained from the measurements below by adding 980.61 to them.)

Measurements Made in August, 1958

0.0005	0.0020	0.0020	0.0025	0.0025	0.0030	0.0035
0.0015	0.0020	0.0020	0.0025	0.0025	0.0030	0.0035
0.0015	0.0020	0.0025	0.0025	0.0030	0.0030	
0.0015	0.0020	0.0025	0.0025	0.0030	0.0030	
0.0020	0.0020	0.0025	0.0025	0.0030	0.0030	

Measurements Made in December, 1959

0.0020	0.0030	0.0035	0.0040	0.0040	0.0045	0.0055
0.0025	0.0030	0.0035	0.0040	0.0040	0.0045	0.0060
0.0025	0.0030	0.0035	0.0040	0.0045	0.0050	
0.0030	0.0030	0.0035	0.0040	0.0045	0.0050	
0.0030	0.0035	0.0040	0.0040	0.0045	0.0050	

(a) Use the data from August to estimate the force of gravity. Also find a 95% confidence interval.

(b) Repeat (a) for the December measurements.

(c) Now compare the measurements made in August to those made in December. Is there a statistically significant difference between the two groups? What is the practical significance of this result?

(d) In between these two sets of measurements it was necessary to change a few key components of the apparatus. Might this have made a difference in the measurements? If so, can you draw any morals for sound scientific experimentation? What if the experimenters had done all their measurements at one time? Might they have mislead themselves about the accuracy of their results? What if other parts of the apparatus were changed?

8-7 A small study was done to compare how well students with different majors do in an introductory statistics course. Seven majors were found: biology, psychology, sociology, business, education, meteorology and economics. At the end of the course, the students were given a special test to measure their understanding of basic statistics. Then a series of t-tests were performed to compare every pair of majors. Thus, biology and psychology majors were compared, biology and sociology majors, psychology and sociology majors, etc., for a total of 21 t-tests.

Simulate this study assuming that all majors do about the same. Assume there are 20 students in each major, and that scores on the test have a normal distribution with $\mu = 12$ and $\sigma = 2$. Use NRANDOM to get a sample for biology majors and put it in c1, then use NRANDOM a second time to get a sample for psychology majors and put it in c2, and so on, for 7 samples.

(a) What is the null hypothesis?

(b) What are the 21 pairs of majors for the 21 t-tests?

(c) Do the 21 t-tests.

(d) In how many of the tests did you reject the null hypothesis at $\alpha = 0.10$?

(e) Since this study was simulated, the true situation is known—there aren't any differences. But you probably did find at least one pair of majors where there was a significant difference. This illustrates the "hazards" of doing a lot of comparisons. Try to think of some other situations where one might do a lot of statistical tests. For example, suppose a pharmaceutical firm had 16 possible new drugs which they wanted to try out in hopes that at least one was better than the present best competing brand. What are the consequences of doing a lot of statistical tests?

8-8   In this section we found evidence that men and women have different pulse rates. But what about the effect of exercise? Does this differ for men and women? Calculate the change in pulse rate ("second pulse rate" minus "first pulse rate") for each man and woman in the experimental group of the **Pulse** study (page 285). These changes give us a measure of the effect of exercise on pulse rate. Compare the changes for men with those for women. Do an appropriate test.

8-9   Let's evaluate the relative effectiveness of various types of visual aids, using the data from the **Cartoon** experiment (page 270). Here we will analyze only the pre-professional data.

(a) The pre-professionals were separated into 2 groups, those who saw color slides and those who saw black and white slides. First, let's check that these two groups have about the same ability as measured by OTIS scores. Do the appropriate t-test to compare their OTIS scores.

(b) Now, using immediate test scores as a measure of learning, see what type of visual material is better. In each of the following cases, do the appropriate t-test for comparing the two scores. Compare

(1)   The effectiveness of black and white cartoon slides with that of black and white realistic slides.

(2)   Color cartoon slides with color realistic slides.

(3)   Black and white slides with color slides. (What are appropriate scores to compare?)

(c)   Would it be appropriate to use all the cartoon scores (whether the person saw color or black and white slides) as one sample, and all the realistic scores (whether color or black and white) as a second sample, and then do a t-test to compare these two samples? Why or why not?

8.3 Other Forms of POOLED and TWOSAMPLE

Both the POOLED and TWOSAMPLE commands have 2 optional arguments, the percent confidence and the alternative hypothesis.

(Continued from pages 138 and 141.)

> POOLED T, **K** PERCENT CONFIDENCE, DATA IN **C**, AND **C**

> TWOSAMPLE T, **K** PERCENT CONFIDENCE, DATA IN **C**, AND **C**

Each command finds a two-sided K percent confidence interval for $(\mu_2 - \mu_1)$, and does a test of H_0: $\mu_1 = \mu_2$ versus H_1: $\mu_1 \neq \mu_2$.

> POOLED T, ALTERNATIVE **K**, DATA IN **C**, AND **C**

> TWOSAMPLE T, ALTERNATIVE **K**, DATA IN **C**, AND **C**

Each command allows one-sided as well as two-sided tests. (The confidence intervals, however, are always two-sided.) The following codes are used for the alternative hypothesis:

$$K = -1 \text{ means } \mu_1 < \mu_2$$
$$K = 0 \text{ means } \mu_1 \neq \mu_2$$
$$K = +1 \text{ means } \mu_1 > \mu_2$$

Note: Both optional arguments can be used, in either order, in the same command.

Example

TWOSAMPLE T 90% CONFIDENCE, ALTERNATIVE −1, DATA IN C3 AND C5

9

Correlation and Regression

Some of the most interesting problems in statistics occur when we try to find a model for the relationship between several variables. The data in Exhibit 9.1 illustrate a common situation. Two exam scores were recorded for 31 students in an elementary statistics course. We might ask questions like the following:

(a) What is the correlation between the scores on the two exams?

(b) If you know someone's score on the first exam, does that help you at all in predicting his score on the second exam?

(c) What is a good prediction of the second exam score for a student who scored a 70 on the first exam?

In this chapter we will see how questions like these can be answered.

9.1 Correlation

There are several ways to measure the association between two variables, x and y. The most common measure is the Pearson product moment correlation coefficient, or just *correlation* for short.

EXHIBIT 9.1

Exam Scores

(a)   Two Exam Scores for 31 Students

Student Number	First Exam Score	Second Exam Score
1	50	69
2	66	85
3	73	88
4	84	70
5	57	84
6	83	78
7	76	90
8	95	97
9	73	79
10	78	95
11	48	67
12	53	60
13	54	79
14	79	79
15	76	88
16	90	98
17	60	56
18	89	87
19	83	91
20	81	86
21	57	69
22	71	75
23	86	98
24	82	70
25	95	91
26	42	48
27	75	52
28	54	44
29	54	51
30	65	73
31	61	52

EXHIBIT 9.1

(b)   Plot of Second Exam Score vs. First Exam Score

```
-- PLOT C2 VS C1

       C2
    100.+
       -
       -
       -                                      *   *      *
       -                                  *
       -                              *       *         *
       -                          *  *           *
    85.+            *          *              *
       -
       -         *                        *   *  *
       -                                *
Second -                         *
Exam  70.+      *     *                      **
Score  -     *
       -
       -        *
       -
    55.+              *
       -           *      *           *
       -  *
       -
       -        *
    40.+
       +---------+---------+---------+---------+---------+C1
      40.               70.              100.
           55.               85.              115.
```

First Exam Score
```
```

+---+
| |
| CORRELATION COEFFICIENT BETWEEN DATA IN C AND C |
| |
| Computes the (linear) correlation coefficient between the two columns |
| of data. The usual Pearson product moment correlation coefficient is |
| used. |
| |
+---+

$$r = \frac{\Sigma(x - \bar{x})\,(y - \bar{y})}{\sqrt{\Sigma(x - \bar{x})^2\ \Sigma(y - \bar{y})^2}}$$

CORRELATION COEFFICIENTS FOR DATA IN C, C,...,C

If more than two columns are specified, Minitab prints a table giving the correlations between all pairs of columns.

Example

CORRELATION C1, C2, C3

Three correlations are given: the correlation between c1 and c2, between c1 and c3, and between c2 and c3.

Suppose we want to compute the correlation coefficient for the data in Exhibit 9.1. All we need to do, once the data have been read into c1 and c2, is say

CORRELATION BETWEEN C1 AND C2.

In this example, Minitab gives the result that the correlation is 0.703.

It is useful to point out that $r^2 = (0.703)^2 = 0.494$ tells us that 49.4% of the variation in the second exam scores can be "explained" or "predicted" through knowledge of the students' first exam scores, using a straight-line prediction equation. Thus the higher the r^2 value, the more useful one variable will be as a predictor of the other.

Exercises

9-1   There are 3 variables in the **Tree** data (page 278): diameter, height, and volume. Find the correlation between each pair (3 correlations in all). Which relationship seems strongest? Which variable would probably be the better predictor of volume?

9-2 (a) Plot weight versus height for all 92 participants in the **Pulse** experiment (page 285). Does weight seem to increase with height? Calculate the correlation between weight and height.

(b) Study the relationship between weight and height separately for
males and females. Plot weight versus height for males and calculate the correlation. Do the same for females. Do the correlations
seem to agree with what you'd expect from the plots?

(c) Compare the 2 plots and 2 correlations in part (b). Is the relationship
stronger for men or for women? Any explanations?

(d) Compare the 2 plots and 2 correlations from part (b) with those from
(a). Can you see why the correlation in (a) is larger than either
correlation in (b)? Look at the plots—perhaps you should even put
the plots for males and females on the same axis.

9.2 Simple Regression: Fitting a Straight Line

Correlation tells us how much association there is between two variables, but regression goes further. It gives us an equation that can be
used to predict one variable from the other. In this section we will show
how to use the REGRESS command to fit a straight line.

Let's look at the data in Exhibit 9.1 again. Suppose we want to predict
a student's score on the second exam from his score on the first exam.
If one student scored 70 on the first exam, we might predict he'd score
about 75 on the second exam. If another student scored 90 on the first
exam, we might predict about a 90 on his second exam. If still another
student scored 55 on the first exam, we might expect a second score of
about 65. In fact, it looks as if we might be able to draw a straight line
on the plot and use it to predict scores on the second exam. Let's suppose
we decide to do that. How would we draw the line? Any line we draw
will miss some of the data. Exhibit 9.2 gives another copy of this plot
with several lines drawn in. Which one looks best?

A method that statisticians usually use to decide which line to choose
is called *least squares*. Statisticians look at all the differences between
what the line predicts and what actually happened for each student. If
a line predicts a second exam score of 79 and the actual score was 88,
then the *deviation* (also called the *residual*) is $88 - 79 = 9$. Suppose
we compute all the deviations for a line, square them, and add them up.

EXHIBIT 9.2

Several Lines for Predicting the Second Exam Score from the First

-- PLOT C2 VS C1

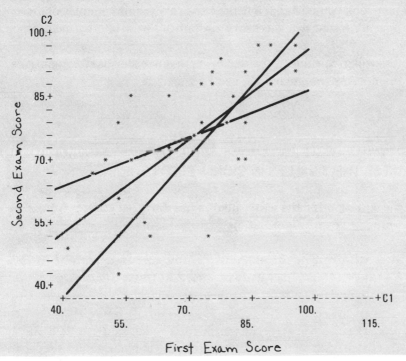

First Exam Score

A line that has a large sum of squared deviations won't be as good as one that has a small sum of squared deviations. The least squares criterion says we should use the line that gives us the smallest sum of squared deviations. The surprising thing is that it's relatively easy to find the equation for that line.

If we're trying to predict y from x, any straight line can be written as y = a + bx where a and b are two numbers that tell us which line we're using. For example, y = 3 + 2x or y = −5 + 0.8x. For the least squares line, the formulas are

$$b = \frac{\Sigma(x - \bar{x}) \, (y - \bar{y})}{\Sigma(x - \bar{x})^2}, \text{ and}$$

$$a = \bar{y} - b\bar{x} \, .$$

These may look complicated, but they are really quite simple compared to the formulas that are necessary to find the best line by most other criteria.

Minitab will give values for a and b, and many other useful quantities, when the REGRESS command is used.

REGRESS THE Y-VALUES IN **C** ON 1 PREDICTOR IN **C**

Gives the equation for the least squares line for predicting y from x, as well as other relevant information.

More general forms of the REGRESS *command are described in Sections 9.4 (page 166), 9.7 (page 181), and 9.10 (page 194).*

Suppose we want to use REGRESS to predict the second exam score from the first exam score. All we need to do, once the data have been read into the worksheet, is say

REGRESS C2 ON 1 PREDICTOR IN COL C1.

This instruction produced the output shown in Exhibit 9.3.

REGRESS Output

Let's look at some of the simpler parts of this output.* First, we are told that the regression equation is y = 22.47 + 0.7546x. This equation corre-

---

* The output discussed here is the full output. On some computers the usual output has been abbreviated. To get the full output, use the command NOBRIEF (page 193) before the first REGRESS command.

EXHIBIT 9.3

Regression Output for Predicting the Second Exam Score from the First

```
-- REGRESS C2 ON 1 PREDICTOR IN COL C1
THE REGRESSION EQUATION IS
Y =      22.47 + 0.7546 X1
```

	COLUMN	COEFFICIENT	ST. DEV. OF COEF.	T-RATIO = COEF./S.D.
	--	22.5	10.2	2.20
X1	C1	0.755	0.142	5.32

```
THE ST. DEV. OF Y ABOUT REGRESSION LINE IS
S =     11.5
WITH ( 31− 2) = 29 DEGREES OF FREEDOM
R-SQUARED = 49.4 PERCENT
R-SQUARED = 47.7 PERCENT, ADJUSTED FOR D.F.
```

ANALYSIS OF VARIANCE

DUE TO	DF	SS	MS = SS/DF
REGRESSION	1	3757.	3757.
RESIDUAL	29	3844.	133.
TOTAL	30	7601.	

ROW	X1 C1	Y C2	PRED. Y VALUE	ST.DEV. PRED. Y	RESIDUAL	ST.RES.
1	50.0	69.0	60.2	3.6	8.8	0.80
2	66.0	85.0	72.3	2.2	12.7	1.13
3	73.0	88.0	77.6	2.1	10.4	0.92
4	84.0	70.0	85.9	2.8	−15.9	−1.42
5	57.0	84.0	65.5	2.8	18.5	1.66
6	83.0	78.0	85.1	2.7	−7.1	−0.63
7	76.0	90.0	79.8	2.2	10.2	0.90
8	95.0	97.0	94.2	4.0	2.8	0.26
9	73.0	79.0	77.6	2.1	1.4	0.13
10	78.0	95.0	81.3	2.3	13.7	1.21
11	48.0	67.0	58.7	3.8	8.3	0.77
12	53.0	60.0	62.5	3.2	−2.5	−0.22

EXHIBIT 9.3 (Cont'd)

13	54.0	79.0	63.2	3.1	15.8	1.43
14	79.0	79.0	82.1	2.4	−3.1	−0.27
15	76.0	88.0	79.8	2.2	8.2	0.72
16	90.0	98.0	90.4	3.4	7.6	0.69
17	60.0	56.0	67.7	2.6	−11.7	−1.05
18	89.0	87.0	89.6	3.3	−2.6	−0.24
19	83.0	91.0	85.1	2.7	5.9	0.53
20	81.0	86.0	83.6	2.5	2.4	0.21
21	57.0	69.0	65.5	2.8	3.5	0.32
22	71.0	75.0	76.0	2.1	−1.0	−0.09
23	86.0	98.0	87.4	3.0	10.6	0.96
24	82.0	70.0	84.3	2.6	−14.3	−1.28
25	95.0	91.0	94.2	4.0	−3.2	−0.29
26	42.0	48.0	54.2	4.6	−6.2	−0.58
27	75.0	52.0	79.1	2.2	−27.1	−2.39
28	54.0	44.0	63.2	3.1	−19.2	−1.73
29	54.0	51.0	63.2	3.1	−12.2	−1.10
30	65.0	73.0	71.5	2.2	1.5	0.13
31	61.0	52.0	68.5	2.5	−16.5	−1.47

sponds to one of the lines in Exhibit 9.2, and, since it is the least squares line, it is impossible to find any straight line that gives a smaller sum of squared deviations than this one. The sum of squared deviations for this line is 3844 (see RESIDUAL SS in analysis of variance table in Exhibit 9.3).

The next block of output gives the values of a and b again, with some additional information. Next comes the analysis of variance table, which gives, as we will see later, a breakdown of the variation in the data.

The last block of output lists each of the x-values and y-values and then gives the y-value predicted by the equation. For example, the first student's first exam score was 50, his second exam score was 69 and his predicted score is 60.2. His deviation is thus y−(predicted y) = 69 − 60.2 = 8.8. This is given under RESIDUAL.

R-Squared (Coefficient of Determination)

The output tells us that, for these data, R-SQUARED = 49.4 PERCENT. Whenever a straight line is fit to a set of data, R^2 is just the square of the ordinary correlation coefficient we discussed in Section 9.1. There we found $r = 0.703$, which when squared gave 0.494 or 49.4 percent, which, of course, is the value given here in the REGRESS output.

R^2 also has two other, more general, interpretations. It is the square of the correlation between the observed y-values and the predicted y-values. And, as we mentioned in Section 9.1, it is the fraction of the variation in y that can be explained by means of the straight-line prediction equation. Look at the analysis of variance table in Exhibit 9.3. The TOTAL SS is a measure of the variation in y about its mean. Here it is 7601. The REGRESSION SS is the amount of this variation which is explained by the regression line. Here it is 3757. Then the fraction of variation explained is $3757/7601 = 0.494$. Thus, we say the regression line explains 49.4% of the observed variation in the second exam score from the first exam score. The RESIDUAL SS is the amount of unexplained variation, and equals TOTAL SS minus the REGRESSION SS.

Exercises

9-3 Refer to the output in Exhibit 9.3.

(a) If a student scored 54 on the first exam, what score would you predict for him to get on the second exam?

(b) How many students got 54 on the first exam? What did they each get on the second exam? Find the residual (deviation) for each of these students.

(c) If a student got 100 on the first exam, what score would you expect him to get on the second exam?

9-4 The following are the mean Scholastic Aptitude Test scores (SAT scores) for 1963 through 1974:

Year (19--)	63	64	65	66	67	68	69	70	71	72	73	74
Verbal	478	475	473	471	467	466	462	461	454	450	445	444
Math	502	498	496	496	495	494	491	488	487	482	481	480

(a)   Plot the verbal SAT scores versus year. Repeat for math scores.

(b)   Fit a regression line using year to predict the verbal SAT scores.

(c)   Fit a regression line using year as a predictor of math SAT scores.

(d)   Draw the 2 regression lines, by hand, on the plots of the data.

(e)   Do both verbal and math scores seem to be changing at about the same rate?

(f)   What is the predicted average SAT score for math in 1970? In 1975? In 2000? Which of these seem to make sense? Repeat for verbal scores.

(g)   The mean SAT scores for 1975 were 434 for verbal and 472 for math. How do these compare with the scores you predicted for 1975 in part (f)?

9-5   Given below are the winning times (in seconds) for the men's 1500-meter run in the Olympics from 1900-1972. (Note: no Olympics were held in 1916, 1940, and 1944 due to wars.)

Year	1900	1904	1908	1912	1920	1924	1928	1932
Time (sec.)	246.0	245.4	243.4	236.8	241.8	233.6	233.2	231.2

Year	1936	1948	1952	1956	1960	1964	1968	1972
Time (sec.)	227.8	229.8	225.2	221.2	215.6	218.1	214.9	216.3

(a)   Plot winning time versus year. Does winning time seem to be changing, according to a straight line, over the years?

(b)   Fit a regression line for predicting winning time from year and draw this line on the plot.

(c)   What winning time would you predict for the 1980 Olympics?

9-6   The following data were collected to study the relationship between the temperature of a battery and its output voltage.

Reading	1	2	3	4	5	6	7	8
Temperature (Kelvin)	283.0	283.0	296.1	296.1	307.0	307.0	318.6	318.6
Voltage	4290	4270	4470	4485	4723	4731	4920	4935

(a) Plot the data and use REGRESS to fit a straight line to estimate the output voltage as a function of temperature. Does the regression line seem to fit the data well?

(b) Do you spot any weakness in the way the experiment was apparently run? (Try drawing the regression line on the data plot.) How would you design such an experiment? Specifically, in what order would you take the 8 readings if you had to do this experiment again?

9-7 (a) How well can you predict the volume of a tree from its diameter? Use the **Tree** data (page 278) to find such an equation for black cherry trees in Pennsylvania.

(b) Plot the data (volume versus diameter) and draw your regression line on it. How does the line seem to fit the data? Do you see any problems?

9.3 Making Inferences from Straight-Line Fits

In this section, we'll see how the output in Exhibit 9.3 can be used to make inferences about a population, if certain conditions are met.

Conditions for Inference

The basic conditions needed before we can make valid inferences from our computations are as follows:

(a) The true relationship between x and y is a *straight line*. This means that for any given value of x, the mean of all corresponding y-values is given by the expression A + Bx. For example, suppose we calculate the mean of all the y's in the population corresponding to x =

1, the mean of all the y's corresponding to x = 2, the mean of all the y's corresponding to x = 3, and so on. Then all these means must fall on a straight line. We will call this line the "true" regression line. Note that the values a and b, discussed in Section 9.2, are the *sample estimates* of the *population values* A and B. For any given value of x, an *observed* y-value can be thought of as the *average value*, (A + Bx), plus a *random quantity*, e. This e is the amount by which that individual y-value deviates from the true regression line.

(b) For all values of x, the e's have the same variance. This is equivalent to saying that the amount of variation in the y's is the same, no matter what the value of x is. This variance is usually called the *variance of y about the regression line*, and is denoted by σ^2. Correspondingly, σ is called the *standard deviation of y about the regression line*.

(c) The e's have mean = 0. This says that we are not favoring y-values that are high (or low) on the average.

(d) The distribution of the e's is *normal* (with mean = 0 and variance = σ^2). This is equivalent to saying that the distribution of the y-values corresponding to any given value of x is normal (with mean = A + Bx and variance = σ^2).

In addition to these conditions concerning the population, there is also another condition that must be met. This concerns how the observations were actually taken.

(e) The e's that are obtained must be independent. In other words, the amount by which each y-value differs from its mean must not be related to the amount by which any other y-value differs from its mean.

Conditions (c) and (e) are the most important and the most difficult to check. Checking for them usually comes back to checking whether the survey or experiment was done properly in the first place. For example, were proper randomization procedures used? Was there any way that the result of one observation could be influenced by another? Was bias or a systematic error present?

Condition (a) is also important. However, there are several techniques that can be used when the true relationship between x and y is not a straight line. In Sections 9.7 and 9.9, we discuss some procedures for checking whether the assumptions of regression hold.

Before going on, we should point out that no problems in the real world will ever meet all these conditions exactly. Nevertheless, the statistical techniques we discuss can still give us some useful insight in many situations, provided these conditions are met to some degree of approximation.

We should point out one more thing. The conditions we just discussed are needed for making valid inferences (i.e., for constructing confidence intervals or doing hypothesis tests). They are not necessary when we just want to fit a line (or curve) to a batch of numbers. Often we're interested in discovering the general trend in some data (as in Exercise 9-4) or the relationship between two variables (for example, does y increase with x or with 1/x?), or we're looking for unusual data points. In these cases, we will use regression as a descriptive technique, and conditions such as normality, or independence may not be too important.

Interpreting the Output

Estimate of σ^2.   Let's begin by looking at THE ST. DEV. OF Y ABOUT REGRESSION LINE (also called "the standard error of estimate") in Exhibit 9.3. This quantity, denoted by s, gives us an estimate of σ^2. It is computed using the formula

$$s = \sqrt{\frac{\Sigma(y - \text{pred.y})^2}{n-2}}.$$

The value s can be thought of as a measure of how much the observed y-values differ from the corresponding average y-value as predicted by the least squares line. It has $(n-2)$ degrees of freedom and is used in all of the formulas for standard deviations of estimated quantities. Thus, *all* t-tests and confidence intervals will be based on this s, and all will have $(n-2)$ degrees of freedom.

Standard Deviation of Coefficients.   Under the conditions of regression, the estimated coefficients a and b each have a normal distribution. The estimated standard deviations of these coefficients are given in the column headed ST. DEV. OF COEF. in Exhibit 9.3. The estimated standard deviation of a is 10.2, and the estimated standard deviation of b is 0.142. The general formula for a t confidence interval is

(quantity) ± (value from t-table) × (estimated s.d. of quantity).

Here we have $31 - 2 = 29$ degrees of freedom. Thus a 95% confidence interval for A (the population value of a) is

$$22.47 \pm 2.045 \ (10.2),$$

which gives the interval 1.61 to 43.33. A 95% confidence interval for B (the population value of b) is similarly given by

$$0.7546 \pm 2.045 \ (0.142),$$

which gives the interval 0.46 to 1.04.

The estimated standard deviations of a and b are also useful for t-tests. For example, a null hypothesis we frequently want to test is that B is zero. We use the general formula

$$t = \frac{b - (\text{hypothesized value})}{(\text{estimated s.d. of b})} .$$

Here we find that

$$t = \frac{0.7546 - 0}{0.142} = 5.32 .$$

This is given in the column headed T-RATIO = COEF/S.D. With 29 degrees of freedom, this value of t is highly significant, giving us evidence that B is probably not zero. This in turn implies that the score on the first exam is a useful predictor of the score on the second exam. (It is useful to note that this t-test is exactly equivalent to testing whether the population correlation is zero.)

A similar t-test of the null hypothesis that A = 0 gives

$$t = \frac{22.47 - 0}{10.2} = 2.20 .$$

This is also statistically significant, although just barely. Thus from a statistical standpoint, both a and b have been shown to be useful in the equation.

Standard Deviation of a Predicted y-Value.   The estimated standard deviations of the predicted y-values are given in the column headed ST.DEV.PRED.Y in Exhibit 9.3. These can be used in a similar manner to get confidence intervals for the *population mean* of all y-values corresponding to any given value of x. For example, a 95%

confidence interval for the average of all y-values in the population whose x-values are equal to 50, is given by

$$60.2 \pm 2.045(3.6) .$$

This gives the interval 52.84 to 67.6. Thus, we can be 95% confident that the mean score on the second exam for all students who score 50 on the first exam is between 53 and 68.

   This tells us how well students with a first exam score of 50 will do, on the average. But how about *one particular individual* who scores 50 on the first exam? Since individuals are never as predictable as averages, we might expect more uncertainty in our prediction. The following calculations give us an interval we can be 95% confident will contain the second exam score of some specified student who gets a 50 on the first exam:

$$60.2 \pm 2.045 \sqrt{(3.6)^2 + (11.5)^2} .$$

This gives the interval 35.54 to 84.85. The 3.6 is the estimated standard deviation of the predicted mean value of y, and s $= 11.5$ is the estimated standard deviation of an individual about the mean value. The 2.045 is, as usual, the value of t for 29 degrees of freedom and 95% confidence. Note that the interval for an individual is larger than the interval for the average. This is something we must always expect. Individuals are less predictable than averages.

   Most texts give the following, slightly different looking, formula for a prediction interval corresponding to a given x-value, say x_0:

$$(\text{pred. } \ddot{y}) \pm t^*s \sqrt{\frac{1}{n} + \frac{(x_0 - \bar{x})^2}{\Sigma(x - \bar{x})^2} + 1} ,$$

where t^* is the appropriate value from a t-table. We can rewrite this formula as

$$(\text{pred. } y) \pm t^* \sqrt{(\text{estimated s.d. of pred. } y)^2 + s^2} ,$$

which is precisely the formula we used in the calculations above.

   The procedure we just used for x $= 50$ will work for any value of x that was in our set of data, such as x $= 66$, x $= 73$, or x $= 84$. But how about a prediction for a value of x that is not in our original set of data? For example, how could we make a prediction for x $= 68$? To get the predicted second score is not too difficult. All we have to do is substitute the 68 into the prediction equation. This gives

$$y = 22.47 + (0.7546)(68) = 73.84 .$$

Getting the estimated standard deviation of this predicted y-value is a little more difficult. We could calculate it, by hand, using a formula given in many textbooks. But, there is a much easier approximate method that is usually good enough. Let's look at the x-values in our set of data that are close to 68. Exhibit 9.4 shows some of the closest. There it's easy to see that for x = 68, the ST.DEV. PRED. Y is about 2.2. This guess is close enough for most purposes. Now we can use the same techniques we used for x = 50 and find a confidence interval for the population mean value of y corresponding to x = 68 as

$$73.84 \pm 2.045(2.2) .$$

Similarly, the prediction interval for a future value of y corresponding to x = 68 is

$$73.84 \pm 2.045 \sqrt{(2.2)^2 + (11.5)^2} .$$

Exercises

In Exercises 9-8 through 9-11 use the output in Exhibit 9.3.

9-8   (a) Calculate a 90% confidence interval for B, the slope of the true regression line.

(b) Find a 95% confidence interval for the average second exam score for all students who get a 90 on the first exam.

9-9   (a) Suppose you got 86 on the first exam. What score would you expect to get on the second exam? Find an interval which you are 95% confident covers your second exam score.

(b) Suppose someone took the first exam and only got a score of 48. Suppose 55 is passing in this course. (The 2 exam scores are averaged to get the course grade.) Do you think this student is likely to pass? (Use a 95% prediction interval to see what score you might expect him to get on the second exam. Then compute his likely averages.)

EXHIBIT 9.4

Some Values of x Near 68, and the Corresponding Standard Deviation of the Predicted Value (Taken from Exhibit 9.3)

x in *Col. 1*	*St. Dev.* *Pred. y*
75.0	2.2
73.0	2.1
68.0	?
66.0	2.2
65.0	2.2

9-10   Find a 95% confidence interval for the mean second exam score for all students who got a score of 77 on the first exam.

9-11   Test the null hypothesis, H_0: B = 0.5 versus the alternative hypothesis H_1: B ≠ 0.5.

9-12   Refer to Exercise 9-5 (page 158) for the 1500-meter race.

(a) Give 95% confidence intervals for the two regression coefficients.

(b) Give a 95% prediction interval for the winning time for the 1976 Olympics.

9-13   (a) We can simulate data from a regression model as follows. To choose a model, we need to specify 3 parameters, A, B, and σ. Suppose we take A = 3, B = 5, and σ = 0.2. Next, we must specify values for the predictor, x. Suppose we take 2 observations at each integer from 1 to 10. First, put the 20 values of x into a column. Then, calculate A + Bx. Now, simulate 20 observations from a normal distribution with μ = 0, σ = 0.2. Add these to A + Bx to get the observed y's. Get a plot and do a regression for these simulated data.

(b) Repeat part (a) using σ = 0.05. Compare the results with those of part (a).

(c) Repeat part (a) using σ = 1.0. Compare the results with those of (a) and (b).

9.4 Multiple Regression

So far, we've described how *one* variable can be used to predict another. For example, how a first exam score can be used to predict a second exam score. But, what if you have two or three, or even more, variables that could help with the prediction? One technique you can use, and the one we will describe in this section, is *multiple regression*. Let's begin with an example.

Many universities use multiple regression to predict how well the various applicants would do if they were admitted to that university. One equation that was recently used at a major northeastern university is

(Pred. freshman grade point ave.) = 0.61813(H.S. ave.) +
0.00137(SAT verbal) + 0.00063(SAT math) − 0.19787

This equation says that the "predicted grade point average" at the end of the freshman year is equal to 0.61813 times the "high school grade point average" plus 0.00137 times the "Scholastic Aptitude Test verbal score," plus 0.00063 times the "Scholastic Aptitude Test mathematics score," minus 0.19787. This prediction equation was an important criterion in deciding who to admit to that university.

This equation was obtained by using multiple regression on the records of previous students. The university had the freshman year GPA for some past students, as well as their high school GPA, and their two SAT scores. They asked, "Which equation best predicts freshman GPA from these other variables?" The procedure they used is very similar to the one we used in Sections 9.2 and 9.3 for simple straight-line predictions.

REGRESS C ON K PREDICTORS IN C,...,C

Calculates and prints out a multiple regression equation,

$$(Pred.\ y) = b_0 + b_1x_1 + b_2x_2 + b_3x_3 + ... + b_kx_k$$

The **Grades** example (page 279) gives some data from another university. Let's suppose we want to develop a similar equation for predicting freshman GPA from SAT scores at that university.

We used the program below to find a prediction equation based on a sample of 100 freshmen. (We used samples A and B from page 280.)

```
READ SAT VERBAL IN C1, SAT MATH IN C2, GPA IN C3
623        509        2.6
454        471        2.3

  .          .          .

  .          .          .

  .          .          .

REGRESS Y IN C3, USING 2 PREDICTORS VERBAL IN C1 AND MATH IN C2
STOP
```

Part of the results of this program are shown in Exhibit 9.5.

Interpreting the Output

The equation for predicting freshman GPA is

(Pred. GPA) = 0.4706 + (0.00356)(SAT verbal) + (0.00016)(SAT math).

We can use this equation to find out how well a student might do who made 500 on both of his SAT scores. We would predict

(Pred. GPA) = 0.4706 + (0.00356)(500) + (0.00016)(500)
$$= 0.4706 + 1.78 + 0.08 = 2.33 .$$

For a student who made 500 on the verbal test and 800 on the math test we would predict

(Pred. GPA) = 0.4706 + (0.00356)(500) + (0.00016)(800) = 2.38 .

Thus a student with scores of 500 and 500 and another student with scores of 500 and 800 have predicted GPA's which differ by only 0.05. This seems to indicate that SAT math scores are not very useful predictors of GPA at that university.

How good is the prediction equation as a whole? Put another way, how much might the GPA's for individual students vary from what we predict? One way to answer this question is to look at the value of R^2. It's 23.5%, which means that our predictions account for only 23.5% of the observed variation in GPA's.

From these results, it appears that SAT scores have only limited value in predicting success in college. We can give several possible reasons why the SAT scores seem to be such poor predictors. First, we don't have results for a random sample of *all* students. All we have is students who were admitted to, and attended, that university. Second, perhaps those students with low SAT scores were advised to take easier courses and thus got higher grades than they ordinarily would. Third, it is possible that tests like the Scholastic Aptitude Test simply don't do a very good job of measuring whatever it takes to make good grades in college.

Notation and Assumptions in Multiple Regression

We'll use just 2 predictors; it should be clear how to generalize to more than 2. We assume the following: (a) the true regression "line" is $y = B_0 + B_1x_1 + B_2x_2$. For any given values of x_1 and x_2, the observed y-value is $B_0 + B_1x_1 + B_2x_2 + e$, where e is a random deviation; (b) for all values of x_1 and x_2, the e's have the same variance, σ^2; (c) the e's have mean $= 0$; (d) the e's have a normal distribution; (e) the e's are independent. We use b_0, b_1, b_2, and s for the estimated values of B_0, B_1, B_2, and σ respectively.

Confidence Intervals and Tests

All the confidence intervals we calculated for straight lines in Section 9.3 can be calculated here in essentially the same way. For example, in Exhibit 9.5 the estimated standard deviation of b_2 is .000851. Since there are 97 degrees of freedom, a 95% confidence interval for B_2 is

$$.000158 \pm (1.99)(0.000851) \text{ or } (-.00154 \text{ to } .00185).$$

Suppose we want a 95% confidence interval for the population mean value of y corresponding to an SAT verbal score of 623 and an SAT math score of 509. Since this pair of scores happens to be in the set of data (it's the first observation on page 280) we used in the regression, we can conveniently read from Exhibit 9.5 that the predicted GPA is 2.770, and the ST.DEV. PRED. Y is 0.142. This means that $2.77 \pm (1.99)(0.142)$ gives a 95% confidence interval for the mean GPA of all students in the population who had an SAT verbal score of 623 and an SAT math score of 509.

For a new individual with these same test scores the prediction interval is

EXHIBIT 9.5

Multiple Regression Output for Predicting College Grades from SAT Scores (Abbreviated Output)

--REGRESS Y IN C3, USING 2 PREDICTORS VERB IN C1 AND MATH IN C2
THE REGRESSION EQUATION IS
$Y = 0.4706 + 0.00356 X1 + 0.00016 X2$

	COLUMN	COEFFICIENT	ST. DEV. OF COEF.	T-RATIO = COEF/S.D.
	--	0.471	0.543	0.87
X1	C1	0.003563	0.000735	4.85
X2	C2	0.000158	0.000851	0.19

THE ST. DEV. OF Y ABOUT REGRESSION LINE IS
$S = 0.502$
WITH (100− 3) = 97 DEGREES OF FREEDOM
R-SQUARED = 23.5 PERCENT
R-SQUARED − 22.0 PERCENT, ADJUSTED FOR D.F.

ANALYSIS OF VARIANCE

DUE TO	DF	SS	MS=SS/DF
REGRESSION	2	7.514	3.757
RESIDUAL	97	24.423	0.252
TOTAL	99	31.936	

FURTHER ANALYSIS OF VARIANCE
SS EXPLAINED BY EACH VARIABLE WHEN ENTERED IN THE ORDER GIVEN

DUE TO	DF	SS
REGRESSION	2	7.514
C1	1	7.505
C2	1	0.009

ROW	X1 C1	Y C3	PRED. Y VALUE	ST.DEV. PRED. Y	RESIDUAL	ST.RES.
1	623.	2.600	2.770	0.142	−0.170	−0.35
2	454.	2.300	2.162	0.154	0.138	0.29
3	643.	2.400	2.872	0.063	−0.472	−0.95
4	585.	3.000	2.668	0.078	0.332	0.67
5	719.	3.100	3.144	0.095	−0.044	−0.09
6	693.	2.900	3.041	0.089	−0.141	−0.29
7	571.	3.100	2.610	0.056	0.490	0.98
8	646.	3.300	2.885	0.072	0.415	0.83
9	613.	2.300	2.764	0.059	−0.464	−0.93
10	655.	3.300	2.915	0.066	0.385	0.77

$$2.77 \pm (1.99) \sqrt{(0.502)^2 + (0.142)^2} \ .$$

If we want to make a prediction for a pair of test scores that did not happen to be in the original set of data, say 600 and 750, we would compute the predicted GPA as

$$(\text{Pred. GPA}) = 0.471 + (0.00356)(600) + (0.000158)(750) = 2.73 \ .$$

To get the approximate ST.DEV. PRED. Y corresponding to this prediction we could make up a little table just as we did in Exhibit 9.4. We could then make an estimate from this table and proceed as before.

We can also do t-tests on the coefficients, just as we did in simple regression. For example, to test H_0: $B_2 = 5$, we form the ratio $t = (b_2 - 5)/(\text{estimated s.d. of } b_2)$. This ratio has a t-distribution with $n - (\text{number of parameters in equation}) = (n - 3)$ degrees of freedom. The t-ratio for H_0: $B_2 = 0$ is given on the output, and is just 0.19. This statistical test indicates that an SAT math score is not a very useful predictor of GPA, as we had conjectured earlier.

Exercises

9-14 Refer to the output in Exhibit 9.5.

(a) Get a 95% confidence interval for B_1, the coefficient of SAT verbal score.

(b) Is B_1 significantly different from zero (use $\alpha = 0.05$)? What does this say about the relationship between SAT verbal score and GPA?

(c) Is your answer to (b) consistent with the low value of R^2? Explain.

9-15 (a) Use the data in sample C from the **Grades** data (page 171) to develop another equation for predicting GPA from SAT scores.

(b) How does this equation compare to the equation in Exhibit 9.5? Compare the estimates of B_0 and B_1, B_2, σ^2 and R^2 for the two equations.

9-16 In Exercise 9-7, we fit an equation for predicting volume of a black cherry tree from its diameter. Suppose we use height as a second predictor.

(a) Find an equation for predicting volume from diameter and height.

(b) Calculate a 95% confidence interval for estimating the average volume for a tree with diameter $= 11.0$ and height $= 66$.

(c) Use the results to Exercise 9-7 to get a 95% confidence interval for the average volume of a tree with diameter 11.0. How does that confidence interval compare to the one in part (b) of this exercise, where you used the height as well as the volume?

(d) How much extra help does height seem to give you when predicting volume?

9.5 A Longer Example of a Multiple Regression Problem

The **Peru** data on page 276 were collected to study the long-term effects of a change in environment on blood pressure. Some questions we might ask of these data are as follows: "What happens to the Indians' blood pressure as they live longer periods in the new environment?" "Does it go up or down?" "Does it change by about the same amount each year?" In this section we will show how *multiple regression* can be used to help answer these questions. We begin by showing what happens when we use just one predictor.

First we need to decide how we should measure "how long" the Indians have lived in their new environment. We could just use the "number of years since migration." But that has problems. Younger people adapt to new surroundings more quickly than older people. A 25-year-old might be able to adapt as well in one year as a 50-year-old could in two years. In this analysis we chose to use the *fraction* of life in the new environment as a measure of "how long" they've lived there. Thus, one year for a 25-year-old and two years for a 50-year-old will both be listed as 1/25 of their life. The data on page 277 were read into C1-C10, with age in C1 and years since migration in C2. Then fraction of life was computed using the instruction

DIVIDE C2 BY C1, PUT IN C15 .

Now let's look at what happens when we plot systolic blood pressure in C9 versus "fraction of life" in C15. Exhibit 9.6 shows this plot as well

EXHIBIT 9.6

Plot of Blood Pressure Versus Fraction of Life Since Migration, and a Portion of the Corresponding Regression Output

- –PLOT C9 VS C15

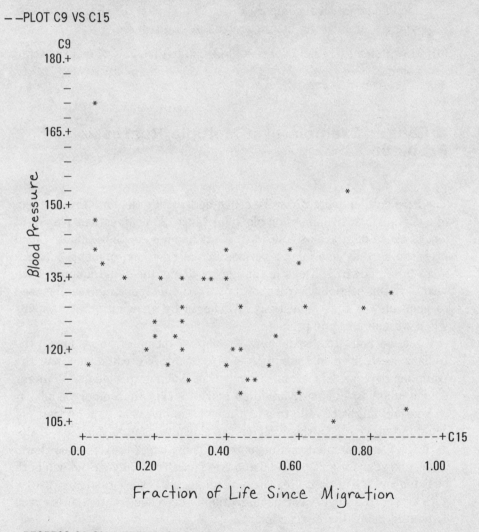

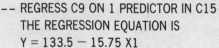

Fraction of Life Since Migration

-- REGRESS C9 ON 1 PREDICTOR IN C15
THE REGRESSION EQUATION IS
Y = 133.5 − 15.75 X1

EXHIBIT 9.6 (Cont'd)

COLUMN		COEFFICIENT	ST. DEV. OF COEF.	T-RATIO = COEF/S.D.
	--	133.50	4.04	33.06
X1	C15	−15.75	9.01	−1.75

THE ST. DEV. OF Y ABOUT REGRESSION LINE IS
S = 12.8
WITH (39− 2) = 37 DEGREES OF FREEDOM
R-SQUARED = 7.6 PERCENT
R-SQUARED = 5.1 PERCENT, ADJUSTED FOR D.F.

ANALYSIS OF VARIANCE

DUE TO	DF	SS	MS=SS/DF
REGRESSION	1	498.	498.
RESIDUAL	37	6033.	163.
TOTAL	38	6531.	

as the result from fitting a straight line to these data. The plot shows that there is virtually no relationship between blood pressure and the fraction of life that was spent in the new environment. The coefficient is negative (−15.75) which suggests that there may be a tendency for blood pressure to decrease with increasing fraction of life in the modern society. However, the t-ratio of −1.75 is not statistically significant. This lack of significance says that from this analysis it appears that it may well have been chance alone operating to give the −15.75 coefficient in the sample. The coefficient in the population may well be zero, in which case there would be no linear association between blood pressure and fraction of life since migration.

There is one outlying point in the data. One person who had just migrated had a much higher blood pressure than any of the others (about 170). This point was checked to see if a blunder had been made in keypunching, typing, or at some other place, but no error was found. Of course, it may just have been a person with abnormally high blood pressure, or he may have been excited when his blood pressure was being taken. Perhaps an error was made when the anthropologist took the blood pressure. In any event, this data point seems to be clearly different from the rest. Another regression was done with this point temporarily set aside. When this was done, there was even less indication of a significant relationship between the two variables.

Taking Weight into Consideration

At this point in the analysis it does not appear that there is any significant relationship between fraction of life since migration and blood pressure. But blood pressure is known to depend greatly on how much the person weighs. What happens if we take weight into consideration in our analysis?

Exhibit 9.7 shows the result of fitting a multiple regression model involving both fraction of life and weight. The relationship can be written as

$$(\text{pred. blood pressure}) = a + b(\text{weight}) + c(\text{fraction of life}).$$

Here, this equation is

$$(\text{pred. blood pressure}) = 60.90 + 1.217 \ (\text{weight})$$
$$- 26.77 \ (\text{fraction of life}).$$

The coefficient for fraction of life since migration is again negative (−26.77). This indicates that blood pressure tends to be lower for those individuals who have lived longer in their new modern low-altitude environment. The t-ratio for the coefficient is now −3.71, which is statistically significant. This tends to rule out the possibility of chance variation producing this result and lends support to the theory about the long-term effects of a change in environment on blood pressure. Of course, it does not prove the theory, since these results could have been caused by the effect of a change in altitude, or some other factor, or with some very small probability, by chance alone.

The equation indicates that a person who has lived half his life in the new environment will have, on the average, a blood pressure which is about 26.77 × 0.5 = 13.4 lower than someone of the same weight who has just moved into modern society. Thus it appears that fraction of life since migration is both *statistically* significant (t-ratio = −3.71) and *practically* significant (13.4 change in blood pressure in 1/2 of life).

The coefficient for weight is positive (+1.217) as we might expect. This indicates that blood pressure tends to increase as weight increases. This coefficient is statistically significant, with a t-ratio equal to 5.21 for testing the null hypothesis that there is no association between blood

EXHIBIT 9.7

Predicting Blood Pressure from Weight and Fraction of Life Since Migration

```
-- REGRESS C9 ON 2 PREDICTORS C3 AND C15
THE REGRESSION EQUATION IS
Y =   60.90 + 1.217 X1 − 26.77 X2
```

	COLUMN	COEFFICIENT	ST. DEV. OF COEF.	T-RATIO = COEF/S.D.
	--	60.9	14.3	4.26
X1	C3	1.217	0.234	5.21
X2	C15	−26.77	7.22	−3.71

```
THE ST. DEV. OF Y ABOUT REGRESSION LINE IS
S = 9.78
WITH ( 39− 3) = 36 DEGREES OF FREEDOM
R-SQUARED = 47.3 PERCENT
R-SQUARED = 44.4 PERCENT, ADJUSTED FOR D.F.
```

ANALYSIS OF VARIANCE

DUE TO	DF	SS	MS=SS/DF
REGRESSION	2	3090.1	1545.0
RESIDUAL	36	3441.4	95.6
TOTAL	38	6531.4	

pressure and weight. Weight is also practically significant, since the equation indicates that a change in weight of 10 kilograms (about 22 pounds) would lead to a $10 \times 1.217 = 12.17$ change in blood pressure.

Weight as a Suppressor Variable

These data demonstrate what some scientists call a "suppressor variable." Here weight was a suppressor variable for fraction of life since migration, since we found no relationship between blood pressure and fraction of life until we took differences in weight into consideration. The explanation seems to be that the migrants' blood pressure would have decreased over time as they stayed longer in their new environment, except that their blood pressure was simultaneously being driven up by

their gaining weight. Increased weight was sending it up, while environmental acclimatization was lowering it. The net effect was an essentially
zero change.

Exercise

9-17   Repeat the analysis we just did but use the data only for the men under
forty years of age. Compare your results to those in the text using all
39 men. Are the two regression equations similar? Discuss the relative
importance of the two predictors—weight and fraction of life—in each
equation.

9.6 Fitting Polynomials

So far, we have talked about fitting straight lines (Sections 9.2 and 9.3)
and about fitting equations with several predictors (multiple regression,
Sections 9.4 and 9.5). Now we will show how to fit curved data like that
shown in Exhibit 9.8. In this section, we will describe how to use
polynomial models. In Section 9.8 we show how transformations give
another, often preferable, method of analysis.

Polynomials are equations that involve powers of the x variable. For
example,

$$y = B_0 + B_1x + B_2x^2 + B_3x^3 + e$$

is the equation for a third-degree polynomial with random variation. The
equation for a second-degree polynomial with random variation is

$$y = B_0 + B_1x + B_2x^2 + e .$$

An Example

The data in Exhibit 9.8 were gathered in conjunction with an environmental impact study to find the relationship between stream depth and
flow rate. (*Flow rate* is the total amount of water that flows past a given
point of the stream in a fixed amount of time.) Data were collected at
seven different sites each on a different stream. The data in Exhibit 9.8
are all from one site. Here we are interested in being able to predict the

EXHIBIT 9.8

Stream Depth and Stream Flow Rate

Depth	Flow Rate
0.34	0.636
0.29	0.319
0.28	0.734
0.42	1.327
0.29	0.487
0.41	0.924
0.76	7.350
0.73	5.890
0.46	1.979
0.40	1.124

-- PLOT FLOW RATE C2 VS DEPTH C1

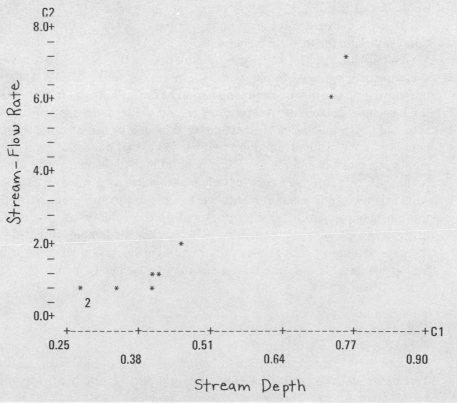

flow rate from the depth of the stream. Obviously, a straight line will not give a very good fit. But a second-degree polynomial might.

All we need to do, to fit a second-degree polynomial, is to compute x^2 and put it in another column. Then we simply regress y on the two predictor variables x and x^2, just as we do in multiple regression. A program that does this is

```
READ X INTO C1, Y INTO C2
```

(data from Exhibit 9.8)

```
MULTIPLY C1 BY C1 PUT IN C3 (X-SQUARED)
REGRESS C2 ON 2 PREDICTORS IN C1 AND C3
```

Some of the output from this program is in Exhibit 9.9. The form of the output is essentially the same as for a straight line. The regression equation is (flow) $= 1.683 - 10.86$(depth) $+ 23.54$(depth)^2. The standard deviation about the regression line is 0.279.

We can do a t-test of the null hypothesis that, in the population, the coefficient of the (depth)^2 term is zero. The data give t $= (23.54-0)/4.27$ $= 5.51$. This is statistically significant, giving us evidence that the population coefficient for (depth)^2 is not zero.

One might ask, "Just what is the 'population' in this case?" To answer this question, we need to imagine the amount of water in this stream fluctuating up and down over a long period of time, but without changing the basic flow pattern of the stream. Then all the measurements of flow rate and depth that *might* be made over this long period of time, is our population. We pretend (but don't really believe) that our set of measurements is a random sample from this population. All we can really hope is that our measurements act just about the same as a random sample would. If all of our measurements were made in the spring, or early in the morning, or just after a storm, or all in the same week, we could be pretty confident they wouldn't act like a random sample. Hopefully, the experimenter took all these factors into consideration when he was taking his data. If not, our inferences may be seriously incorrect.

Exercise

9-18   In Exercise 9-7, we fit the equation (volume) $= B_0 + B_1$ (diameter) to the **Tree** data. In Exercise 9-16, we added height as a second predictor and fit the equation, (volume) $= B_0 + B_1$ (diameter) $+ B_2$ (height). In this exercise, use just diameter to predict volume, but now fit the quadratic equation, (volume) $= B_0 + B_1$ (diameter) $+ B_2$ (diameter)^2.

(a) How well does this quadratic fit compare to the straight line of Exercise 9-7?

(b) Does a quadratic equation seem a reasonable choice from a theoretical standpoint? Consider the geometry of diameter versus volume for a tree.

(c) Compare the quadratic equation to the two-variable equation of Exercise 9-16. How well does each fit?

(d) It is more expensive to measure the height of a tree than its diameter. Based on this information, what equation would you use to predict the volume of a tree?

9.7 Interpreting Residuals in Simple and Polynomial Regression

Whenever we fit a model to a set of data, we should *always* look at the residuals because we never know for sure that we have the right model. *Residuals* are the difference between the observed data and the values predicted by the equation. Thus, they tell us how the model missed in fitting the data. For example, in Exhibit 9.9, for the first observation, the stream depth is 0.340, the observed flow rate is 0.636, and the predicted flow rate is 0.711. Thus the first residual is $(0.636 - 0.711) = -0.075$. We always look at residuals in terms of the quantity we are trying to predict. Here we are trying to predict flow rate, so we look at how much we missed in predicting flow rate. The second residual is -0.193. These, and all the other residuals, are listed in the column headed RESIDUAL.

Let's look at them a little more closely. Is -0.075 a big residual? How about -0.193? It's difficult to say from just looking at the plain residual. To make the residuals easier to look at and think about, we standardize them. Minitab divided each residual by an estimate of its standard deviation, giving the *standardized residuals*. These standardized residuals are listed in the column headed ST. RES. Usually they vary between -2 and $+2$. Any residual outside this range is automatically cause for

EXHIBIT 9.9

Part of Output of Program to Fit Second-Degree Polynomial to Stream Data

– –MULTIPLY C1 BY C1, PUT IN C3 (X-SQUARED)
– – REGRESS C2 ON 2 PREDICTORS IN C1 AND C3
THE REGRESSION EQUATION IS
Y = 1.683 − 10.86 X1 + 23.54 X2

	COLUMN	COEFFICIENT	ST. DEV. OF COEF.	T-RATIO = COEF/S.D.
	--	1.68	1.06	1.59
X1	C1	−10.86	4.52	−2.40
X2	C3	23.54	4.27	5.51

THE ST. DEV. OF Y ABOUT REGRESSION LINE IS
S = 0.279
WITH (10 − 3) = 7 DEGREES OF FREEDOM
R-SQUARED = 99.0 PERCENT
R-SQUARED = 98.7 PERCENT, ADJUSTED FOR D.F.

ANALYSIS OF VARIANCE

DUE TO	DF	SS	MS=SS/DF
REGRESSION	2	54.1055	27.0527
RESIDUAL	7	0.5465	0.0781
TOTAL	9	54.6520	

FURTHER ANALYSIS OF VARIANCE
SS EXPLAINED BY EACH VARIABLE WHEN ENTERED IN THE ORDER GIVEN

DUE TO	DF	SS
REGRESSION	2	54.1055
C1	1	51.7386
C3	1	2.3669

ROW	X1 C1	Y C2	PRED. Y VALUE	ST.DEV. PRED. Y	RESIDUAL	ST.RES.
1	0.340	0.636	0.711	0.103	−0.075	−0.29
2	0.290	0.319	0.512	0.148	−0.193	−0.82
3	0.280	0.734	0.487	0.163	0.247	1.09

EXHIBIT 9.9 (Cont'd)

4	0.420	1.327	1.273	0.134	0.054	0.22
5	0.290	0.487	0.512	0.148	−0.025	−0.11
6	0.410	0.924	1.186	0.128	−0.262	−1.05
7	0.760	7.350	7.022	0.214	0.328	1.82
8	0.730	5.890	6.296	0.183	−0.406	−1.92
9	0.460	1.979	1.667	0.157	0.312	1.35
10	0.400	1.124	1.104	0.122	0.020	0.08

suspicion that something has gone wrong. Here we don't see any outside that interval, so we don't have any grounds for suspicion yet, but we need to check some other things too.

Exhibit 9.10 shows what happens when we fit an inadequate model to the stream-flow data. The data in Exhibit 9.10(a) are curved but we tried to represent them with a straight line anyhow. Here it's easy to see that the equation wasn't a good fit. For low x-values the observed y-values are above the straight line; for middle x-values they are below the straight line; and for the largest x-value the observed y is above the line. This means the residuals will be positive for low values of x; negative for middle values of x; and positive again for the high value of x. This pattern shows up nicely in a plot of residuals versus x, as shown in Exhibit 9.10(b). It doesn't really make any difference here whether we plot standardized residuals or regular residuals. The picture will still look about the same. To make it easy to do plots such as this, there is a version of the REGRESS command which allows you to store the standardized residuals.

REGRESS C, K PRED. C,...,C, PUT ST. RES. IN C, PRED. Y IN C

If one extra column is specified, the standardized residuals are stored in it. If two extra columns are specified, the standardized residuals are stored in the first, and the predicted y-values are stored in the second.

EXHIBIT 9.10

Illustration of Pattern in Residuals When the Wrong Model is Fit to the Data

(a)   Plot of the Data

-- PLOT C2 VS C1

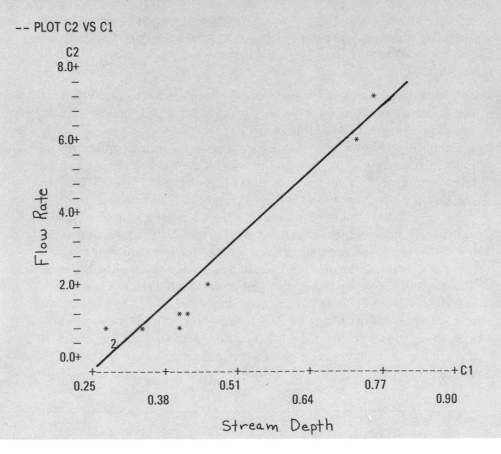

To get the residual plot in Exhibit 9.10(b), we used the following program:

READ X INTO C1, Y INTO C2

(data from page 177)

EXHIBIT 9.10 (Cont'd)

(b)   Plot of Residuals Versus Depth

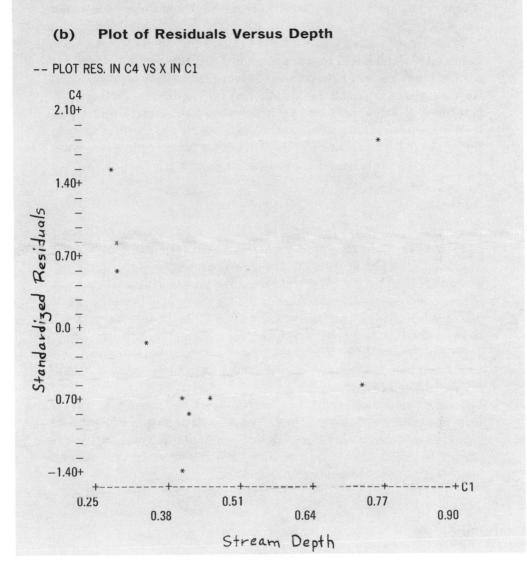

-- PLOT RES. IN C4 VS X IN C1

```
    C4
  2.10+
     -
     -                                                          *
     -
     -        *
  1.40+
     -
     -
     -
     -        x
  0.70+
     -        *
     -
     -
  0.0  +
     -           *
     -
     -
  0.70+
     -              *      *
     -                 *
     -
     -
 -1.40+                 *
     +----------+----------+---------+      -----+--------+ C1
        0.25        0.51                     0.77
             0.38            0.64                    0.90
```

Stream Depth

REGRESS C2 ON 1 PRED. IN C1, STORE STAND. RES. IN C4
PLOT RES. IN C4 VS. X IN C1
STOP

Patterns like those in Exhibit 9.10(b) frequently show up better in plots of the residuals than in plots of the original data. The plots help us know when the model we have fit to the data is not good enough. Whenever we get a strong pattern like this, we know we've used a poor model.

What happens when we fit a second-degree polynomial, as we did in Exhibit 9.9? Exhibit 9.11 contains a residual plot for this fit. Is there any pattern here? For example, do low x-values tend to have low residuals? How about the residuals for middle and high values? Are there any patterns that would indicate our model wasn't adequate? In this plot, we don't see any. It appears that the model we fit was okay, at least as far as *this* plot was concerned. There are other types of plots we should do, but we'll stop here and leave those to Section 9.9.

Summary

If we fit a straight line to data when the basic relationship between x and y is a curve, then a plot of the standardized residuals versus x will be curved. (The plot of y versus x will also be curved but the curvature may not be as apparent.) We might then fit a second-degree polynomial. If the residual plot after this fit is no longer curved (and no other problems are indicated) we probably have a good fit. If the residual plot still shows curvature, we could try fitting a third-degree, or even higher degree, polynomial. As a general rule, however, it's better to use a transformation, as discussed in Section 9.8, than to use polynomials of degree higher than two or three.

Residual plots also help us spot *outliers*—observations that are far from the majority of the data or far from the fitted equation. Outliers should always be checked for possible errors, and in some cases temporarily set aside to see whether they have any effect on the practical interpretation of the results of our analysis.

Exercises

Exercises 9-19 through 9-22 involve stream-flow data from two different sites.

9-19   Here are the data from site 3.

Flow Rate	.820	.500	.433	.215	.120	.172	.106	.094	.129	.240
Stream Depth	.96	.92	.90	.85	.84	.84	.82	.80	.83	.86

EXHIBIT 9.11

Residuals from Second-Degree Polynomial Fit to Stream-Flow Data

-- PLOT RES. IN C4 VS X IN C1

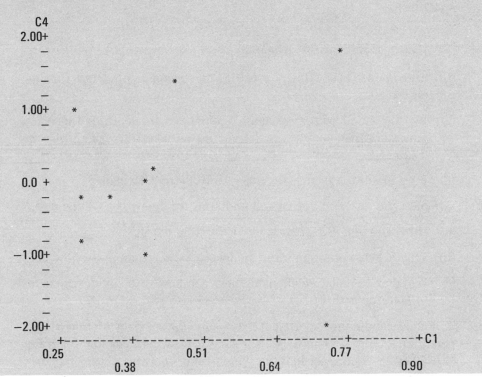

(a) Plot flow rate versus stream depth.

(b) Fit a straight line for predicting flow rate from stream depth. Draw this line on the plot.

(c) Find a 95% confidence interval for the slope, B.

(d) Find a 95% confidence interval for the intercept, A.

9-20 (a) Plot the standardized residuals from the straight-line fit in Exercise 9-19 versus stream depth. Does the plot indicate any lack of fit, or any other problems? Explain.

(b) Fit a quadratic model to the data from site 3. Does it fit any better? Explain.

9-21 Here are the data from site 4.

Flow Rate	.352	.320	.219	.179	.160	.113	.043	.095	.278
Stream Depth	.71	.72	.64	.64	.67	.61	.56	.73	.72

(a) Plot flow rate versus stream depth.

(b) Fit a line for predicting flow rate from stream depth. Draw this line on the plot.

(c) Plot the standardized residuals against stream depth. Is there any indication that another model should be used? Anything else indicated?

(d) Fit a quadratic model. Does it fit any better? Explain.

9-22 Compare the analyses for sites 3 and 4 on the following points:

(a) How well you can predict flow rate from depth;

(b) Whether or not a quadratic model fits better than a straight line;

(c) Whether a similar relationship between flow rate and depth seems to hold for both sites.

9-23 A simple pendulum experiment from physics consists of releasing a pendulum of a given length (L), allowing it to swing back and forth for, say, 50 cycles, and recording the time it takes to swing these 50 cycles. Data from 5 trials of this experiment are given below.

Trial	1	2	3	4	5
Length (L)	175.2	151.5	126.4	101.7	77.0
Time for 50 Cycles	132.5	123.4	112.8	101.2	88.2

(a) Let T be the average time per cycle. Compute T for each trial. Plot T versus L and fit a straight line for predicting T from L. How well can you predict time per cycle from pendulum length?

(b) Are there any indications that a higher-degree polynomial should be used? Fit a better model if one seems needed.

9-24   In Exercise 9-13 (Section 9.3) we simulated data from a regression equa-
        tion. Repeat those simulations and each time plot the standardized
        residuals versus x. This should give you some idea of how a residual plot
        looks when the correct model is fit.

9-25   Let's use simulation to look at some residual plots when the wrong
        model is fit.

   (a) Use the model $y = 3x^2 + 10 + e$, with $\sigma = 0.1$. Take one observation
        at each of the following values of x: 0, .1, .2, .3, .4, .5, .6, .7, .8, .9,
        1.0. Now fit the line $y = a + bx$ and get a residual plot. Is there any
        pattern?

   (b) Repeat part (a) using $\sigma = 0.5$.

9.8 Using Transformations

Rather than fit a polynomial to curved data, it is often preferable to try
a few transformations to see if a simpler model can be found. The basic
idea behind the use of transformations is to analyze some function of
x or y, such as $\sqrt{y}$, $-1/y$, or $\log(x)$, rather than x or y itself.[*]
    We can use the stream-flow data from Exhibit 9.8 as an example.
Obviously, when we plot y (stream flow) versus x (depth), we don't get
a straight line. But what if we plotted $\sqrt{y}$ versus x? Or y versus $-1/x$?
Or $\sqrt{y}$ versus $\sqrt{x}$? Perhaps one of these will give an approximately
straight line.
    Exhibit 9.12 shows this same stream-flow data plotted several differ-
ent ways using a variety of transformations.
    Several of these plots seem to be reasonably close to straight lines,
although none overwhelm us with their straightness. Clearly y versus
x is not a straight line. Neither is y versus $\sqrt{x}$. Perhaps $\sqrt{y}$ versus x
is close enough to use. In this case we might decide to predict $\sqrt{y}$, using
x as the predictor variable. The resulting equation would be

$$\sqrt{y} = a + b\,x\,.$$

[*] We use $-1/y$ rather than $1/y$. If we used $1/y$, the scale would reverse itself since large
values of y give small values of $1/y$ and small values of y give large values of $1/y$. When
we use $-1/y$, the scale doesn't reverse itself since small values of y give small values of
$-1/y$, and so on.

EXHIBIT 9.12

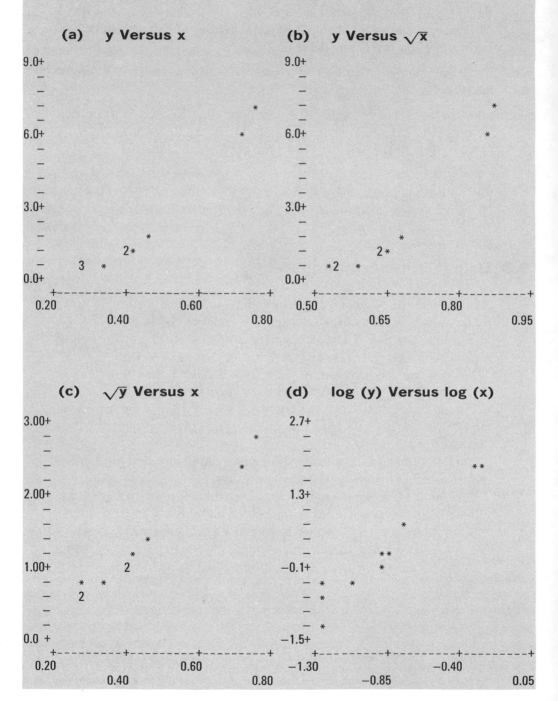

Transformations of Stream-Flow Data

(a)   y Versus x

(b)   y Versus √x̄

(c)   √ȳ Versus x

(d)   log (y) Versus log (x)

EXHIBIT 9.12 (Cont'd)

      (e)   log (y) Versus x   **(f)   −1/y Versus −1/x**

```
2.7+                                    0.7+
   -                                       -
   -                    * *                -                              **
   -                                       -
1.3+                                    -0.7+                        *
   -                                       -                      *
   -              *                        -                    **
   -                                       -                *
   -          **                           - .
-0.1+          *                         -2.1+          *
   -       *     *                          -
   -       *                                -
   -                                        -
   -     *                                  -          *
-1.5+                                     -3.5+
   +---------+---------+---------+        +---------+---------+---------+
   0.20      0.40     0.60      0.80      -4.00    -3.00    -2.00    -1.00
```

Suppose the x-values are in C1 and the y-values are in C2. Then a program to do this regression is

```
SQRT OF C2 PUT IN C3
REGRESS C3 ON 1 PREDICTOR IN C1
```

The output from this program is a little tricky since Minitab always assumes we fitted "y" to "x." So it tells us that the best equation is

$$y = -0.558 + 4.16 \ x .$$

Of course, this really means

$$\sqrt{\text{flow}} = -0.558 + (4.16)(\text{depth}) .$$

Thus if the depth was .7, we would predict $\sqrt{\text{flow}}$ as

$$-0.558 + 4.16 \ (.7) = 2.354, \text{ or}$$
$$\text{flow} = (2.354)^2 = 5.54.$$

Another plot that looks fairly good is log(y) versus log(x). In this case, regressing log(y) would give the equation

$$\log(y) = a + b \log(x).$$

Either of these might do for prediction purposes. In addition, they *might* give us some idea of a good *theoretical* model for the relationship between stream-flow rate and depth. Using a polynomial might be equally good for prediction purposes over the range of the data, but it probably wouldn't work very well outside the range of the data, or give us much theoretical insight.

How to Choose Which Transformations to Try

The process of deciding which transformations to try is not as hit-or-miss as it might at first seem. All of the transformations on y we have mentioned, $\sqrt{y}$, log(y), and $-1/y$, have the effect of pulling in the upper end of the scale. Furthermore, they are ordered. The weakest transformation is $\sqrt{y}$. Next comes log(y), while $-1/y$ has the biggest effect.

The procedure can be summarized as follows: Suppose you plot y versus x and the line curves up like the plot in panel (a) of Exhibit 9.12. Then to get a straight line, you need to shrink the upper end of the y-scale. First try $\sqrt{y}$ versus x. If this isn't strong enough, try log(y) versus x. If the line still curves up, try $(-1/y)$ versus x. Usually one of these will work fairly well.

If the line curves down, like the one in panel (e) of Exhibit 9.12, then you need to shrink the upper end of the x-scale. First try $\sqrt{x}$, then log(x), and finally $-1/x$. After a while you can begin to guess pretty well which transformation will be needed.

Sometimes it helps to transform both scales. The pair of transformations that seems to work best for the stream-flow data is to use the log on both scales. That is, plot log(y) versus log(x). Engineers have a saying—"Anything is a straight line when you plot it on log-log paper." While their saying is, of course, not true in all cases, it does work surprisingly often.

Effect of Transformations on Assumptions

The conditions necessary for inference in regression were listed in Section 9.3 (page 159). Whenever we make a transformation, we have some effect on the validity of the conditions. If we have a straight line, and take the logarithm of x or y, we won't have a straight line any more. If y has the same variance for all values of x, then log(y) and $\sqrt{y}$ won't. If y is normally distributed, then log(y) and $\sqrt{y}$ won't be.

But, on the other hand, if some of these conditions aren't met before we transform the data, they may be afterward. Sometimes a transformation will help with one of these conditions, but mess up another. Surprisingly often, a transformation that helps with one condition will help with the others.

To summarize, our advice is to use transformations as you would use any other statistical technique—not blindly, but with a healthy skepticism that says, "I know none of these assumptions are met exactly, and I know that some are more important than others. I will check them all, particularly the most important ones, and always use the results of my analysis as guidance, not as gospel."

Exercises

9-26   In Exercise 9-23, you fit a line to some pendulum data. A residual plot indicates a curve in the data—a curve which may not have been apparent in a data plot. You then probably fit a quadratic. This gives a residual plot with no apparent pattern (of course, with just 5 observations, it's difficult to do a very precise analysis). It is known from physics that the correct relationship is $T = (2\pi/\sqrt{g})\sqrt{L}$, where $g = 981$ cm/sec.^{2} (at the latitude where the experiment was done). Thus if we fit a straight line of T versus $\sqrt{L}$, we should find $A = 0$ and $B - 2\pi/\sqrt{981} = 0.201$.

(a)   Fit the model $T = A + B\sqrt{L} + e$. How well does it fit compared to a quadratic model? If you didn't know any physics, could you decide between these two models based on these data?

(b)   Do your estimates of A and B seem close to the theoretical values?

(c)   Now test H_0: $A = 0$ and H_0: $B = 0.201$ (use $\alpha = 0.05$). Are the results of these tests consistent with your answers in (b)? Explain.

9-27   An experiment was run in which a tumor was induced in a laboratory animal. The size of the tumor was recorded as it grew.

Number of Days After Induction	Size of Tumor (cc)
12	.085
14	1.25
16	1.90
19	4.75
21	5.45
23	7.53
26	14.5
28	16.7
30	21.0
33	27.1
35	30.3
37	40.5
41	51.4

Investigate the relationship between time and tumor size. Is the relationship linear? Can it be "linearized" by an appropriate transformation?

9.9 More about Residuals

When we fit a straight line, we plot residuals versus our single predictor. In multiple regression, where there are several predictors, the basic residual plot is residuals versus the predicted y-values. (Recall from Section 9.7, that Minitab can store the predicted y-values.) Curvature in this plot can come from any of a number of sources—the need for a squared term, such as x_1^2, x_2^2, x_3^2, or the need for an interaction term such as x_1x_2, or the need for a transformation such as $\sqrt{x}$ or $1/x$. The residuals versus each predictor can be plotted to see which predictor(s) need to be modified.

It is also useful to plot the residuals versus the order in which the data were gathered. (This is often the order in which it's given to you.) Patterns here indicate a change over time— a change in chemistry, a change in personnel, etc. Changes such as these were probably not intended and indicate problems with the experiment or survey.

Two assumptions of regression are deviations that have a normal distribution and equal variances (conditions (d) and (b) of Section 9.3).

A histogram of the residuals will give a rough check on normality. Lack of equal variances can often be spotted in the residual plots. For example, if a plot of residuals versus x_1 fans out, then variance is increasing with the value of x_1. In general, if any residual plot fans out (or in), inequality of variances is indicated.

As pointed out in Section 9.8, a transformation of y affects the residuals—both normality and equal variance. Often transformations are used precisely to make residuals normal when they originally were not, or to get equal variances. On the other hand, an inappropriate transformation on y can destroy normality or equal variances. Thus you should always check residual plots and a residual histogram.

9.10 More about Minitab and Regression

There are four control commands which affect REGRESS. They are BRIEF and its opposite NOBRIEF, and NOCONSTANT and its opposite CONSTANT.

> ## BRIEF
>
> When BRIEF is in effect, the amount of output from all REGRESS commands which follow it will be minimized. Only the regression equation, table of coefficients, R^2, R^2 – adjusted, estimated standard deviation, and analysis of variance table are printed. Once in effect, BRIEF remains in effect until the command NOBRIEF is encountered.
>
> ## NOBRIEF
>
> Restores the full output, as described in this chapter, from the REGRESS command.

NOCONSTANT

Tells Minitab to fit, in all REGRESS commands that follow, a regression equation with no constant (intercept) term. Thus, if there are k predictors, Minitab fits the equation

$$y = b_1 x_1 + b_2 x_2 + \dots + b_k x_k$$

The command NOCONSTANT remains in effect until the command CONSTANT is encountered.

CONSTANT

Tells Minitab to return to fitting the usual regression equation, with a constant term, i.e.,

$$y = b_0 + b_1 x_1 + b_2 x_2 + \dots + b_k x_k$$

Weighted regression can be done using the following form of the REGRESS command:

REGRESS Y'S IN **C**, USING WEIGHTS IN **C**, ON **K** PREDICTORS

IN **C, C,...,C**

The procedure is to put the weights you want to use in a column, then specify this as a second column before the K on the REGRESS command.

10

Analysis of Variance

10.1 One-Way Analysis of Variance

In Chapter 8 we showed how t-tests could be used to compare data from two different populations. But what if we want to compare more than two? To be more explicit, let's consider an example.

The flammability of children's sleepwear has received a lot of attention in the last few years. Standards are being developed to ensure that manufacturers don't sell children's pajamas that burn easily. But a problem always arises in cases like this. How do you test the flammability of a particular garment? The shape of the garment might make a difference. How tightly it fits might be important. Of course, the flammability of clothing can't be tested on children. Perhaps an asbestos manikin could be used. But how should the material be lighted? Different people putting a match to identical cloth will probably get different answers. The list of difficulties is endless, but the problem is real, and important.

One procedure that has been developed to test flammability is called the *Vertical Semi-Restrained Test*. There are a lot of details to the test, but basically it involves holding a flame under a standard-size piece of cloth which is loosely held in a metal frame. The dryness of the fabric, its temperature, the height of the flame, how long the flame is held under the fabric, and so on, are all carefully controlled. After the flame is removed and the fabric stops burning, the length of the charred portion of the fabric is measured and recorded.

Once we have a proposed way to test flammability, one important question is, "Will the laboratories of the different garment manufacturers all be able to get about the same results if they apply the same test to the same fabric?" In 1974 a study was conducted to answer this question. A small part of the data is in Exhibit 10.1.

These data are plotted in Exhibit 10.2. This plot tells us a lot by itself. Even within a given laboratory, the char-length varies from specimen to specimen. All of the specimens are supposedly identical since they were cut from the same bolt of cloth. But there probably were still some differences between them. In addition, the test conditions probably differed slightly from specimen to specimen—the tautness of the material, the exact time the flame was held under the specimen, and so on. We must expect some variation even within a laboratory. The variation within the laboratory can be thought of as simply random error. There are several other names for it—*within group variation, unexplained variation, residual variation,* or *variation due to error.*

There is a second possible source of variation in the data—that due to differences between labs. This variation is called *between group variation, variation due to factor,* or *variation explained by the factor.* Here the factor under study is laboratory. Sometimes the word *treatment* is used instead of factor. If we look at the plot again, we see some variation among the 5 labs. Lab 4 got mostly low values whereas labs 2 and 5 got mostly high values. Instead of using a plot, we could compare the sample means for the 5 labs. These are given in Exhibit 10.1. The 5 sample means do vary from lab to lab, but again some variation is to be expected. The question is, "Do the 5 sample means differ any more than we'd expect from just random variation?" Put another way, "Is the *between group variation* significantly greater than the *within group variation?*" Analysis of variance is a statistical procedure that gives an answer to this question.

The One-Way Analysis of Variance Procedure

In one-way analysis of variance, we want to compare the means of several populations. We assume that we have a random sample from each population, that each population has a normal distribution, and that all of the populations have the same variance, σ^2. (In practice, the normality assumption is not too important, the equal variances assumption is not important if the sample sizes for the different samples are about the same, but the assumption of a random sample is very important.) The main question is, "Do all of the populations have the same mean?" Suppose we have r populations, and that μ_1 is the mean of the first

EXHIBIT 10.1

Part of Data Obtained in an Interlaboratory Study of Fabric Flammability Measurements

Length of Charred Portion of Fabric

	Laboratory				
	1	*2*	*3*	*4*	*5*
	2.9	2.7	3.3	3.3	4.1
	3.1	3.4	3.3	3.2	4.1
	3.1	3.6	3.5	3.4	3.7
	3.7	3.2	3.5	2.7	4.2
	3.1	4.0	2.8	2.7	3.1
	4.2	4.1	2.8	3.3	3.5
	3.7	3.8	3.2	2.9	2.8
	3.9	3.8	2.8	3.2	3.5
	3.1	4.3	3.8	2.9	3.7
	3.0	3.4	3.5	2.6	3.5
	2.9	3.3	3.8	2.8	3.9
Sample Means	3.34	3.60	3.30	3.00	3.65

population, μ_2 is the mean of the second population, μ_3 of the third, and so on. Then the null hypothesis of no differences is

$$H_0: \mu_1 = \mu_2 = \mu_3 = ... = \mu_r .$$

To test this null hypothesis, we can use Minitab's analysis of variance one-way command.

AOVONEWAY ON DATA IN C, C,...,C

Performs a one-way (one-factor) analysis of variance on the data. The first column contains a sample from the first population (sometimes called group, or level), the second column contains a sample from the second population, the third column from the third population, and so on. (The sample sizes need not be equal.)

The output gives the following: (1) a plot of the data; (2) an analysis of variance table; (3) the sample size, sample mean, and standard deviation corresponding to each population (or factor level); (4) the pooled estimate, $s_p = \sqrt{\text{mean square error}}$, of the common standard deviation, σ; (5) a display of individual 95% confidence intervals for each population mean. Each confidence interval is calculated by

$$\bar{x}_i - t^* \, s_p / \sqrt{n_i} \text{ to } \bar{x}_i + t^* \, s_p / \sqrt{n_i} \,,$$

where $\bar{x}_i$ and n_i are the sample mean and sample size corresponding to population i, and t^* is the value from a t-table corresponding to 95% confidence and the degrees of freedom associated with the mean square error.

The output discussed here is the full output. On some computers this output has been abbreviated. To get the full output, put the command NOBRIEF (page 326) before the first analysis of variance command.

The following program was used to analyze the flammability data from Exhibit 10.1:

```
SET DATA FROM FIRST LAB INTO C1
2.9, 3.1, 3.1, 3.7, 3.1, 4.2, 3.7, 3.9, 3.1, 3.0, 2.9
SET DATA FROM SECOND LAB INTO C2
2.7, 3.4, 3.6, 3.2, 4.0, 4.1, 3.8, 3.8, 4.3, 3.4, 3.3
SET DATA FROM THIRD LAB INTO C3
3.3, 3.3, 3.5, 3.5, 2.8, 2.8, 3.2, 2.8, 3.8, 3.5, 3.8
SET DATA FROM FOURTH LAB INTO C4
3.3, 3.2, 3.4, 2.7, 2.7, 3.3, 2.9, 3.2, 2.9, 2.6, 2.8
SET DATA FROM FIFTH LAB INTO C5
4.1, 4.1, 3.7, 4.7, 3.1, 3.5, 7.8, 3.5, 3.7, 3.5, 3.9
AOVONEWAY ON DATA IN C1-C5
STOP
```

EXHIBIT 10.2

Plot of Flammability Measurements for 5 Laboratories

```
-- PLOT C21 C20

     C21
  4.40+
      -           *
      - *                                       *
      -
      -           *                             2
  4.00+           *
      - *                                       *
      -
      -           2         2
      - 2                                       2
  3.60+           *
      -                     3                   3
      -           2                   *
      -
      -           *         2         2
  3.20+           *         *         2
      - 4                                       *
      - *
      -
      - 2                             2
  2.80+                     3         *         *
      -           *                   2
      -
      -                               *
      -
  2.40+
        +---------+---------+---------+---------+---------+ C20
      1.00                3.00                5.00
                2.00                4.00                6.00
```

Length of Charred Portion

Laboratory

The output is in Exhibit 10.3. The first part is a plot of the data, much like the one we used in Exhibit 10.2.

The second part of the output is an analysis of variance table. The total sum of squares is broken down into two sources—the variation due to differences between the 5 labs and the variation due to random error

EXHIBIT 10.3

Output from AOVONEWAY Command—Analysis of Flammability Data

– –AOVONEWAY ON DATA IN C1-C5

	ALL DATA	C1	LEVEL C2	C3	C4	C5
4.80+						
—						
—						
—	1		1			
—	5	1	1			3
4.00+	1		1			
—	6	1	2	2		1
—	5	2	1			2
—	6			3		3
—	8		3	2	3	
3.20+	4		1	1	2	
—	6	5				1
—	4	2			2	
—	8		1	3	3	1
—	1				1	
2.40+						

ANALYSIS OF VARIANCE

DUE TO	DF	SS	MS=SS/DF	F-RATIO
FACTOR	4	2.987	0.747	4.53
ERROR	50	8.233	0.165	
TOTAL	54	11.219		

LEVEL	N	MEAN	ST. DEV.
C1	11	3.336	0.452
C2	11	3.600	0.460
C3	11	3.300	0.371
C4	11	3.000	0.286
C5	11	3.645	0.432
POOLED ST. DEV. =	0.406		

EXHIBIT 10.3 (Cont'd)

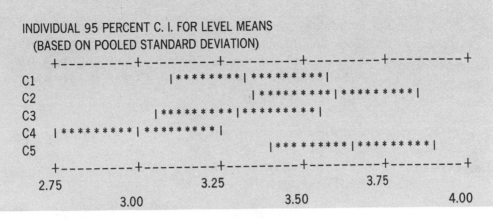

INDIVIDUAL 95 PERCENT C. I. FOR LEVEL MEANS
(BASED ON POOLED STANDARD DEVIATION)

within a lab. Thus, (SS TOTAL) = (SS FACTOR) + (SS ERROR). In this
example, $11.219 = 2.987 + 8.233$. Each sum of squares has a certain
number of degrees of freedom associated with it. These will be used
when we do tests. The degrees of freedom also add up, (DF TOTAL) = (DF
FACTOR) + (DF ERROR).

The third column gives the mean square due to the factor (difference
among labs) and the mean square due to error (variation within labs).
Each mean square is just the ratio of the corresponding sum of squares
and degrees of freedom. The last column gives the quotient of these two
mean squares (F-RATIO) = (MS FACTOR)/(MS ERROR). This F-RATIO is a
useful test statistic. If it is large, then MS FACTOR must be much larger
than MS ERROR. That is, the variation between the labs is much greater
than the variation due to random error. So we would reject the null
hypothesis that the labs all have the same average char-length. How
large the F-RATIO must be is determined by the critical value from an
F-table. To use an F-table, we need the degrees of freedom for the
numerator of the F-ratio and the degrees of freedom for the denominator of the F-ratio. Here the numerator has 4 degrees of freedom and
denominator 50. The corresponding value from an F-table, using $\alpha =
0.05$, is about 2.6. Since 4.53 is greater than 2.6, we reject the null
hypothesis and conclude we have significant evidence that there is some
difference among the 5 labs.

The next table contains some other useful information, such as the
sample size, sample mean, and sample standard deviation corresponding

to each level. (In the usual analysis of variance terminology, each population is called "a level of the factor.")

Following this table is the pooled estimate of the common standard
deviation, σ. This pooled estimate is used to construct confidence intervals for each of the 5 population means. These confidence intervals are
displayed in the next table. Here, we see that lab 4 seems to have a low
mean value, much lower than labs 2 and 5.

Exercises

10-1   In a simple pendulum experiment a weight (bob) is suspended at the end
of a length of string. The top of the string is supported by some sort
of stable frame. Under ideal conditions the time (T) required for a single
cycle of the pendulum is related to the length (L) of the string by the
equation

$$T = \left(\frac{2\pi}{\sqrt{g}}\right)\sqrt{L},$$

where, as usual, $\pi = 3.1415...$, and g is the pull (acceleration) of gravity.
If the time required for a cycle and the length of the pendulum are
measured, then this equation can be solved to give an estimate of g.
In theory, neither the length of the pendulum nor the type of bob should
have any effect on the estimate of g. In practice, however, things that
are not supposed to make any difference often do. So it is always a good
practice, when doing an experiment, to vary things that are not supposed
to matter. Therefore, the experiment was run using four different
lengths and two types of bobs.

The following data were obtained by college professors during a short
course on the use of statistics in physics and chemistry courses.

| | Length of Pendulum (cm) | | | |
	60	70	80	90
	924	994	970	1000
Heavy	973	969	975	1017
Bob	955	968	970	1055

	60	70	80	90
	966	973	985	960
Light	949	997	999	1041
Bob	955	988	994	962

(a) Do a one-way analysis of variance to see if length affects the estimate of g. Use the data obtained with the heavy bob.

(b) Repeat part (a), using the data obtained with the light bob.

(c) Does length appear to effect the estimate? In what way? Is the effect the same for the two bobs?

10-2 Very small amounts of some minerals (for example, manganese and titanium) are important to a good diet. But how do you know if you have enough? Measurement of these very small amounts is quite difficult. The National Bureau of Standards (NBS) sometimes does very careful chemical analyses of such materials, then sells pieces of the material together with an accurate chemical analysis so that interested researchers can evaluate their own ability to measure the same material. In one such study, NBS measured the amount of manganese in cow liver. They made two measurements on each of 11 different samples and got the following results. Do a one-way analysis of variance to see if there is a statistically significant difference among the 11 different samples.

Manganese (parts per million)

Sample	1	2	3	4	5	6	7	8	9	10	11
Measure- ment 1	10.02	10.41	10.25	9.41	9.73	10.07	10.09	9.85	10.02	9.92	9.7
Measure- ment 2	10.03	9.79	9.80	10.17	10.75	9.76	9.38	9.99	9.51	10.01	10.0

10.2 The ONEWAY Command

The ONEWAY command does exactly the same thing as the AOVONEWAY command. The only difference is in how the data are stored in the worksheet.

> ## ONEWAY ANALYSIS OF VARIANCE ON DATA IN **C**, LEVEL NOS.
>
> ### IN C
>
> Does the same analysis and has the same output as AOVONEWAY. The only difference is the input. All data for all groups (levels) are put into one column. A second column says what group each value belongs to.
>
> ### Example
>
> Suppose we have the following data:
>
> | | | | |
> |---|---|---|---|
> | *Group 1* | 5.2, | 1.8 | |
> | *Group 2* | 2.3, | 1.0, | 1.6 |
> | *Group 3* | 2.1, | 2.2 | |
>
> The following program does a one-way analysis of variance:
>
> ```
> READ DATA INTO C1, LEVELS INTO C2
> 5.2  1
> 1.8  1
> 2.3  2
> 2.1  3
> 1.0  2
> 1.6  2
> 2.2  3
> ONEWAY ANALYSIS OF VARIANCE, DATA IN C1, LEVELS IN C2
> STOP
> ```
>
> The numbers used for levels (group numbers) must be integers.

Sometimes it is more convenient to use ONEWAY than AOVONEWAY. For example, in the **Cartoon** experiment (page 270), suppose we want to compare the immediate cartoon scores for the 3 different levels of education (pre-professional, professional, student). The following program is probably the simplest way:

READ DATA INTO C1-C9

(data from page 272)

ONEWAY FOR IMMED. CARTOON IN C6, ED. LEVEL IN C3
STOP

Exercises

10-3   When you exercise, your pulse rate goes up. Does a person's usual level
       of physical activity have any effect on this increase? To investigate this,
       use the data from the **Pulse** experiment (page 285) for the people who
       ran in place.

   (a) Do a one-way analysis of variance using the "second pulse rate"
        data. Is there a significant difference between activity levels? What
        is the practical significance of these results? (Note: Be careful to
        use only those students who did run in place.)

   (b) Repeat the analysis of part (a), but instead of using the "second
        pulse rate" data, use the change in pulse rate (i.e., "second pulse
        rate" minus "first pulse rate"). Interpret these results.

   (c) How do the analyses of (a) and (b) compare?

10-4   Steelmakers find that small differences in the amount of oxygen in steel
       make an important difference in the quality of the steel they produce.
       Since small amounts of oxygen are difficult to measure accurately, the
       National Bureau of Standards agreed to make very careful measure-
       ments on some homogeneous material, then sell samples to steel manu-
       facturers who could use them to check whether their own instruments
       were making accurate measurements. The Bureau of Standards took a
       long "homogeneous" steel rod and cut it up into 4-inch lengths. They
       randomly selected 20 of these 4-inch pieces. These pieces were labelled
       1 through 20. Then they made two very careful measurements of the
       amount of oxygen in each piece of rod.

Measurements of Oxygen in 20 Pieces of a Steel Rod

Date of Measurement	Piece Number	Amount of Oxygen (parts per million)
January 14 (Day 1)	17	5.6
	11	5.9
	10	6.8

Measurements of Oxygen in 20 Pieces of a Steel Rod (Cont'd)

Date of Measurement	Piece Number	Amount of Oxygen (parts per million)
	15	7.5
	5	4.7
	6	4.0
	19	4.4
January 15 (Day 2)	4	6.6
	7	4.9
	1	5.5
	13	4.9
	3	6.3
	18	4.2
	9	3.3
	14	4.8
January 16 (Day 3)	16	6.1
	12	5.3
	8	5.2
	2	4.3
	11	4.0
	19	6.2
	17	5.1
	9	3.3
January 17 (Day 4)	13	5.4
	18	6.1
	2	5.7
	10	6.1
	4	5.7
	20	4.6
	7	5.7
	6	4.4
	12	4.1
January 21 (Day 5)	16	6.3
	15	7.5
	8	6.1
	14	6.4
	3	5.1
	20	5.7
	5	3.8
	1	3.8

Note: On a given date, the measurements were made in the order listed.

Bear in mind when analyzing these data that finding and measuring quantities as small as 5 parts of oxygen in a million parts of steel is a very difficult process, and is subject to a wide variety of unsuspected sources of error.

In the following analysis, it will probably help if you use a variable which specifies the date of measurement (perhaps just 1, 2, 3, 4, 5) and a variable which specifies the order in which the measurements were made on each day (perhaps 1,2,...,7 for day 1; 1,2,...,8 for day 2; etc.).

(a) Is there statistically significant evidence that the 20 pieces are not homogeneous? (Try doing a one-way analysis of variance using the piece number as the "level.")

(b) Is there any evidence of day to day variation in the measurements? (Use day number as the level.)

(c) Plot the data in a variety of ways. There is a major unsuspected source of error in these measurements. See if you can find a plot that shows how it affects the measurements, then make a conjecture about what the problem might be.

(d) There are (at least) two important morals that can be learned from these data, one concerning the statistical aspects of planning experiments, and one concerning analysis of data. Can you think of what they might be?

10.3 Two-Way Analysis of Variance

Two-way analysis of variance is very much like one-way analysis of variance, except the data are grouped by two different classifications, rather than just one. Exhibit 10.4 shows a typical example. These data were obtained in an experiment where the primary interest was in comparing several different methods of freezing meat loaf. Meat loaf was to be baked, then frozen for a time, and finally compared by expert tasters.

Eight loaves could be baked in the oven at one time. But some parts of an oven are usually hotter or differ in some other important way from other parts. If this were the case, then loaves baked in one part of the oven might taste better than those baked in other parts, and differences between the freezing methods might be masked. So, a preliminary test

EXHIBIT 10.4

Drip Loss in Meat Loaves

	Batch		
Oven Position	1	2	3
1	7.33	8.11	8.06
2	3.22	3.72	4.28
3	3.28	5.11	4.56
4	6.44	5.78	8.61
5	3.83	6.50	7.72
6	3.28	5.11	5.56
7	5.06	5.11	7.83
8	4.44	4.28	6.33

Oven Positions On One Shelf

5	6	7	8
4	3	2	1

Front of Shelf

Note: Thermometers to measure the temperature of the loaves were inserted in the four corner loaves (1, 4, 5, 8) and in one central loaf (7).

was conducted to see if there was any noticeable difference between the oven positions. Eight loaves were mixed and baked at once and then analyzed. A second batch of 8 loaves was mixed, baked, and analyzed, and then a third batch. Percentage of drip loss was measured for each meat loaf (i.e., the amount of liquid which dripped out of the meat loaf during cooking divided by the original weight of the meat loaf).

In this example the two classifications (or factors) are "oven position" (which corresponds to rows in the table) and "batch" (columns in the table). There are 8 different levels of oven position and 3 different levels of batch. Thus there are $8 \times 3 = 24$ cells in the table and each cell has one observation in it.

Exhibit 10.5 gives a plot of these data using the LPLOT command (see

EXHIBIT 10.5

Letter Plot of Drip Loss Versus Oven Position

A denotes batch 1
B denotes batch 2
C denotes batch 3

-- LPLOT C1 VS C2, USING CODES IN C3

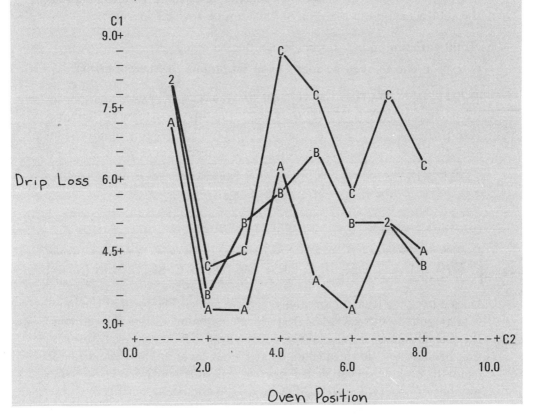

program in Exhibit 10.6). The letters are useful here because they tell us which loaf was in which batch. All of the A's were in the first batch, the B's in the second batch, and the C's in the third. (The 2's are a little confusing but we can figure out that the one at the top left stands for a B and a C, and the other 2 stands for an A and a B.)

We connected the letters by hand, to help us see better. Here it seems obvious that there was some systematic difference between the 3 batches. The readings for batch 1 are the lowest at almost every position while those for batch 3 are almost always the highest. Thus, part of the variation in the data seems to be due to differences between batches. It also appears that oven position makes a difference. All the readings for position 1 are pretty high. Those for 2 and 3 are low, and so on. So part of the variation seems to be due to differences between oven position.

Now, just as we did in one-way analysis of variance, we can express the total variation in the data as the sum of several sources:

(Total variation in data) = (variation due to batch) +

(variation due to oven position) + (variation due to random error).

If the variation due to batch is much greater than the random variation, we'll have evidence that there is a significant difference between batches. And if the variation due to oven position is much greater than random variation, we'll have evidence that there is a difference between the 8 oven positions.

TWOWAY AOV, OBS. IN **C**, FIRST FACTOR IN **C**, SECOND IN **C**

Does a two-way (two-factor) analysis of variance. The form of the input is analogous to ONEWAY. The first column contains all the observations; the second column says what level of the first factor (row) each observation belongs to; the third column says what level of the second factor (column) each observation belongs to. All cells must have the same number of observations (i.e., the experiment must be balanced).

The output includes the usual analysis of variance table, cell means and factor level means, a table of residuals, and an individual 95% confidence interval for the mean of each factor level. Exactly what's printed out depends on whether you have one observation per cell or more than one.

As in AOVONEWAY, the output may have been abbreviated on some computers. Use NOBRIEF (page 326) to get the full output.

EXHIBIT 10.6

Program to Do a Plot and Two-Way Analysis of Variance of the Meat Loaf Data of Exhibit 10.4

```
READ DRIP LOSS INTO C1, OVEN POSITION INTO C2, BATCH INTO C3
7.33    1.    1.
3.22    2.    1.
3.28    3.    1.
6.44    4.    1.
3.83    5.    1.
3.28    6.    1.
5.06    7.    1.
4.44    8.    1.
8.11    1.    2.
3.72    2.    2.
5.11    3.    2.
5.78    4.    2.
6.50    5.    2.
5.11    6.    2.
5.11    7.    2.
4.28    8.    2.
8.06    1.    3.
4.28    2.    3.
4.56    3.    3.
8.61    4.    3.
7.72    5.    3.
5.56    6.    3.
7.83    7.    3.
6.33    8.    3.
LPLOT C1 VS C2, USING CODES IN C3
TWOWAY ANALYSIS DATA IN C1, CLASSIFICATIONS IN C2 AND C3
STOP
```

Exhibit 10.6 gives a program that does the analysis for the meat loaf data.

Output from the TWOWAY command is in Exhibit 10.7. The breakdown of the variation is given in the analysis of variance table. The sum

EXHIBIT 10.7

Two-Way Analysis of Variance of Meat Loaf Data

```
-- TWOWAY AOV ON DATA IN C1, POSITION IN C2, BATCH IN C3
ANALYSIS OF VARIANCE
```

DUE TO	DF	SS	MS=SS/DF
C2	7	40.396	5.771
C3	2	16.259	8.130
ERROR	14	9.290	0.664
TOTAL	23	65.945	

```
OBSERVATIONS
ROWS ARE LEVELS OF C2                    COLS ARE LEVELS OF C3
```

	1	2	3	ROW MEANS
1	7.33	8.11	8.06	7.83
2	3.22	3.72	4.28	3.74
3	3.28	5.11	4.56	4.32
4	6.44	5.78	8.61	6.94
5	3.83	6.50	7.72	6.02
6	3.28	5.11	5.56	4.65
7	5.06	5.11	7.83	6.00
8	4.44	4.28	6.33	5.02
COL. MEANS	4.61	5.46	6.62	5.56

```
POOLED ST. DEV. =    0.815
```

of squares due to oven position is 40.396 and has 7 degrees of free-dom associated with it. The sum of squares due to batch is 16.259 and has 2 degrees of freedom associated with it. The sum of squares due to random error is 9.290 and has 14 degrees of freedom associated with it. So the three respective mean squares are $40.396/7 = 5.771$, $16.259/2 = 8.130$, and $9.290/14 = 0.664$. There are two tests we can do.

To see if there is a significant difference between the 8 oven positions, we form the F-ratio, (MS position)/(MS error) $= 5.771/0.664 = 8.74$, and

EXHIBIT 10.7 (Cont'd)

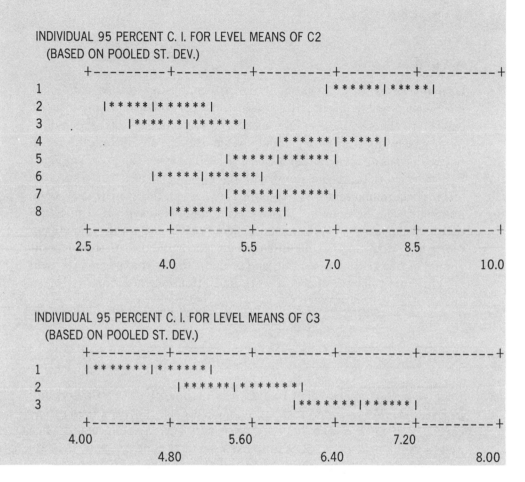

INDIVIDUAL 95 PERCENT C. I. FOR LEVEL MEANS OF C2
(BASED ON POOLED ST. DEV.)

```
         +---------+---------+---------+---------+---------+
1                                      |******|*****|
2           |*****|******|
3             |*****  **|******|
4                               |******|*****|
5                    |*****|******|
6           |*****|******|
7                    |*****|******|
8             |******|*****|
         +---------+---------+---------+---------+---------+
      2.5            5.5                 8.5
            4.0                7.0                   10.0
```

INDIVIDUAL 95 PERCENT C. I. FOR LEVEL MEANS OF C3
(BASED ON POOLED ST. DEV.)

```
         +---------+---------+---------+---------+---------+
1          |*******|******|
2              |******|********|
3                      |********|******|
         +---------+---------+---------+---------+---------+
      4.00            5.60                7.20
            4.80                6.40                  8.00
```

compare it to the value from an F-table, corresponding to 7 degrees of freedom in the numerator and 14 in the denominator. Here the F-table value is 2.76, for $\alpha = 0.05$. Since $8.74 > 2.76$, we have evidence that drip loss varies among the 8 oven positions. This agrees with what we observed in the LPLOT of Exhibit 10.5.

To see if there is a significant difference between batches, form the F-ratio, (MS batch)/(MS error) $= 8.130/0.664 = 12.32$, and compare it to the value from an F-table, corresponding to 2 degrees of freedom in the numerator and 14 degrees of freedom in the denominator. Here the table value is 3.74, for $\alpha = 0.05$. Since $12.32 > 3.74$, we have evidence that drip loss varies from batch to batch. Again, this is what we observed in the LPLOT.

A Further Look

In many cases an analysis of variance would stop at this point, but whenever possible it will pay us to look deeper to learn as much as we can. Here the significant difference between batches was expected—quality usually varies from batch to batch. But the significant difference between positions warranted a closer look. The experimenter happened to notice that the three positions with the lowest drip loss were the three *without* thermometers. Even though unexpected, this was quite reasonable, since the hole made by the thermometer allowed some juices to escape. One obvious solution would have been to put a thermometer in every loaf, then they would all have been the same. But then hindsight should be better than foresight, and perhaps the next experimenter will benefit from this one's careful work and attention to details.

Exercise

10-5   Four young men each spent two days in an office and two days riding in a taxi cab. At the end of each day, measurements were taken of the carbon monoxide in their lungs. Days 1 and 3 were spent in the office and days 2 and 4 were spent in taxis. Two of the men, A and B, were non-smokers, C was a light smoker and D was a heavy smoker.

Carbon Monoxide in Lungs

Day	Person			
	A	B	C	D
1	11	14	21	63
2	13	11	28	75
3	12	14	16	47
4	23	26	26	65

Do a two-way analysis of variance. What does this analysis tell you?

10.4 Two-Way Analysis of Variance: Testing for Interaction

In an analysis of variance, when there is more than one observation per cell, it is convenient to test whether there is any "interaction" between the two factors. In this section, we'll show how this can be done, but first let's take a closer look at the meaning of "interaction" as used in the analysis of variance.

Interaction

Let's begin with an example where it is convenient to suppose we know the population means almost exactly. So, we won't need to worry about random variation for a moment.

Mean Annual Incomes for Full-Time Workers, 1973

	Years of Schooling					
	7 or Less	*8*	*9-11*	*12*	*13-15*	*16 or More*
Males	7,870	9,113	9,976	11,574	13,678	17,882
Females	4,408	5,098	5,428	6,514	7,323	9,834
Difference	3,462	4,018	4,548	5,060	6,355	8,048
Ratio	1.78	1.79	1.84	1.78	1.80	1.82

When we plot the male and female salaries as we have in Exhibit 10.8, we see that the amount of difference between male and female workers *depends* on the other factor, the number of years of schooling. For example, among persons with "7 or less" years of schooling, the difference is $3,462 while among persons with, say, "16 or more" years of schooling, the difference is $8,048. Clearly the differences are not constant, but depend upon education.

This is the meaning of *interaction*. We say that two factors interact whenever the differences between the population means for one factor depend upon the level of the other factor. When random variation is

EXHIBIT 10.8

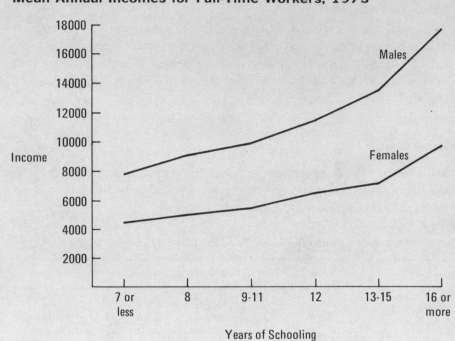

Mean Annual Incomes for Full-Time Workers, 1973

present too, it is usually more difficult to spot interactions. Then the statistical test described on the following pages is useful.

Removable Interaction

Before leaving the annual-incomes example, we would like to point out an interesting feature of the data. That is, while the *differences* between males and females are not constant, the *ratios* essentially are. According to these figures, males earn about 1.8 times as much as females with the same education. The ratios aren't exactly constant, but are close enough to being constant for almost any practical purpose. Thus, we are able to remove the interaction that was present in the differences, by looking at the ratios. The mathematically sophisticated reader will recognize that, if we analyzed the logarithm of the incomes, there would be essentially no interaction present in the data. Some might argue that this is cheating, but we think not. Re-expressing the original measurement scale is a very useful and helpful analytical procedure that is, unfortunately, just beyond the scope of this book.

An Example

Now that we have taken a glimpse at the meaning and interpretation of interaction in an example where we knew the population means, let's take a look at the more common case where we don't.

The **Integration** data (page 287) provides us with a convenient example. There are two factors—"race" and "integrated or segregated" —each of which has two levels. The output from a two-way analysis of variance of these data is shown in Exhibit 10.9. This output is similar to the output in Exhibit 10.7, with a few exceptions. The ANALYSIS OF VARIANCE table for the meat loaf data broke down the total sum of squares into three sources—oven position, batch, and error. Since the **Integration** data has replicates (more than one observation per cell), we can investigate a fourth possible source of variation—the interaction between the two factors. Thus we have

$$(\text{SS TOTAL}) = (\text{SS integration, in } c2) + (\text{SS race, in } c3) +$$
$$(\text{SS interaction between } c2 \text{ and } c3) + (\text{SS ERROR}).$$

Here, the interaction sum of squares is 266.8, with 1 degree of freedom. So the mean square for interaction is $266.8/1 = 266.8$. We can do an F-test to see if this is significant by using $F = (\text{MS } c2{}^*c3)/(\text{MS ERROR}) = 266.8/18.8 = 14.19$. The corresponding value from an F-table, using 1 and 196 degrees of freedom and $\alpha = 0.05$, is 3.84. Since $14.19 > 3.84$, there is statistically significant evidence that the two factors interact. We can also see evidence of this interaction in the table of CELL MEANS in Exhibit 10.9. Among blacks, the mean is higher for integrated (17.08) than segregated (14.54) children. Among whites, this is reversed (12.94 versus 15.02). Put another way, black children are *more* ethnocentric than white children under integration, but *less* ethnocentric under segregation.

Exercises

10-6   An experiment was done to see whether the damage to corn, wheat, dried milk, and other stored crops due to a beetle called Trogoderma

EXHIBIT 10.9

Two-Way Analysis of Variance of Integration Data

-- TWOWAY AOV ON DATA IN C1, INTEGRATION IN C2, RACE IN C3

ANALYSIS OF VARIANCE

DUE TO	DF	SS	MS=SS/DF
C2	1	2.6	2.6
C3	1	167.4	167.4
C2 * C3	1	266.8	266.8
ERROR	196	3689.9	18.8
TOTAL	199	4126.8	

CELL MEANS

ROWS ARE LEVELS OF C2   COLS ARE LEVELS OF C3

	Blacks 1	*Whites* 2	ROW MEANS
1 *Integrated*	17.08	12.94	15.01
2 *Segregated*	14.54	15.02	14.78
COL. MEANS	15.81	13.98	14.90

CELL STANDARD DEVIATIONS

ROWS ARE LEVELS OF C2   COLS ARE LEVELS OF C3

	1	2
1	3.69	5.02
2	3.89	4.62

POOLED ST. DEV. =   4.34

INDIVIDUAL 95 PERCENT C. I. FOR LEVEL MEANS OF C2
   (BASED ON POOLED ST. DEV.)

```
        +---------+---------+---------+---------+---------+
 1          | * * * * * * * * * * * * * * * | * * * * * * * * * * * * |
 2             | * * * * * * * * * * * * * | * * * * * * * * * * * * * |
        +---------+---------+---------+---------+---------+
      13.50               14.50               15.50
            14.00               15.50               16.00
```

EXHIBIT 10.9 (Cont'd)

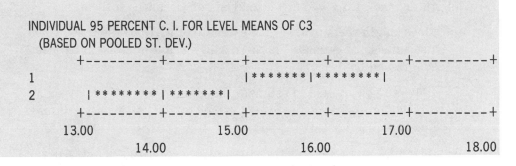

INDIVIDUAL 95 PERCENT C. I. FOR LEVEL MEANS OF C3
(BASED ON POOLED ST. DEV.)

Glabrum could be reduced. The idea was to lure male adult beetles to inoculation sites where they would pick up disease spores which they would then carry back to the remaining population for infection. The experiment consisted of two factors, "sex attractant or none" and "disease pellet present or not." The dependent variable was the fraction of larvae failing to reach adulthood. Here are the results:

Larvae Fraction	Attractant = 1 None = 2	Disease = 1 None = 2
.979	1	1
.743	1	1
.775	1	1
.885	1	1
.312	2	1
.293	2	1
.188	2	1
.388	2	1
.222	1	2
.189	1	2
.143	1	2
.262	1	2
.239	2	2
.253	2	2
.159	2	2
.241	2	2

(a) Do a two-way analysis of variance.

(b) Interpret the results.

10-7   The pendulum data of Exercise 10-1 (page 202) involves two factors—length and bob. Do a two-factor analysis of variance on the data.

(a) Does length seem to affect the estimate of g? Does the type of bob used affect the estimate? Is there a significant interaction between length and bob?

(b) Suppose you wanted to estimate the acceleration of gravity using a pendulum. What do the results in part (a) tell you about designing such an experiment?

10-8   A substantial percentage of the potatoes raised in this country never have a chance to reach the table. Instead they fall victim to potato rot while being stored for later use. To find out what could be done to reduce this loss, an experiment was carried out at the University of Wisconsin. Potatoes were injected with a bacteria known to cause rot, then stored under a variety of conditions. After 5 days the diameter of the rotted portion on each potato was measured (in millimeters).

Three factors were varied in this experiment: (1) the amount of bacteria injected into the potato (1 = low amount, 2 = medium amount, 3 = high amount); (2) the temperature during storage (1 = 10°C, 2 = 16°C); (3) the amount of oxygen during storage (1 = 2%, 2 = 6%, 3 = 10%).

Potato Rot Data

Bacteria	Temp.	Oxygen	Rot	Bacteria	Temp.	Oxygen	Rot
1	1	1	7	2	2	1	17
1	1	1	7	2	2	1	18
1	1	1	9	2	2	1	8
1.	1	2	0	2	2	2	3
1	1	2	0	2	2	2	23
1	1	2	0	2	2	2	7
1	1	3	9	2	2	3	15
1	1	3	0	2	2	3	14
1	1	3	0	2	·2	3	17
1	2	1	10	3	1	1	13
1	2	1	6	3	1	1	11
1	2	1	10	3	1	1	3
1	2	2	4	3	1	2	10
1	2	2	10	3	1	2	4

Potato Rot Data (Cont'd)

Bacteria	Temp.	Oxygen	Rot	Bacteria	Temp.	Oxygen	Rot
1	2	2	5	3	1	2	7
1	2	3	8	3	1	3	15
1	2	3	0	3	1	3	2
1	2	3	10	3	1	3	7
2	1	1	2	3	2	1	26
2	1	1	4	3	2	1	19
2	1	1	9	3	2	1	24
2	1	2	4	3	2	2	15
2	1	2	5	3	2	2	22
2	1	2	10	3	2	2	18
2	1	3	4	3	2	3	20
2	1	3	5	3	2	3	24
2	1	3	0	3	2	3	8

These data should probably be analyzed using a three-way analysis of variance. But you can discover most of what's going on by using several two-way analyses, and some plots and tables.

(a) Do a two-way analysis of variance using bacteria and temperature as the two factors (ignore oxygen for the moment). Next do a two-way analysis using bacteria and oxygen. Also do a two-way analysis using temperature and oxygen. How do each of the three factors influence amount of rot? Do any of the factors appear to interact?

(b) The factors that can be controlled, to some extent, by the food supplier are temperature and oxygen. Analyze these two factors at each of the three levels of bacteria (i.e., do 3 two-way analyses—a separate one for each bacteria level.) Do temperature and oxygen seem to have the same effect at each level?

(c) What recommendations would you give to someone who was storing potatoes?

10-9 Use two-way analysis of variance to continue the study of the **Cancer** data begun in Exercises 2-16 (page 35) and 7-9 (page 131). Let band be one factor and cancer the other factor.

(a) Investigate the relationship between AKP and these two factors.

(b) Repeat part (a) using P.

(c) Repeat part (a) using LDH.

11

Chi-Square Tests and Contingency Tables

The chi-square distribution arises in many different ways in the theory of statistics. In this chapter we discuss its use in situations where we want to test whether the observed frequencies of events agree with theoretical predictions.

11.1 Multinomial Data (Goodness-of-Fit Test)

Some people working with the Missouri Department of Conservation wanted to learn about the migration habits of Canadian geese. They banded over 18,000 geese, all from one flock, and classified them by age and sex. Information on the bands asked all hunters who shot one of these geese to send the band to a central office and tell where they shot the goose. Exhibit 11.1 gives a count of those bands that were returned from geese shot outside the normal migration route for this flock.

An important question was, "Are the geese returned in the same proportion as they were banded?" Of course, we don't expect the percentages to be *exactly* the same for banded and returned geese. But if the four groups do not differ in their migratory habits (nor in their vulnerability to hunters), there shouldn't be "too much" difference between the distribution of banded and returned geese. The chi-square test gives us a way of testing whether or not the amount of deviation between the expected and observed distributions could readily be due to chance.

EXHIBIT 11.1

Canadian Geese Bands Returned from Areas Outside Normal Migration Route

Age and Sex	Number Banded	Proportion Banded	Number Returned	Expected Number Returned
Adult Males	4144	0.2264	17	25.36
Adult Females	3597	0.1965	21	22.01
Yearling Males	5034	0.2750	38	30.80
Yearling Females	5531	0.3021	36	33.84
Totals	18,306	1.0000	112	112.01

Minitab does not have a special command to do this test, but we can write a little program ourselves.

```
SET EXPECTED NUMBERS INTO C1
25.36   22.01   30.80   33.84
SET OBSERVED NUMBERS INTO C2
17   21   38   36
SUBTRACT C1 FROM C2, PUT DIFFERENCES INTO C3
MULT C3 BY C3, PUT IN C4
DIVIDE C4 BY C1, PUT IN C5
SUM C5 (CHISQUARE)
PRINT C1-C5
```

The output from this program is given in Exhibit 11.2. The computed value of chi-square is 4.62 which does not appear very large when compared with tables of the chi-square distribution with 3 degrees of freedom. In fact, there is about a 20% chance of getting a value this large or larger. Thus, even though the numbers look quite different for the banded geese than those returned, deviations like this will occur just by chance variation. Thus, based on these data, we cannot conclude that there is any more of a tendency for one type of goose to stray (or be shot) than another.

EXHIBIT 11.2

Output of Program to Calculate Chi-Square Goodness-of-Fit Test

```
-- SET EXPECTED NUMBERS INTO C1
   COLUMN C1
   COUNT  4
   25.3600    22.0100    30.8000    33.8400
-- SET OBSERVED NUMBERS INTO C2
   COLUMN C2
   COUNT  4
   17.    21.    38.    36.
-- SUBTRACT C1 FROM C2, PUT DIFFERENCES INTO C3
-- MULT C3 BY C3, PUT IN C4
-- DIVIDE C4 BY C1, PUT IN C5
-- SUM C5 (CHISQUARE)
   SUM    =    4.6232
-- PRINT C1-C5
   COLUMN        C1          C2          C3          C4          C5
   COUNT         4           4           4           4           4
   ROW
     1         25.3600      17.      -8.35999     69.8893     2.75589
     2         22.0100      21.      -1.00999      1.0201     0.04635
     3         30.8000      38.       7.20001     51.8402     1.68312
     4         33.8400      36.       2.16000      4.6656     0.13787
```

Exercises

11-1   Test whether each group of geese (adult male, adult female, yearling male, yearling female) was equally likely to be banded. That is, test the null hypothesis that the proportion of geese in each group is 0.25.

11-2   Suppose we were only interested in comparing yearlings with adults. Then there were $4144 + 3597 = 7741$ adults and $5034 + 5531 = 10{,}565$ yearlings banded. Is there a significant difference between the ages banded and returned?

11-3   The following table gives accidental deaths from falls, by month, for the year 1970.

Month	Number of Deaths from Falls
Jan	1688
Feb	1407
Mar	1370
Apr	1309
May	1341
Jun	1338
Jul	1406
Aug	1446
Sep	1322
Oct	1363
Nov	1410
Dec	1526

(a) Do accidental deaths due to falls seem to occur equally often in all 12 months? Do a chi-square goodness-of-fit test.

(b) Can you give some reasons for the result in part (a)? What patterns do you see in the data?

11-4   Several years ago, an article in the *Washington Post* told about a high school boy named Edward who made 17,950 coin flips and "got 464 more heads than tails and so discovered that the United States Mint produces tail-heavy pennies."

(a) Is this result statistically significant? Calculate the observed and expected number of heads and tails and do a chi-square goodness-of-fit test.

(b) The statistician W. J. Youden called Edward and asked how he had done this experiment. Edward explained that he had tossed 5 pennies at a time and his younger brother had recorded the results as Edward called them out. Here's what was recorded:

Number of Heads in 5 Tosses	Number of Times Found
0	100
1	524
2	1080
3	1126
4	655
5	105
Total Tosses	3590

Use the BINOMIAL PROBABILITIES command to compute the theoretical probabilities of each of these 6 possible outcomes (0-heads, 1-head,...,5-heads) if $p = 0.5$. Then test the null hypothesis that Edward's data came from a binomial distribution with $p = 0.5$ (i.e., that the observed number of times found agrees with the binomial probabilities). Try to interpret any discrepancies that seem significant.

11-5   Suppose we count the number of days in a week on which at least 0.01 inch of precipitation falls. Can we model this by a binomial distribution? Below we give some data collected in State College, Pennsylvania, during the years 1950-1969. All the observations are from the same month, February. This gives us (4 weeks in Feb) $\times$ (20 years) $=$ (80 weeks in all).

Number of Precipitation Days in a Week	0	1	2	3	4	5	6	7
Number of Weeks in Which This Occurred	3	12	17	25	14	5	4	0

(a)   Use these data to estimate $p =$ the probability of precipitation on a given day.

(b)   Test to see if a binomial distribution with $n = 7$ and p as estimated in part (a) fits the data.

(c)   Does your answer to part (b) agree with what you'd expect of rainfall data? Explain.

11.2 Computing Chi-Square for Contingency Tables

A Penn State graduate student in art education once did a study involving the relationship between being an artist and believing in extrasensory perception (ESP). He got the following results:

	Believe in ESP	Believe More-or-Less	Do Not Believe
Artists	67	41	6
Non-Artists	129	183	32

A type of question that is frequently asked of such data is, "Is there any association between being an artist and belief in ESP?" Another version of the same question is, "Do artists and non-artists seem to have about the same degree of belief in ESP?" The chi-square technique is the one most frequently used to test the null hypothesis that there is no association, or equivalently, that the distribution of ESP beliefs is the same among artists as among non-artists.

The chi-square test compares the observed frequencies in the table with those we would expect if there were no relationship between the two variables. The test statistic is

$$x^2 = \Sigma \left[\frac{(\text{observed-expected})^2}{\text{expected}} \right].$$

This can be computed in Minitab with the CHISQUARE command.

CHISQUARE ANALYSIS OF THE TABLE IN COLUMNS C, C,...,C

Performs a chi-square test for association on the table of frequencies given in the specified columns. The table, row and column totals, expected cell frequencies, and the chi-square value are all printed out.

Example

To analyze the table of frequencies

5	3	6
2	10	9

use the program:

```
READ C1 C2 C3
       5  3  6
       2 10  9
CHISQUARE ANALYSIS ON C1 C2 C3
STOP
```

A program to do this for the ESP data is

```
READ TABLE INTO C1-C3
  67    41    6
 129   183   32
CHISQUARE FOR DATA IN C1-C3
STOP
```

The output from this program is given in Exhibit 11.3. The overall χ^2 value is 15.94, which is highly significant ($p < 0.005$). This provides strong evidence that the distribution of ESP beliefs among artists is different from that among non-artists.

Note that the output also gives the cell by cell contributions to the overall χ^2 value. In this case the largest contribution, 6.80, comes from the "artists who believe in ESP" cell. The observed count is 67 but the expected count if the null hypothesis were true is only 48.8. So many more artists than expected believe in ESP.

Exercises

11-6 Two researchers at Penn State studied the relationship between infant mortality and environmental conditions in Dauphin County, Pennsylvania. This county has one large city, Harrisburg. As a part of the study, the researchers recorded, for each baby born in Dauphin County during the year 1970, in what season the baby was born, and whether or not the baby died before one year of age. These data are given below.

Infant Deaths and Births for Dauphin County, 1970

	Jan Feb Mar	*Apr May Jun*	*Jul Aug Sep*	*Oct Nov Dec*
		Season of Birth		
Died Before One Year	14	10	35	7
Lived One Year	848	877	958	990

EXHIBIT 11.3

Output of Program to Test the Distribution of Belief in ESP in Artists and Non-Artists

```
-- READ TABLE INTO C1-C3
   COLUMN  C1        C2        C3
   COUNT    2         2         2
   ROW
     1       67.      41.       6.
     2      129.     183.      32.
```

```
-- CHISQUARE FOR DATA IN C1-C3
```

EXPECTED FREQUENCIES ARE PRINTED BELOW OBSERVED FREQUENCIES

	C1	C2	C3	TOTALS
1	67	41	6	114
	48.8	55.8	9.5	
2	129	183	32	344
	147.2	168.2	28.5	
TOTALS	196	224	38	458

TOTAL CHI SQUARE =

$$6.80 \; + \; 3.90 \; + \; 1.26 \; +$$
$$2.25 \; + \; 1.29 \; + \; 0.42 \; +$$
$$= 15.94$$

DEGREES OF FREEDOM = (2−1) X (3−1) = 2

(a) Is an infant more likely to die if he's born in one season than another? Which season has the highest risk? The lowest risk?

(b) Newspapers reported severe air pollution, covering the entire east, during the end of July. Air pollution, especially during the end of pregnancy and in the first few days after birth, is suspected of increasing the risk of an infant's death. Is this observation consistent with the data and analysis in part (a)?

(c)   Since environmental conditions, as well as socio-economic conditions, are different for Harrisburg and the surrounding countryside, separate analyses were done for Harrisburg and the rest of the county. Repeat the analysis of part (a) for the separated data. What are your conclusions now?

Data for Harrisburg

	Season of Birth			
	Jan Feb Mar	Apr May Jun	Jul Aug Sep	Oct Nov Dec
Died Before One Year	6	6	25	3
Lived One Year	306	334	347	369

Data for Dauphin County Excluding Harrisburg

	Season of Birth			
	Jan Feb Mar	Apr May Jun	Jul Aug Sep	Oct Nov Dec
Died Before One Year	8	4	10	4
Lived One Year	542	543	611	621

11-7   Mark Twain has been credited in numerous places with the authorship of ten letters published in 1861 in the *New Orleans Daily Crescent*. The letters were signed "Quintus Curtius Snodgrass." Did Twain really write these letters? In a 1963 paper, Claude S. Brinegar used statistics to compare the Snodgrass letters to works known to be written by Mark Twain. We present some of his very interesting analyses in this exercise.

There are many statistical tests of authorship. The one Brinegar used is quite simple in concept—just compare the distributions of word lengths for the two authors. If these distributions are very different, we'll conclude that the two authors are probably two different people. Of course, in using this type of test, we must assume that the distribution of word lengths is about the same in all works written by the same author. Parts (a), (b), and (c) below attempt to provide some check on this assumption.

The ten Snodgrass letters were first divided into three groups. Then the number of 2-letter words was recorded in each group, the number of 3-letter words in each group, the number of 4-letter words, and so on. One-letter words were omitted. There are only two such words, "I" and "a," and the use of "I" tends to characterize content (work written in first person or not) more than an unconscious style. The data are in Exhibit 11.4. Data for Mark Twain were obtained from letters he wrote to friends at about the same time the Snodgrass letters appeared. They are given in Exhibit 11.5. Exhibit 11.5 also contains data from two other works of Mark Twain written at a later time than the letters. These will

EXHIBIT 11.4

Word Counts for Quintus Curtius Snodgrass Letters

Word Length	First Three Letters	Second Three Letters	Last Four Letters
2	997	831	857
3	1026	828	898
4	856	669	777
5	565	420	446
6	366	326	300
7	318	293	285
8	258	183	197
9	186	150	129
10	96	94	86
11	63	49	40
12	42	30	29
13 and over	25	25	11
Totals	4798	3898	4055

EXHIBIT 11.5

Word Counts for Known Mark Twain Writings

Word Length	Two Letters from 1858 and 1861	Four Letters from 1863	Letter from 1867	Sample from Roughing It, 1872	Sample from Following the Equator, 1897
2	349	1146	496	532	466
3	456	1394	673	741	653
4	374	1177	565	591	517
5	212	661	381	357	343
6	127	442	249	258	207
7	107	367	185	215	152
8	84	231	125	150	103
9	45	181	94	83	92
10	27	109	51	55	45
11	13	50	23	30	18
12	8	24	8	10	12
13 and over	9	12	8	9	9
Totals	1811	5794	2858	3031	2617

be used to see if word-length distribution seems to remain the same throughout a person's writings.

(a) Compare the three groups of Snodgrass letters to see if they are consistent in word-length distribution.

First compare them graphically. To make the numbers comparable, change the frequencies into relative frequencies (proportions). Then plot each column versus word length. Put all three plots on the same axes by using MPLOT. Do the distributions look similar?

Next do a chi-square test of the null hypothesis that all three sets of letters have the same word-length distribution. Is there any evidence that they differ?

(b) Next compare the three groups of Mark Twain letters written at about the same time as the Snodgrass letters. Do both a plot and a chi-square test, as in part (a). Is there any evidence that these three writings differ in word-length distribution?

(c) Now compare Mark Twain's writings over a large span of years. The samples from *Roughing It* and *Following the Equator* were taken for this purpose. First combine the three columns of Mark Twain letters into one column of "early works." Compare the "early," "middle," and "late" samples for Mark Twain. Do both a plot and chi-square test as in part (a). Is there any evidence that the word-length distribution changed over the years?

(d) Finally, now that we've checked the authors for consistency, let's compare the Twain and Snodgrass works. As in part (c), combine the three columns of Twain's early works into one column. Also combine the three columns of Snodgrass letters into one column. Finally compare Twain's work with the Snodgrass letters. Do both a plot and a chi-square test. Do you think Mark Twain wrote the Snodgrass letters?

(e) In what ways do the two authors differ, as far as word-length distribution is concerned? Examine both the plot and chi-square output from part (d) to find out. Does the chi-square output tell you anything the plot doesn't or vice versa?

11.3 Making Contingency Tables

Most textbook problems on contingency tables start with the table already made up, as we did in the preceding section. But in practice, the first job is usually to make up the table. Exhibit 11.6 shows some data that were gathered in an introductory statistics class. The year in college, type of major, and political preference were recorded for 84 students.

Suppose we want to make a contingency table giving us the relationship between political preference and year in school. The first student is a sophomore Democrat; the second a freshman "other"; and the third a senior Republican. We could "easily" go down this list of 84 students and make up a table giving the counts we are interested in. But if we had a lot more data, this would be a very time consuming (and error prone) activity. Instead we could use Minitab's TABLE command to make up the table.

EXHIBIT 11.6

Data from Class Survey

Code for major: 1 = behavioral science,
                2 = biological science, 0 = other
Code for political preference: 1 = Democrat, 2 = Republican,
                0 = other

Student	Yr.	Maj.	Pol. Pref.	Student	Yr.	Maj.	Pol. Pref.
1	2	0	1	43	3	2	2
2	1	0	0	44	3	2	1
3	4	0	2	45	2	1	2
4	3	2	0	46	3	2	0
5	2	1	0	47	2	2	2
6	4	2	0	48	2	1	1
7	4	2	1	49	2	1	1
8	2	1	1	50	2	1	1
9	3	1	1	51	1	2	0
10	3	0	1	52	1	0	1
11	3	1	1	53	3	2	0
12	1	1	0	54	4	2	1
13	2	2	0	55	2	0	1
14	1	2	2	56	3	1	1
15	4	2	0	57	3	1	0
16	2	1	1	58	3	1	2
17	2	1	1	59	3	0	2
18	4	2	1	60	3	1	1
19	3	2	0	61	4	2	2
20	3	2	0	62	2	1	1
21	3	2	1	63	2	2	1
22	2	2	2	64	3	1	0
23	2	1	0	65	3	0	2
24	3	1	1	66	1	0	1
25	2	0	1	67	1	0	1
26	3	1	2	68	3	0	1
27	2	2	2	69	2	2	1
28	1	2	1	70	2	0	2
29	3	1	1	71	3	2	2
30	4	0	2	72	3	0	0
31	3	2	1	73	2	2	2

EXHIBIT 11.6 (Cont'd)

Student	Yr.	Maj.	Pol. Pref.	Student	Yr.	Maj.	Pol. Pref.
32	4	2	1	74	4	0	0
33	3	0	0	75	2	2	0
34	4	1	0	76	3	0	0
35	2	1	2	77	2	2	1
36	3	1	0	78	3	0	2
37	3	1	1	79	3	1	1
38	2	1	1	80	4	1	1
39	4	1	1	81	4	1	0
40	3	1	1	82	3	2	1
41	2	1	1	83	2	2	1
42	3	1	0	84	3	2	1

TABLE USE CODES IN **C** FOR ROWS, CODES IN **C** FOR COLS.

Prints out a two-way table from the data, using the first named column for the row classification and the second named column for the column classification. The codes in both columns should be integers.

Example

```
READ   C1   C2
 −1    0
 −1    3
  0    1
  0    1
  0    1
```

```
  0   0
 −1   3
TABLE C1 VS C2
```

The following table is printed out:

```
ROW CLASSIFICATION - C1 COLUMN CLASSIFICATION - C2
          |   0   |   1   |   3   | TOTALS
 ------- |-------|-------|-------|-------
    −1  |   1   |   0   |   2   |   3
 ------- |-------|-------|-------|-------
     0  |   1   |   3   |   0   |   4
 ------- |-------|-------|-------|-------
 TOTALS |   2   |   3   |   2   |   7
```

Since there are 7 rows of data in the worksheet, the total count in the table is 7. c1 contains the codes −1 and 0, so there are two rows in the table. c2 contains the codes 0, 1, 3, so there are three columns in the table.

The following program could be used with the data in Exhibit 11.6 to give us a breakdown of political preference by year in college:

```
READ DATA INTO COLS C1-C4
  1   2   0   1
  2   1   0   0
  .   .   .   .

  .   .   .   .

  .   .   .   .
 84   3   2   1
TABLE C4 VS C2 (POLITICAL PREF. VS YEAR)
STOP
```

Part of the output from this program is given in Exhibit 11.7. In all there were 4 freshmen Democrats, 1 freshman Republican, and so on.

EXHIBIT 11.7

Table of Political Preference Versus Year in College

-- TABLE C4 VS C2 (POLITICAL PREF. VS YEAR)
ROW CLASSIFICATION - C4   COLUMN CLASSIFICATION - C2

		1		2		3		4	I TOTALS
Other	0	3		4		12		5	24
Dem.	1	4		16		16		6	42
Rep.	2	1		7		7		3	18
TOTALS	I	8		27		35		.14	84

Exercises

11-8   Using the data in Exhibit 11.6, make a contingency table of

(a)   Major versus Political Preference.

(b)   Major versus Year in School.

11-9   Using the **Cartoon** data (page 270), make a contingency table that gives the relationship between "education" and whether or not a person took the delayed test. (Hints: You could use either variable 8 or 9. You could use the RECODE command (page 323), or you could combine some hand and computer work.)

11.4 Making the Table and Computing Chi-Square

The TABLE command forms the table, but does not do the chi-square test. If you wish to do both, the CONTINGENCY TABLE command can be used.

CONTINGENCY TABLE ANALYSIS ON DATA IN **C** VS **C**

Forms a table from the data in the same way that the command TABLE
does and then performs a chi-square test on the table in the same way
that the command CHISQUARE does.

For example, by changing the TABLE instruction on page 236 to

CONTINGENCY TABLE OF C4 VS C2 (POL. PREF. VS YEAR)

we got the output in Exhibit 11.8. (We'll discuss the message given at
the end of the output in the next section.)

Exercise

11-10 (a)   In the **Cancer** data (page 289) is the result of the band test (variable
4) associated with whether the patient has cancer or not (variable
3)?

(b)   When the judges see the band (band = 1), what percentage of the
patients have cancer? What percentage have cancer when they don't
see the band?

11.5 Tables with Small Expected Frequencies

The output in Exhibit 11.8 has the message

NOTE: 5 CELLS WITH EXPECTED FREQUENCIES LESS THAN 5

This indicates that the chi-square analysis done on this table may not
be quite appropriate. As with many statistical tests, the chi-square test

EXHIBIT 11.8

Chi-square Test for Independence of Political Preference and Year in College

```
-- CONTINGENCY TABLE OF C4 VS C2 (POL. PREF. VS YEAR)
   EXPECTED FREQUENCIES ARE PRINTED BELOW OBSERVED FREQUENCIES
   ROW CLASSIFICATION - C4          COLUMN CLASSIFICATION - C2
              |   1   |   2   |   3   |   4   | TOTALS
      --------|-------|-------|-------|-------|-------
        0  |   3   |   4   |  12   |   5   |    24
           |  2.3  |  7.7  |  10.0 |  4.0  |
      --------|-------|-------|-------|-------|-------
        1  |   4   |  16   |  16   |   6   |    42
           |  4.0  |  13.5 |  17.5 |  7.0  |
      --------|-------|-------|-------|-------|-------
        2  |   1   |   7   |   7   |   3   |    18
           |  1.7  |  5.8  |  7.5  |  3.0  |
      --------|-------|-------|-------|-------|-------
   TOTALS  |   8   |  27   |  35   |  14   |    84
   TOTAL CHI SQUARE =
              0.22  +  1.79  +  0.40  +  0.25  +
              0.0   +  0.46  +  0.13  +  0.14  +
              0.30  +  0.25  +  0.03  +  0.0   +
                          = 3.98
   DEGREES OF FREEDOM = ( 3–1) X ( 4–1) = 6
   NOTE: 5 CELLS WITH EXPECTED FREQUENCIES LESS THAN 5
```

is an approximate test. In this case approximation becomes better and better as the expected cell frequencies increase. Consequently, if too many cells have expected frequencies that are too small, a chi-square analysis should not be done. A good, but conservative, rule of thumb is that not more than 20% of the cells should have expected cell frequencies less than 5, and no cell should have an expected frequency less than 1. The table in Exhibit 11.8 has 12 cells. So, no more than $0.2 \times 12 = 2.4$ cells should have expected frequencies less than 5. But, as the message says, and as we can see ourselves from the table, there are 5 such cells.

There are several procedures we can follow with tables having too many small expected frequencies.

Combining Cells

We can try to combine cells so that we reduce the number of rows and/or columns. For example, if we combine columns 1 and 2 in Exhibit 11.7 into one level called "lower classmen," and combine columns 3 and 4 into one level called "upper classmen," we get the following 3 × 2 table:

	Lower Classmen	Upper Classmen
Other	7	17
Dem.	20	22
Rep.	8	10

Now, if no more than 1 cell in this smaller table has expected frequency less than 5, we can comfortably do the chi-square analysis. The smaller table was read into the worksheet and a second analysis done. In this case, no cell had expected frequency less than 5, so the chi-square approximation is probably good enough. Of course, we have changed our analysis slightly. Now we are testing the null hypothesis: there is no relationship between a student's political preference and whether he is an upper or lower classman. Before we were testing the null hypothesis: there is no relationship between a student's political preference and whether he is a freshman, sophomore, junior, or senior. We do not have quite enough data here to analyze the larger 3 × 4 table. So, if we want to get something out of the data, we can try looking at a table with fewer levels.

Eliminating Rows or Columns

Another way we could handle the problem is to remove one or more levels of a classification, eliminating levels that contain few observations. In the political preference table, we could omit the first column, corresponding to freshmen. This leads to the following table:

	Sophomore	Junior	Senior
Other	7	7	3
Dem.	4	12	5
Rep.	16	16	6

This table provides an analysis relevant to students above the freshmen level. Here, however, the omission doesn't help much. There are still too many cells with small expected frequencies.

12

Nonparametric Statistics

There are several reasons why it may be more appropriate to use nonparametric procedures instead of the normal theory (parametric) procedures described in Chapters 7, 8, 9, and 10. These reasons include the following:

(a) Populations Not Normal. To be strictly valid, the procedures in Chapters 7, 8, 9, and 10 require that we have random samples from *normal* populations. If the samples do not come from normal populations, these procedures may be more or less invalid, depending on the particular application. For example, if we construct a 95% t confidence interval from non-normal data, the real confidence may be only 93%, not 95% as we had planned. Another, and usually more serious, problem with using normal theory methods on non-normal data is loss in efficiency. Loosely speaking, a more efficient procedure makes better use of the data and enables us to get a better estimate or test with a smaller sample size. Some nonparametric procedures are more efficient than normal theory procedures if we are sampling from a non-normal population.

(b) Ordinal Data. Many statisticians believe that only nonparametric procedures should be used on *ordinal* data. A common example of ordinal data is that obtained from questionnaires having response categories, such as 1 = strongly agree, 2 = agree, 3 = disagree, and 4 = strongly disagree. With ordinal data we know how to order the response categories but we may not want to assume that the difference between a "1" and a "2" is the same as that between a "2" and a "3," or between a "3" and a "4," and so on. If we want to assume all these differences *are* the same, then we have *interval* data, and most statisticians would agree that normal theory techniques might be appropriate. However, there is still a lot of controversy on this subject.

(c) Concern about Occasional "Outliers." Normal theory methods are quite sensitive to even a few extreme, or outlying, observations. As a simple example, consider the five numbers: 3, 7, 9, 10, 11. Normal theory would have us use their *mean* while most of the methods in this chapter would instead use the *median*. The median of these numbers is 9 and the mean is 8. But what would happen if one of the observations had been measured or recorded incorrectly? Suppose the 11 had been recorded as a 61. Then the median would remain unchanged but the mean would be more than doubled, to 18. The median, and the other procedures described in this chapter, are more *resistant* than normal theory methods to distortion by a few gross errors.

12.1 Sign Tests—One Sample

Suppose we want to show that the median height, η (Greek letter eta), of all students who take an introductory statistics course at Penn State is over 5 feet 7 inches (67.5 inches). (Perhaps this is the average height of calculus students and we want to show that statistics students are taller.) Our null hypothesis in this case would be $H_0 : \eta = 67.5$ and our alternative hypothesis $H_1 : \eta > 67.5$. Now we need a sample of students. One such sample is recorded in the **Pulse** experiment (page 285). If $\eta = 67.5$, then roughly half the students in the sample should be taller than 67.5 inches and half shorter. Of course in any given sample, we wouldn't expect exactly a 50-50 split, but it shouldn't be too far off. Suppose we scan through the heights. We see that 59 of them are over 67.5 and the remaining 33 are under. Thus well over half the students in our sample are taller than 67.5 inches. What do we conclude? Do we have evidence that $\eta > 67.5$ or are we likely to get as many students as this over 67.5 just by chance alone, even if $\eta = 67.5$?

Suppose we had a large population of students. Half would be taller than the median and half shorter. If we picked one student at random, we would have a 50-50 chance that he would be taller than the median.

If we picked another at random we'd again have a 50-50 chance. If we picked 92 students, we could count how many were taller than the median. If we look at it right, this is just like a binomial distribution. On each trial (drawing a student at random) we have a 50-50 chance of a "success" (taller than the median). Since we're drawing our sample at random, the observations are independent, so our count of the number of successes has a binomial distribution with n = 92 and p = 1/2.

In our example we found that 59 students (X = 59) were taller than our hypothesized median, $\eta = 67.5$. Suppose that our 92 students are a random sample of students who take an introductory statistics course. We can use the binomial distribution to find the probability that 59 or more students in a random sample of 92 students will be taller than the median. The output in Exhibit 12.1 gives P(59 or more $\geq$ median) = 0.0044. That is, if $\eta = 67.5$ inches and we had a random sample, there would be only a very small chance of getting results this extreme. Thus we are led to suspect that perhaps the population median is greater than 67.5 inches.

Here we found the value of X by hand. However, if the data set is very large, or if the data are in the computer for other reasons (such as making a histogram) it may help to use Minitab's SIGNS command.

SIGNS OF C

Finds and prints the number of negative, zero, and positive values in the column.

Example

If c3 contains the values 4, 7, −2, 0, 1, the command SIGNS OF c3 will print the summary

1 NEGATIVE VALUES   1 ZERO VALUES   3 POSITIVE VALUES

SIGNS OF C, PUT IN C

This form of the command prints the summary and, in addition, stores a column as follows: If a value in the first named column is positive, Minitab puts a +1 in the corresponding row of the second column. If a value is negative, it puts a −1, and if a value is 0, it puts a 0.

Example
SIGNS OF C3, PUT IN C5

C3	*C5*
4	1
7	1
−2 →	−1
0	0
1	1

The following is a program to do calculations for the sign test on height:

READ DATA INTO C1-C8

(data from **Pulse** experiment)

SUBTRACT 67.5 FROM C6, PUT DIFFERENCES INTO C20
SIGNS OF C20

(Notice that if a value in C8 is greater than 67.5, the corresponding row of C20 will be positive; if it's less than 67.5, C20 will be negative, and if equal to 67.5, C20 will be zero.) The output for the SIGNS command is

-- SIGNS OF C20
33 NEGATIVE VALUES   0 ZERO VALUES   59 POSITIVE VALUES

We finish the test by hand using a binomial table as before.

EXHIBIT 12.1

Binomial Probabilities Used for a Sign Test and Confidence Interval

-- BINOMIAL PROBABILITIES FOR N = 92 AND P = .5
BINOMIAL PROBABILITIES FOR N = 92 AND P = 0.500000

K	P(X = K)	P(X LESS OR = K)
28	0.0001	0.0001
29	0.0001	0.0003
30	0.0003	0.0006
31	0.0006	0.0012
32	0.0011	0.0023
33	0.0021	0.0044
34	0.0036	0.0080
35	0.0060	0.0140
36	0.0095	0.0235
37	0.0144	0.0379
38	0.0208	0.0587
39	0.0288	0.0875
40	0.0382	0.1257
41	0.0484	0.1741
42	0.0588	0.2329
43	0.0684	0.3012
44	0.0761	0.3773
45	0.0812	0.4585
46	0.0830	0.5415
47	0.0812	0.6227
48	0.0761	0.6988
49	0.0684	0.7671
50	0.0588	0.8259
51	0.0484	0.8743
52	0.0382	0.9125
53	0.0288	0.9413
54	0.0208	0.9621
55	0.0144	0.9765
56	0.0095	0.9860
57	0.0060	0.9920

EXHIBIT 12.1 (Cont'd)

58	0.0036	0.9956
59	0.0021	0.9977
60	0.0011	0.9988
61	0.0006	0.9994
62	0.0003	0.9997
63	0.0001	0.9999
64	0.0001	1.0000

In the data set of 92 students, no student was exactly 67.5 inches tall. What happens if we get "ties"? For example, suppose we test $H_0 : \eta = 68$ versus $H_1 : \eta > 68$. In this case the SIGNS command tells us that there are 33 negative (below 68), 49 positive (above 68), and 10 zero (equal to 68). The usual procedure is to discard the ties and apply the sign test to the remaining data. So we have n = 82 observations remaining, with 49 positives. Using the BINOMIAL PROBABILITIES command with n = 82 and p = 1/2, we get $P(X \geq 49) = 0.0485$.

Other Alternate Hypotheses

We just saw how to do a sign test for $H_0 : \eta = 67.5$ versus $H_1 : \eta > 67.5$. Here, we'll briefly illustrate the other two possibilities.

Suppose we want to test $H_0 : \eta = 70.5$ versus $H_1 : \eta < 70.5$. That is, suppose our alternative hypothesis is "less than" instead of "greater than." Again we count the number of observations above and below the hypothesized median, 70.5, discarding any ties. For the **Pulse** data it turns out to be 32 above and 60 below. Now let X denote the number of observations below 70.5. Then, if $\eta = 70.5$, X has a binomial distribution with n = 92 and p = 1/2. Using the output in Exhibit 12.1, we get $P(X \geq 60) = 0.0023$. So only 0.23% of the time we can expect to get as many as 60 out of 92 below 70.5 if $\eta = 70.5$.

Finally, suppose we want to do a two-tailed sign test. For example, suppose we test $H_0 : \eta = 68.5$ versus $H_1 : \eta \neq 68.5$. Here there are 49 above and 43 below. We then find the one-tailed probability corresponding to the *larger* of these two values (if they're equal, either will do). Here the number above is the larger. So we calculate $P(X \geq 49) = 0.3012$.

The attained significance of the two-tailed test is then twice this value, or 2(0.3012) = 0.6024. Thus over 60% of the time we can expect to get a split this extreme or more so, that is with 49 or more on one side or the other of the median.

Exercises

12-1   Consider the OTIS scores from the **Cartoon** experiment (page 270). The national median of all OTIS scores is 100.

(a)   Do the OTIS scores for the pre-professionals differ significantly from the national median? Do a sign test.

(b)   Repeat part (a) for the professionals.

(c)   Repeat part (a) for the students.

12-2   The data below were collected in a chemistry class, and are the results of a titration to determine the acidity of a solution.

0.123	0.109	0.110	0.109	0.112	0.109	0.110	0.110
0.110	0.112	0.110	0.101	0.110	0.110	0.110	0.110
0.106	0.115	0.111	0.110	0.107	0.111	0.110	0.113
0.109	0.108	0.109	0.111	0.104	0.114	0.110	0.110
0.110	0.113	0.114	0.110	0.110	0.110	0.110	0.110
0.090	0.109	0.111	0.098	0.109	0.109	0.109	0.109
0.111	0.109	0.108	0.110	0.112	0.111	0.110	0.111
0.111	0.107	0.111	0.112	0.105	0.109	0.109	0.110
0.110	0.109	0.110	0.104	0.111	0.110	0.111	0.109
0.110	0.111	0.112	0.123	0.110	0.109	0.110	0.109
0.110	0.109	0.110	0.110	0.111	0.111	0.109	0.107
0.120	0.133	0.107	0.103	0.111	0.110	0.122	0.109
0.108	0.109	0.109	0.114	0.107	0.104	0.110	0.114
0.107	0.101	0.111	0.109	0.110	0.111	0.110	0.126
0.110	0.109	0.114	0.110	0.110	0.110	0.110	0.110
0.111	0.107	0.110	0.107				

(a)   The instructor knew the correct value for this solution was 0.110. Do a two-sided sign test of the null hypothesis $H_0 : \eta = 0.110$. (This is a check to see if the class is "biased"—that is, to see if it tends to be systematically too high or systematically too low.)

(b)   Make a histogram of the data. Make the first midpoint at 0.090 (the minimum of the data) and the interval width 0.001. Do you think the population is symmetric? If it is, then $\eta = \mu$.

(c)   A distribution is called "heavy tailed" if there is a higher probability
of very extreme values than in a normal distribution. Does the
histogram of part (b) give any indication that the distribution of
titration results from this class is heavy tailed? (It may help to
compare your histogram with those of normal populations in Exhibit
6.1 on page 108.)

12.2 Sign Confidence Intervals—One Sample

In Section 4.2 (page 87) we showed how the interval between the smallest and largest observation in a sample of size n = 3 could be used to
construct a 75% confidence interval for the population median. Suppose
instead of a sample of size 3, we had a sample of size n = 5. Then there
would be a $(1/2)^5 = 1/32 = 0.03125$ chance that all 5 observations would
be greater than the population median, in which case our interval would
fail to catch it. Similarly, there is a $(1/2)^5 = 0.03125$ chance that all 5
would fall below the population median, in which case we'd also miss.
In all other cases (e.g., 4 above and 1 below, or 2 above and 3 below)
we'd catch the median in our interval. Then the probability of a miss is
$0.03125 + 0.03125 = 0.0625$. So the probability of a catch is 0.9375.

Too Much Confidence

But what if we had a sample of size 14. In that case there's a $(1/2)^{14}$
$= 0.00006$ chance that all 14 observations would fall above the median
and a $(1/2)^{14} = 0.00006$ chance they'd all fall below the median. So the
probability of a miss is 0.0012 and the probability of a catch is 0.99982.
In short, we could be *very* confident that the interval between the extremes of the sample would catch the median. But this interval is likely
to be quite long. For example, we might wind up saying something like,
"I am 99.98% confident that the median family income in the United
States is somewhere between $750 and $48,000 per year."

Maybe we can trade a little confidence for a much shorter interval.
What if instead of making our interval run from the very smallest
observation to the very largest, we had it run from the second smallest
to the second largest, or from the third smallest to the third largest, or
whatever seems most appropriate for the sample size.

As an example, suppose we had a sample of size n = 10, and made our interval go from the second smallest to the second largest observation. What are our chances of catching the median with this interval? Let's use X to denote the number of observations that fall below the population median, η. If $X = 0$, then all 10 observations are above η and our interval misses. If $X = 1$, our interval also misses, since the bottom end of it (the second largest observation) is above η. Similarly, if $X = 9$ or 10, our interval misses η, since now the interval is entirely below η. In all other cases ($X = 2, 3, 4, 5, 6, 7, 8$) our interval covers η. Again we can use the binomial distribution to determine the confidence of our interval. This time X has a binomial distribution with $n = 10$ and $p = 1/2$. The output we need is in Exhibit 12.2. The interval misses when $X = 0$, 1, 9, or 10, which has probability $0.0010 + 0.0098 + 0.0098 + 0.0010 = 0.0216$. So our confidence is $1 - 0.0216 = 0.9784$, or about 97.8%. In a similar way, we can calculate the confidence associated with other intervals. For example, the interval which goes from the third smallest to the third largest has confidence equal to $1 - P(X = 0, 1, 2, 8, 9,$ or $10) = 1 - 0.1094 = 0.8906$. The interval which goes from the fourth smallest to the fourth largest has confidence equal to $1 - P(X = 0, 1, 2, 3, 7, 8, 9,$ or $10)$. Notice that for $p = 1/2$ the binomial distribution is symmetric, so $P(X = 0, 1, 2,$ or $3) = P(X = 7, 8, 9,$ or $10)$. Thus we can also calculate our confidence as $1 - 2P(X = 0, 1, 2, 3) = 1 - 2P(X \leq 3)$. In general, we can write that the interval from the d-th smallest to the d-th largest observation will have confidence $1 - 2P(X \leq d-1)$.

An Example

Suppose we want to calculate a 95% confidence interval using the height data discussed in Section 12.1. Now what we need to do is reverse the procedure we just described—we have the confidence and we want to find the interval. Our interval will go from the d-th smallest to the d-th largest. We must find the value of d. Since we want 95% confidence, we have $.95 = 1 - 2P(X \leq d-1)$. Then $P(X \leq d-1) = (1 - .95) = 0.05$. Here X has a binomial distribution with $p = 1/2$ and $n = 92$. Exhibit 12.1 contains output from the corresponding BINOMIAL PROBABILITIES command. Scanning down, we find $P(X \leq 36) = 0.0235$ and $P(X \leq 37) = 0.0379$. We want 0.0250. This is one characteristic of nonparametric methods—we can't get exactly the confidence we want. So we'll settle for the closest value, 0.0235, which gives $1 - 2(0.0235) = 0.953$. Then $d - 1 = 36$, so $d = 37$. Exhibit 12.3 contains the 92 observations in order. The 37th smallest observation is 68 and the 37th largest is 70. So the interval from 68 to 70 gives a 95.3% confidence interval for η.

EXHIBIT 12.2

Binomial Probabilities Used for a Sign Confidence Interval

BINOMIAL PROBABILITIES FOR N = 10 AND P = 0.500000

K	P(X = K)	P(X LESS OR = K)
0	0.0010	0.0010
1	0.0098	0.0107
2	0.0439	0.0547
3	0.1172	0.1719
4	0.2051	0.3770
5	0.2461	0.6230
6	0.2051	0.8281
7	0.1172	0.9453
8	0.0439	0.9893
9	0.0098	0.9990
10	0.0010	1.0000

Efficiency

If your population is symmetric, then the population mean μ and the population median η are the same number. Suppose we take a sample from such a population. How would you estimate μ? You could use the sample mean. You could also use the sample median, since it is an estimate of η and $\eta = \mu$. For any specific sample of data, these two estimates would probably differ slightly. Is one estimate better than the other?

The same question can be asked of confidence intervals. If you are sampling from a symmetric population, should you use normal theory methods (a t confidence interval) or nonparametric methods (such as a sign confidence interval) to get a confidence interval for $\mu = \eta$? Both methods give an interval which covers μ 95% (or whatever confidence you've chosen) of the time. Then how could they differ? The answer is, in length. For some populations, a t confidence interval is much shorter, on the average, than a sign confidence interval. For such populations we say the t interval is more efficient than the sign interval. For other populations, it is reversed. For those populations we say the sign interval is more efficient than the t interval. If you are sampling from a normal

EXHIBIT 12.3

The 92 Heights from the Pulse Experiment, in Order

```
-- ORDER C6, PUT IN C6
-- PRINT C6
   COLUMN   C6
   COUNT    92
```

61.0000	61.7500	62.0000	62.0000	62.0000
62.0000	62.7500	63.0000	63.0000	63.0000
63.0000	64.0000	64.0000	65.0000	65.0000
65.0000	65.0000	65.5000	66.0000	66.0000
66.0000	66.0000	66.0000	66.0000	66.0000
66.0000	67.0000	67.0000	67.0000	67.0000
67.0000	67.0000	67.0000	68.0000	68.0000
68.0000	68.0000	68.0000	68.0000	68.0000
68.0000	68.0000	68.0000	69.0000	69.0000
69.0000	69.0000	69.0000	69.0000	69.0000
69.0000	69.0000	69.0000	69.5000	70.0000
70.0000	70.0000	70.0000	70.0000	70.0000
71.0000	71.0000	71.0000	71.0000	71.0000
71.0000	71.5000	72.0000	72.0000	72.0000
72.0000	72.0000	72.0000	72.0000	72.0000
73.0000	73.0000	73.0000	73.0000	73.0000
73.0000	73.0000	73.5000	73.5000	74.0000
74.0000	74.0000	74.0000	74.0000	75.0000
75.0000	75.0000			

population, a t confidence interval is shorter, on the average, than a sign interval. However, if you are sampling from a "heavy tailed" population (see Exercise 12-2b), then a sign interval is shorter, on the average, than a t interval.

Exercises

12-3   Using the output in Exhibits 12.1 and 12.3, find (as close as possible) a 90% sign confidence interval for η. Find a 99% sign confidence interval.

12-4   The data from a second titration experiment are given below.

0.109	0.111	0.110	0.110	0.105
0.110	0.111	0.110	0.110	0.111
0.109	0.111	0.109	0.112	0.109
0.109	0.111	0.110	0.112	0.112
0.109	0.110	0.110	0.109	0.113
0.108	0.105	0.110	0.109	0.109
0.110	0.110	0.110	0.104	0.109
0.110	0.111			

(a) Make a histogram. Do you think $\mu = \eta$? It will be if the population is symmetric. Exercise 12-2 gives us some more information about the shape of the distribution for titration data. What did you conclude there?

(b) Find (as close as possible) a 95% sign confidence interval for η.

(c) Find a 95% confidence interval for μ using normal theory methods and compare it to the sign confidence interval in part (a).

(d) Repeat parts (a) and (b) using 90% confidence intervals.

12-5   The following is a sample (which we got by simulation) from a normal distribution:

$$62, 60, 65, 70, 60, 67, 61, 66, 64, 64, 62, 63$$

(a) Calculate an approximately 95% sign confidence interval for η (the closest confidence will be 96.1).

(b) Find a 96.1% t confidence interval using the TINTERVAL command. Compare these two intervals.

(c) Now suppose a mistake was made in recording the last observation and 36 was recorded instead of 63. Repeat parts (a) and (b).

(d) Repeat part (c), only now suppose the last observation was mistakenly recorded as 630.

12-6   We can use simulation to get a feel for how well sign confidence intervals work in various cases. If your data came from a normal population, a t confidence interval is the best way to estimate $\mu = \eta$. But how much worse might a sign confidence interval be? Simulate a sample of size n $= 10$ from a normal distribution with $\mu = 50$, $\sigma = 8$. Get both a sign confidence interval and a t confidence interval. In both cases use 89.1% confidence. Do both intervals cover μ? Which is narrower? Repeat this for a total of 6 intervals. How do the two procedures compare? Which one seems to give shorter confidence intervals on the average?

12-7   (a)   Repeat Exercise 12-6, except simulate data from a Cauchy distribution. (How to do this is explained on page 82.) This gives an example of data from a very "heavy tailed" distribution.

(b)   Repeat Exercise 12-6, except simulate data from a uniform distribution (Use URANDOM described on page 82). A uniform distribution is an example of a distribution that has very "skinny tails."

12.3 Sign Methods—Paired Samples

With paired data, usually all we need to do is take the differences, then use an appropriate single-sample procedure. For example, if we refer back to the cholesterol data on page 135, we could use the program below to do a sign test of the null hypothesis that there is no change. The program also allows us to compute a 95% confidence interval for the median amount of change in cholesterol between 2 days and 4 days after a heart attack.

```
READ TWO-DAY LEVELS INTO C1 AND FOUR-DAY LEVELS INTO C2

(data from page 135)

SUBTRACT C1 FROM C2, PUT DIFFERENCES IN C3
SIGNS OF C3
ORDER C3
PRINT C3
BINOMIAL PROBABILITIES FOR N = 28, P = 0.5
STOP
```

Exercises

12-8   The job of President of the United States is a very demanding, high pressure job. This might cause premature deaths of Presidents. On the other hand, only vigorous people are going to run for President so Presidents might tend to live longer than other people. We list below the "modern" (since Lincoln) Presidents who died by September 1975, the number of years they lived after inauguration, and the life expectancy of a man the same age as the President was on his first inauguration.

Longevity of U.S. Presidents

	Life Expectancy After First Inauguration	Actual Years Lived After First Inauguration
Andrew Johnson	17.2	10.3
Ulysses S. Grant	22.8	16.4
Rutherford B. Hayes	18.0	15.9
James A. Garfield	21.2	.5
Chester A. Arthur	20.1	5.2
Grover Cleveland	22.1	23.3
Benjamin Harrison	17.2	12.0
William McKinley	18.2	4.5
Theodore Roosevelt	26.1	17.3
William H. Taft	20.3	21.2
Woodrow Wilson	17.1	10.9
Warren G. Harding	18.1	2.4
Calvin Coolidge	21.4	9.4
Herbert C. Hoover	19.0	35.6
Franklin D. Roosevelt	21.7	12.1
Harry S. Truman	15.3	27.7
Dwight D. Eisenhower	14.7	16.2
John F. Kennedy	28.5	2.8
Lyndon B. Johnson	19.3	9.2

(a) Do a sign test of the null hypothesis that being President has no effect on length of life.

(b) Find an approximately 95% confidence interval for the median difference between the expected and attained life span of Presidents.

(c) If our main interest is the effect of stress on length of life, then perhaps we should not include the Presidents who were assassinated (Garfield, McKinley, and Kennedy). Carry out the analysis of (a) and (b) without these three Presidents.

(d) We have, perhaps, stretched the use of statistics rather far here, as we often must in real problems. Comment on this statement, paying particular attention to the assumptions needed for a sign test.

EXHIBIT 12.4

Population of the Fifty Largest Cities in the United States

	1970	1960
New York	7896000	7782000
Chicago	3369000	3550000
Los Angeles	2810000	2479000
Philadelphia	1950000	2003000
Detroit	1514000	1670000
Houston	1233000	938000
Baltimore	906000	939000
Dallas	844000	680000
Washington	757000	764000
Cleveland	751000	876000
Indianapolis	746000	747000
Milwaukee	717000	741000
San Francisco	716000	740000
San Diego	697000	573000
San Antonio	654000	588000
Boston	641000	697000
Memphis	624000	498000
St. Louis	622000	750000
New Orleans	593000	628000
Phoenix	582000	439000
Columbus	540000	471000
Seattle	531000	557000
Jacksonville	529000	201000
Pittsburg	520000	604000
Denver	515000	494000
Kansas City	507000	476000
Atlanta	497000	487000
Buffalo	463000	533000
Cincinnati	451000	503000
Nashville	448000	171000
San Jose	447000	204000
Minneapolis	434000	483000
Fort Worth	393000	356000
Toledo	383000	318000
Newark	382000	405000
Portland	380000	373000
Oklahoma	368000	324000
Louisville	362000	391000

EXHIBIT 12.4 (Cont'd)

	1970	*1960*
Oakland	362000	368000
Long Beach	359000	344000
Omaha	347000	302000
Miami	335000	292000
Tulsa	330000	262000
Honolulu	325000	294000
El Paso	322000	277000
St. Paul	310000	313000
Norfolk	308000	305000
Birmingham	301000	341000
Rochester	296000	319000
Tampa	278000	275000

12-9   Exhibit 12.4 gives the population for the 50 largest cities in the United States in 1960 and 1970. We want to answer the question, "Are the cities declining in population?" Two procedures we could use are (1) a paired sign test, and (2) a paired t-test.

(a)   State the null hypothesis and alternative for these two tests.

(b)   Do the sign test.

(c)   Do the t-test.

(d)   Compare the results from parts (b) and (c).

(e)   Which procedure seems more appropriate for these data? You might consider what would happen if one city had a very large change in population between 1960 and 1970. You might also think about the assumptions of the t-test and the sign test and to what extent they are met with these data.

12-10 Consider the data in Exercise 12-9. From 1960 to 1970 the United States as a whole had a 13.3% increase in population. Perhaps we should take this into account in our analysis. For each city, calculate what the population would have been in 1970 if that city had a 13.3% increase over its 1960 population. Compare these numbers to the actual 1970 population. Do both a t-test and a sign test. Compare your results to those in Exercise 12-9.

12.4 Two-Sample Rank Procedures

In this section we study a nonparametric procedure for comparing the medians of two populations. We assume (1) we have two random samples taken independently of each other, and (2) the populations have the same shape (in particular, the variances must be equal).

Our null hypothesis is that the population medians are equal and our alternative is that one population is shifted from the other as shown below.

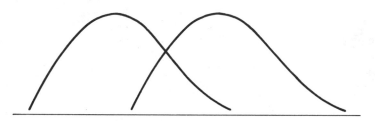

Since we assume the two populations have the same shape, this procedure is analogous to the pooled t procedures discussed in Section 8.2.

This procedure was introduced by Wilcoxon and further developed by Mann and Whitney. To avoid confusion with another test developed by Wilcoxon, discussed in the next section, we chose the name MANN-WHITNEY for the Minitab command.

An Example

The data in Exhibit 12.5 are from a study on Parkinson's disease, which, among other things, affects a person's ability to speak. Eight of the people in this study had had one of the most common operations to treat the disease. Overall, this operation seemed to improve the patients' condition, but how did it affect their ability to speak? Each patient was given several tests. The results of one of these tests are shown in Exhibit 12.5. Unlike most of the data we've seen so far, the scores from this speech test probably are not interval data. They are, however, ordered— the higher the score, the more problems with speaking.

First we'll show how to do a two-sample rank test by hand, then how to do it with Minitab. We begin by combining the two samples. Then we rank the combined sample, giving rank 1 to the smallest observation, rank 2 to the second smallest, etc. This procedure is illustrated in Exhibit 12.6. Whenever we have two or more observations that are tied, we

EXHIBIT 12.5

Speaking Ability for Patients in Study of Parkinson's Disease

Patients Who Had Operation	Patients Who Did Not Have Operation
2.6	1.2
2.0	1.8
1.7	1.8
2.7	2.3
2.5	1.3
2.6	3.0
2.5	2.2
3.0	1.3
	1.5
	1.6
	1.3
	1.5
	2.7
	2.0

assign the average rank to each. For example, the three observations that equal 1.3 are tied for ranks 2, 3, and 4. We therefore give each the rank $(2 + 3 + 4)/3 = 3$. Similarly, the two observations of 1.5 are both given rank $(5 + 6)/2 = 5.5$. Next we sum all the ranks corresponding to the observations in the first sample. This sum is usually denoted by W. Here $W = 126.5$.

If there is no difference between the two populations, then the average value of W is $n_1(n_1 + n_2 + 1)/2$, where n_1 = number of observations in the first sample and n_2 = number of observations in the second sample. Here this average is $8(8 + 14 + 1)/2 = 92$. If W is much larger than 92, then many numbers in the first sample must have been large. In that case, we might suspect that the first population has a larger median. If W is much smaller than 92, then many numbers in the first sample must have been small, so we might suspect that the first population has a smaller median than the second. To finish the test we compare the value of W to a table of critical values (using either a special table or a normal approximation).

All of this work is done by Minitab's MANN-WHITNEY command.

EXHIBIT 12.6

Two-Sample Rank Test, Done by Hand

First Sample	Ranks	Second Sample	Ranks
		1.2	1
		1.3	3
		1.3	3
		1.3	3
		1.5	5.5
		1.5	5.5
		1.6	7
1.7	8		
		1.8	9.5
		1.8	9.5
2.0	11.5	2.0	11.5
		2.2	13
		2.3	14
2.5	15.5		
2.5	15.5		
2.6	17.5		
2.6	17.5		
2.7	19.5	2.7	19.5
3.0	21.5	3.0	21.5
Sum of Ranks =	126.5		

MANN-WHITNEY TEST AND CONFIDENCE INTERVAL, SAMPLES

IN C AND C

Given independent random samples from two populations with population medians η_1 and η_2, this command

(a) Performs a two-sample rank test of the null hypothesis $H_0 : \eta_1 =
     \eta_2$ against the two-sided alternative hypothesis $H_1 : \eta_1 \neq \eta_2$. The
     test statistic, W, and the attained significance level of the test are
     printed out.

(b) Finds a 95% confidence interval for $\eta_1 - \eta_2$, using the two-sample
     rank method. The closest confidence to 95% is used.

(c) Prints a point estimate for $\eta_1 - \eta_2$, using two-sample rank methods.

The following program was used to analyze the Parkinson's disease
data:

SET OPERATION SAMPLE INTO C1

(data)

SET NO OPERATION SAMPLE INTO C2

(data)

MANN-WHITNEY ON DATA IN C1, C2
STOP

The output in Exhibit 12.7 gives W. It also says the attained significance
of the two-sided test is 0.0204. This means the chance of observing two
samples as separated as those in Exhibit 12.5, when in fact the two
populations have the same median, is only 0.0204. We therefore strongly
suspect that the two populations differ.

    Let's look for a moment at the practical significance of these results.
The test says there is statistically significant evidence that the two
populations differ. If we look at the data in Exhibit 12.5, we see the
direction of this difference—the patients who had the operation have
more severe speech problems than those who did not have the operation.

EXHIBIT 12.7

Two-Sample Rank Procedures on Parkinson's Disease Data

-- MANN-WHITNEY ON DATA IN C1, C2
     C1   N = 8   MEDIAN = 2.5500
     C2   N = 14   MEDIAN = 1.7000

A POINT ESTIMATE FOR ETA1-ETA2 IS 0.7000
A 94.8 PERCENT C.I. FOP. ETA1-ETA2 IS (0.2000, 1.2000)

TEST OF ETA1 = ETA2 VS. ETA1 N.E. ETA2
W = 126.5
THE TEST IS SIGNIFICANT AT 0.0204

This, of course, does not prove that the operation causes difficulties in speaking. Maybe the operation was only done on patients who were already in poor condition.

The output in Exhibit 12.7 also contains a confidence interval and a point estimate. Both of these are calculated using procedures developed from the two-sample rank test. Let's look first at the point estimate of $\eta_1 - \eta_2$. The most obvious way to estimate $\eta_1 - \eta_2$ is to take the difference of the corresponding two sample medians. However, in most applications where we want to use two-sample rank procedures, the following more complicated technique works a little "better." Take the first number from the first sample and subtract it from each number in the second sample. This will give 14 differences. Repeat this for each value in the first sample until you have all possible differences between the two samples. If there are n_1 numbers in the first sample and n_2 in the second sample, then you will need to calculate n_1 times n_2 differences. Here this is $8 \times 14 = 112$ differences. Finally, find the median of all these differences. That median is our point estimate of $\eta_1 - \eta_2$.

The confidence interval is calculated, using all of these differences, in much the same way as we calculated sign confidence intervals in Section 12.2. We take the interval from the d-th smallest difference to the d-th largest difference, where d is found using special tables.

Exercises

12-11 (a) By hand, compute the W statistic of a two-sample rank test, using the following data:

Sample A	10	7	6	12	14
Sample B	8	4	6	11	

Use Minitab's MANN-WHITNEY command to check your answer.

(b) By hand, compute the point estimate for the difference of the two population medians, using two-sample rank procedures. Compare your answer to Minitab's.

12-12 A study was done at Penn State to see how much one type of air pollution, ozone, damages azalea plants. Eleven varieties of azaleas were included in the study. We will look at data from just two varieties. During week 1, ten plants of each variety were fumigated with ozone. A short time later each plant was measured for leaf damage. The procedure was repeated four more times, each time using new plants.

Leaf Damage for Variety A

Week 1	Week 2	Week 3	Week 4	Week 5
1.58	1.09	0.00	2.22	.20
1.62	1.03	0.00	2.40	.40
2.04	0.00	.07	2.47	.34
1.28	.46	.18	1.85	0.00
1.43	.46	.40	2.50	0.00
1.93	.85	.20	1.20	0.00
2.20	.30	.63	1.33	.10
1.96	.90	.63	2.40	.06
2.23	0.00	.56	2.23	.17
1.54	0.00	.26	2.57	.25

Leaf Damage for Variety B

Week 1	Week 2	Week 3	Week 4	Week 5
1.29	0.00	.78	.40	0.00
.70	.20	.64	0.00	.40
1.93	0.00	1.00	.20	.47
.98	.98	.42	.40	0.00
.94	0.00	.97	.14	0.00
1.06	.62	2.43	.44	0.00
.94	.67	.65	1.23	0.00
1.65	0.00	0.00	.35	0.00
.70	0.00	.30	.17	0.00
.35	0.00	0.00	.20	0.00

(a) Compare the first week's data for the two varieties, using a two-sample rank test. Does there appear to be any difference in the two varieties' susceptibility to ozone damage?

(b) Repeat the test of part (a) for each of the 4 other weeks. Overall how do the two varieties compare?

(c) Susceptibility to ozone varies with weather conditions, and weather conditions vary from week to week. Does this seem to show up in the data? One simple way to look for a "week effect" is to calculate the median leaf damage for all 20 plants sprayed during week 1, the median for week 2, etc. Do these 5 medians seem to be very different? Of course, we'd like to be able to test to see if there is any difference between weeks. One relevant test is a nonparametric analysis of variance test, which is discussed in books on nonparametric statistics.

(d) Another way we could test for a "week effect" is to use a contingency table analysis (discussed in Section 11.2). First form a contingency table as follows: for each week count the number of damaged plants and the number of undamaged plants (a plant is undamaged if its leaf damage is 0.00); form a table which has 2 rows, corresponding to damaged and undamaged, and 5 columns, corresponding to the 5 weeks. Then do a chi-square test for association between damage and week. Do the results agree with what was indicated in part (c)?

12-13 An early version of this book was tested in two classes. At the end of the term, a questionnaire was given to each class. One question was,

"How many exercises in Chapter 2 did you try to do?" The results were as follows:

	Class A	Class B
(a) None	40	0
(b) One or two	6	13
(c) Three or four	5	17
(d) Five or six	1	3
(e) More than six	1	1

Is there evidence that the two classes did a significantly different number of exercises? To analyze these data, we must first convert the outcomes a, b, c, d, e to numbers. Suppose we choose 1 for a, 2 for b, etc. Then the data for Class A consists of forty 1's, six 2's, five 3's, one 4, and one 5. Class B is converted to numbers the same way. Then use the appropriate nonparametric procedures to compare the two classes.

12-14 Do migratory birds store, then gradually use up a layer of fat as they migrate? To investigate this question, two samples of migratory song sparrows were caught, one sample on April 5 and one sample on April 6. The amount of stored fat on each bird was subjectively estimated by an expert. Here are the results.

	Number of Birds in Class	
Fat Class	*Found on April 5*	*Found on April 6*
0	0	3
1−	0	1
1	0	11
1+	2	6
2−	0	1
2	10	9
2+	9	2
3−	7	2
3	6	1
3+	4	0
4−	1	0
4	2	0

Do an appropriate test to see if there is evidence that migratory birds use up a layer of fat as they migrate. (Note: You will have to convert the data to numbers as we did in Exercise 12-13.)

12.5 Other Nonparametric Procedures

In this section we briefly discuss some other nonparametric procedures.

Rank Correlation, Spearman's Rho

One measure of the correlation between two variables is the Pearson product moment correlation, discussed in Section 9.1. Another is Spearman's rho rank correlation. Spearman's rho is computed in the same way as Pearson's, but uses the ranks of the data instead of the actual values.

RANK THE VALUES IN **C**, PUT RANKS INTO **C**

Puts the number 1 next to the smallest value in the column, the number 2 next to the second smallest value, the number 3 next to the third smallest value, and so on. Ties are assigned the average rank.

Example

RANK C1 PUT RANKS INTO C2

c1	*c2*
0.5	3.5
2.0	6
2.5 →	7
−0.5	1
−0.3	2
1.5	5
0.5	3.5

The following program could be used to compute Spearman's rho for the exam scores in Exhibit 9.1:

```
READ FIRST EXAM INTO C1, SECOND EXAM INTO C2
```

(data from page 149)

```
RANK THE FIRST EXAM IN C1, PUT RANKS INTO C11
RANK THE SECOND EXAM IN C2, PUT RANKS INTO C12
CORRELATION BETWEEN C11 AND C12
STOP
```

Runs Test

The runs test examines a sequence of data for patterns. Patterns can occur in data if certain values tend to clump together, or if there is a general upward (or downward) trend in the data, or if the sequence starts out high and stays high for a while then suddenly jumps down to low values. Runs tests are designed to see if the data depart from being a list of random, independent observations all from the same population.

The runs test built into Minitab counts the number of times the sequence data values cross over some central value. If there is a pattern in the data, this count will probably be too low. Very high values of this count usually mean the data is too regular and has perhaps been "faked."

RUNS ABOVE AND BELOW **K** FOR DATA IN **C**

Performs a (two-sided) runs test on the data. A *run* is one or more observations in a row greater than K, or one or more in a row less than or equal to K.

Example

```
SET DATA INTO C1
1 1 4 6 1 3 2 2 5 4 4 8 6 7 8
RUNS ABOVE AND BELOW 3 FOR DATA IN C1
```

Here there are two runs above 3 and two below 3, as indicated by

$$1\,\overline{1}\,4\,\overline{6}\,1\,3\,2\,\overline{2}\,\overline{5}\,4\,4\,8\,6\,7\,8$$

The total number of runs (here 4) is compared to the expected number of runs from a random sequence (of 14 observations in which 6 are below 3 and 8 are above 3).

Minitab prints the number of runs, the expected number of runs, and the standard deviation under the assumption of randomness. The attained significance is also printed.

(A normal approximation is used to calculate the attained significance. In any case when this approximation is not valid, Minitab prints a message. You must then refer to special tables.)

Wilcoxon Signed Rank Procedures

With the sign test in Section 12.1 we only kept track of whether each observation was bigger or smaller than some hypothesized value. We kept no information about how *much* bigger it was. If the distribution from which we are sampling is symmetric (but not necessarily normal), then we can use the Wilcoxon test, which is often more efficient.

Suppose we have a set of data and our null hypothesis is that the population median is, say, 16. Then the Wilcoxon test is carried out as follows:

a)   Subtract 16 from each data value.

b)   Rank these differences ignoring signs (i.e., rank the absolute values or magnitudes), giving the smallest difference rank 1, the next smallest the rank 2, and so on.

c)   Add up the ranks corresponding to all the original data values that were bigger than 16. Call this sum W.

If most of the data values were larger than 16, then W will be large. If most were smaller, W will be small. If 16 was about in the middle of the data (and therefore a reasonable candidate for the population median), W will be intermediate. The value of W can then be compared with tabled critical values.

In Minitab this is all done automatically for you with the WILCOXON command.

WILCOXON TEST AND CONFIDENCE INTERVAL FOR MEDIAN =

K, DATA IN C

Given a random sample from a symmetric population with the median η, this command

(a) Performs a signed rank test of $H_0 : \eta = \text{K}$ versus $H_1 : \eta \neq \text{K}$. The test statistic W and the attained significance level are printed out.

(b) Prints a 95% confidence interval for η, using signed rank proce-dures. (The closest possible confidence to 95% is used.)

(c) Prints a point estimate for η, using signed rank procedures.

A normal approximation (with continuity correction) is used.

One way to find the Wilcoxon confidence interval and point estimate is from the "Walsh averages." Simply take all pairs of numbers in your sample including each number paired with itself. For each pair, x_i, x_j, calculate the Walsh average $(x_i + x_j)/2$. Then order all these averages. The point estimate is the median of the Walsh averages and the confidence interval is found by going from the d-th smallest to the d-th largest average, where d is found from special tables. (Minitab also has a command, WALSH, which forms the Walsh averages from a set of data—see page 325.)

APPENDIXES

APPENDIX A
Extended Examples

The examples given here are used in various places throughout the handbook. Each example consists of an explanation of the experiment or survey and the data which were collected.

Cartoon

When educators make an instructional film, they have two objectives. Will the people who watch the film learn the material as efficiently as possible? Will they retain what they have learned?

To help answer these questions, an experiment was conducted to evaluate the relative effectiveness of *cartoon* sketches and *realistic* photographs, in both *color* and *black and white* visual materials. A short instructional slide presentation was developed. The topic chosen for the presentation was the behavior of people in a group situation, and in particular, the various roles or character types that group members often assume. The presentation consisted of a five-minute lecture on tape, accompanied by 18 slides. Each role was identified with an animal. Each animal was shown on two slides: once in a cartoon sketch and once in a realistic picture. All 179 participants saw all of the 18 slides, but a randomly selected half of the participants saw them in black and white while the other half saw them in color.

After they had seen the slides, the participants took a test *(immediate test)* on the material. The 18 slides were presented in a random order, and the participants wrote down the character type represented by that slide. They received two scores: one for the number of cartoon characters they correctly identified and one for the number of realistic characters they correctly identified. Each score could range from 0 to 9, since there were nine characters.

Four weeks later, the participants were given another test *(delayed test)* and their scores were again computed. Some participants did not show up for this delayed test, and their scores were given a "missing value" code of —9.

The primary participants in this study were pre-professional and professional personnel at three hospitals in Pennsylvania involved in an in-service training program. A group of Penn State undergraduate students were also given the test as a comparison. All participants were given the OTIS Quick Scoring Mental Ability Test which yielded a rough estimate of their natural ability.

All of these data are described below.

Description of Cartoon Data

Variable	Description
1	Identification number.
2	0 = black and white; 1 = color (no participant saw both).
3	Education: 0 = pre-professional; 1 = professional; 2 = college student.
4	Location: 1 = hospital A; 2 = hospital B; 3 = hospital C; 4 = Penn State student.
5	OTIS Score: from about 70 to about 130.
6	Score on cartoon test given immediately after presentation. Possible scores are 0, 1, 2, ..., 9.
7	Score on realistic test given immediately after presentation. Possible scores are 0, 1, 2, ..., 9.
8	Score on cartoon test given four weeks (delayed) after presentation. Possible scores are 0, 1, 2, ..., 9 (—9 is used for a missing observation).
9	Score on realistic test given four weeks (delayed) after presentation. Possible scores are 0, 1, 2, ..., 9 (—9 is used for a missing observation.

Some questions that are of interest here are as follows: Is there a difference between color and black and white visual aids? Between cartoon and realistic? Is there any difference in retention? Does any difference depend on educational level or location? Does adjusting for OTIS score make any difference?

The data are given below. They have been partially sorted so that various parts may be easily studied separately.

				Variable				
1	*2*	*3*	*4*	*5*	*6*	*7*	*8*	*9*
1	0	0	1	107	4	4	−9	−9
2	0	0	2	106	9	9	6	5
3	0	0	2	94	4	2	3	0
4	0	0	2	121	8	8	6	8
5	0	0	3	86	5	5	−9	−9
6	0	0	3	99	7	8	7	5
7	0	0	3	114	8	9	5	4
8	0	0	3	100	2	1	−9	−9
9	0	0	3	85	3	2	−9	−9
10	0	0	3	115	8	7	8	5
11	0	0	3	101	7	6	−9	−9
12	0	0	3	84	7	5	−9	−9
13	0	0	3	94	4	3	−9	−9
14	0	0	3	87	1	3	2	0
15	0	0	3	104	9	9	5	6
16	0	0	3	104	5	6	−9	−9
17	0	0	3	97	6	5	−9	−9
18	0	0	3	91	1	0	−9	−9
19	0	0	3	83	4	4	−9	−9
20	0	0	3	93	0	1	−9	−9
21	0	0	3	92	2	2	−9	−9
22	0	0	3	91	5	2	3	1
23	0	0	3	88	2	1	−9	−9
24	0	0	3	90	5	4	4	3
25	0	0	3	103	6	2	−9	−9
26	0	0	3	93	9	9	8	4
27	0	0	3	106	2	0	6	3
28	1	0	1	98	3	3	−9	−9
29	1	0	1	103	6	5	2	2
30	1	0	2	109	5	4	1	2
31	1	0	2	107	8	8	−9	−9
32	1	0	2	108	8	8	7	6
33	1	0	2	107	3	2	−9	−9
34	1	0	3	87	6	4	2	2
35	1	0	3	113	5	4	4	4
36	1	0	3	80	0	3	1	1
37	1	0	3	91	5	6	−9	−9
38	1	0	3	102	8	9	5	5
39	1	0	3	83	4	1	2	1
40	1	0	3	108	9	9	−9	−9
41	1	0	3	86	4	4	−9	−9
42	1	0	3	96	6	3	−9	−9
43	1	0	3	101	5	3	−9	−9
44	1	0	3	97	6	3	4	4

				Variable				
1	2	3	4	5	6	7	8	9
45	1	0	3	88	3	1	2	0
46	1	0	3	104	4	2	2	0
47	1	0	3	87	7	3	−9	−9
48	1	0	3	86	1	1	−9	−9
49	1	0	3	90	6	5	4	1
50	1	0	3	102	6	2	−9	−9
51	1	0	3	105	2	2	−9	−9
52	1	0	3	115	7	8	−9	−9
53	1	0	3	88	4	3	−9	−9
54	1	0	3	111	8	8	−9	−9
55	1	0	3	95	5	4	−9	−9
56	1	0	3	104	5	5	−9	−9
57	0	1	1	79	7	4	6	4
58	0	1	1	82	3	2	−9	−9
59	0	1	1	123	8	8	7	5
60	0	1	1	106	9	7	8	6
61	0	1	1	125	9	9	4	3
62	0	1	1	98	7	6	−9	−9
63	0	1	1	95	7	7	4	4
64	0	1	2	129	9	9	7	7
65	0	1	2	90	7	6	3	5
66	0	1	2	111	6	2	3	1
67	0	1	2	99	4	5	3	1
68	0	1	2	116	9	7	7	7
69	0	1	2	106	8	7	6	4
70	0	1	2	107	8	5	−9	−9
71	0	1	2	100	7	6	2	1
72	0	1	2	124	8	9	3	5
73	0	1	3	98	6	7	1	1
74	0	1	3	124	9	6	6	5
75	0	1	3	84	1	4	−9	−9
76	0	1	3	91	8	3	−9	−9
77	0	1	3	118	6	6	3	4
78	0	1	3	102	6	4	−9	−9
79	0	1	3	95	7	4	−9	−9
80	0	1	3	90	4	3	−9	−9
81	0	1	3	86	1	0	−9	−9
82	0	1	3	104	6	4	−9	−9
83	1	1	1	111	9	9	6	3
84	1	1	1	105	1	0	−9	−9
85	1	1	1	110	1	0	0	0
86	1	1	1	80	0	0	0	0
87	1	1	1	78	4	1	1	1
88	1	1	2	120	9	9	−9	−9

				Variable				
1	*2*	*3*	*4*	*5*	*6*	*7*	*8*	*9*
89	1	1	2	110	9	6	6	5
90	1	1	2	107	8	6	−9	−9
91	1	1	2	125	7	8	−9	−9
92	1	1	2	117	9	9	−9	−9
93	1	1	2	126	8	8	5	5
94	1	1	2	98	4	5	−9	−9
95	1	1	2	111	8	6	−9	−9
96	1	1	2	110	8	7	−9	−9
97	1	1	2	120	9	7	−9	−9
98	1	1	2	114	8	7	6	4
99	1	1	2	117	6	7	−9	−9
100	1	1	3	105	7	6	−9	−9
101	1	1	3	97	6	6	−9	−9
102	1	1	3	86	1	1	−9	−9
103	1	1	3	111	7	5	−9	−9
104	1	1	3	93	1	0	−9	−9
105	1	1	3	115	8	7	−9	−9
106	1	1	3	102	2	3	5	2
107	1	1	3	111	7	3	4	4
108	1	1	3	82	1	1	−9	−9
109	1	1	3	117	8	5	4	3
110	0	2	4	132	9	9	−9	−9
111	0	2	4	113	7	8	−9	−9
112	0	2	4	130	9	7	1	4
113	0	2	4	122	9	9	6	4
114	0	2	4	133	9	9	−9	−9
115	0	2	4	103	7	5	3	0
116	0	2	4	118	9	9	−9	−9
117	0	2	4	119	9	9	7	8
118	0	2	4	97	8	8	6	4
119	0	2	4	123	9	9	7	4
120	0	2	4	113	8	7	6	6
121	0	2	4	110	8	7	3	5
122	0	2	4	119	8	7	6	6
123	0	2	4	116	5	7	−9	−9
124	0	2	4	113	8	6	5	5
125	0	2	4	128	9	9	−9	−9
126	0	2	4	113	8	5	4	2
127	0	2	4	110	5	7	−9	−9
128	0	2	4	114	7	6	5	5
129	0	2	4	132	9	8	4	6
130	0	2	4	110	7	8	2	5
131	0	2	4	122	7	7	4	2
132	0	2	4	123	9	9	6	7

				Variable				
1	*2*	*3*	*4*	*5*	*6*	*7*	*8*	*9*
133	0	2	4	131	9	9	7	7
134	0	2	4	131	9	9	8	8
135	0	2	4	121	9	8	7	8
136	0	2	4	125	9	8	−9	−9
137	0	2	4	101	6	6	4	6
138	0	2	4	120	8	9	6	7
139	0	2	4	99	9	6	−9	−9
140	0	2	4	128	8	9	8	7
141	0	2	4	129	8	6	5	2
142	0	2	4	125	8	6	7	4
143	0	2	4	107	8	8	8	5
144	0	2	4	102	8	7	6	4
145	0	2	4	125	9	8	−9	−9
146	1	2	4	129	8	8	−9	−9
147	1	2	4	122	3	0	2	3
148	1	2	4	124	7	6	6	7
149	1	2	4	115	8	8	−9	−9
150	1	2	4	117	8	6	5	2
151	1	2	4	132	7	6	5	7
152	1	2	4	109	8	5	5	5
153	1	2	4	107	9	5	9	2
154	1	2	4	116	8	7	6	5
155	1	2	4	118	8	5	6	5
156	1	2	4	124	9	9	6	7
157	1	2	4	102	9	5	5	2
158	1	2	4	110	9	7	7	7
159	1	2	4	119	7	5	2	4
160	1	2	4	99	3	2	4	0
161	1	2	4	102	7	8	5	6
162	1	2	4	115	7	7	−9	−9
163	1	2	4	105	8	6	3	0
164	1	2	4	104	7	6	−9	−9
165	1	2	4	112	7	7	−9	−9
166	1	2	4	117	9	9	6	5
167	1	2	4	108	9	9	−9	−9
168	1	2	4	135	8	8	8	8
169	1	2	4	133	8	8	7	7
170	1	2	4	105	6	4	5	3
171	1	2	4	124	7	7	9	8
172	1	2	4	112	9	9	9	8
173	1	2	4	128	9	9	9	9
174	1	2	4	96	8	8	7	6
175	1	2	4	110	8	8	4	5
176	1	2	4	108	8	8	6	8

				Variable				
1	*2*	*3*	*4*	*5*	*6*	*7*	*8*	*9*
177	1	2	4	125	7	6	8	8
178	1	2	4	111	4	3	4	1
179	1	2	4	103	4	3	2	1

Peru

Some anthropologists recently did a study to determine the long-term effects of a change in environment on blood pressure. In this study they measured the blood pressure of a number of Indians who had migrated from a very primitive environment in the high Andes mountains of Peru into the main stream of Peruvian society and a much lower altitude.

A previous study in Africa had suggested that migration from a primitive society to a modern one might increase blood pressure at first, but that the blood pressure would tend to decrease back to normal over time.

The anthropologists also measured the height, weight, and a number of other characteristics of the subjects. A portion of their data is given below. All of these data are for males over 21 who were born at a high altitude, and whose parents were both born at a high altitude. The skin-fold measurements were taken as a general measure of obesity. Systolic and diastolic blood pressure are usually studied separately. Systolic is often a more sensitive indicator.

Description of Peru Data

Variable	*Description*
1	Age in years
2	Years since migration
3	Weight in kilograms (1 kg = 2.2 lb.)
4	Height in millimeters (1 mm = 0.039 in.)
5	Chin skin fold in millimeters
6	Forearm skin fold in millimeters
7	Calf skin fold in millimeters
8	Pulse rate in beats per minute
9	Systolic blood pressure
10	Diastolic blood pressure

				Variable					
1	2	3	4	5	6	7	8	9	10
21	1	71.0	1629	8.0	7.0	12.7	88	170	76
22	6	56.5	1569	3.3	5.0	8.0	64	120	60
24	5	56.0	1561	3.3	1.3	4.3	68	125	75
24	1	61.0	1619	3.7	3.0	4.3	52	148	120
25	1	65.0	1566	9.0	12.7	20.7	72	140	78
27	19	62.0	1639	3.0	3.3	5.7	72	106	72
28	5	53.0	1494	7.3	4.7	8.0	64	120	76
28	25	53.0	1568	3.7	4.3	0.0	80	108	62
31	6	65.0	1540	10.3	9.0	10.0	76	124	70
32	13	57.0	1530	5.7	4.0	6.0	60	134	64
33	13	66.5	1622	6.0	5.7	8.3	68	116	76
33	10	59.1	1486	6.7	5.3	10.3	72	114	74
34	15	64.0	1578	3.3	5.3	7.0	88	130	80
35	18	69.5	1645	9.3	5.0	7.0	60	118	68
35	2	64.0	1648	3.0	3.7	6.7	60	138	78
36	12	56.5	1521	3.3	5.0	11.7	72	134	86
36	15	57.0	1547	3.0	3.0	6.0	84	120	70
37	16	55.0	1505	4.3	5.0	7.0	64	120	76
37	17	57.0	1473	6.0	5.3	11.7	72	114	80
38	10	58.0	1538	8.7	6.0	13.0	64	124	64
38	18	59.5	1513	5.3	4.0	7.7	80	114	66
38	11	61.0	1653	4.0	3.3	4.0	76	136	78
38	11	57.0	1566	3.0	3.0	3.0	60	126	72
39	21	57.5	1580	4.0	3.0	5.0	64	124	62
39	24	74.0	1647	7.3	6.3	15.7	64	128	84
39	14	72.0	1620	6.3	7.7	13.3	68	134	92
41	25	62.5	1637	6.0	5.3	8.0	76	112	80
41	32	68.0	1528	10.0	5.0	11.3	60	128	82
41	5	63.4	1647	5.3	4.3	13.7	76	134	92
42	12	68.0	1605	11.0	7.0	10.7	88	128	90
43	25	69.0	1625	5.0	3.0	6.0	72	140	72
43	26	73.0	1615	12.0	4.0	5.7	68	138	74
43	10	64.0	1640	5.7	3.0	7.0	60	118	66
44	19	65.0	1610	8.0	6.7	7.7	74	110	70
44	18	71.0	1572	3.0	4.7	4.3	72	142	84
45	10	60.2	1534	3.0	3.0	3.3	56	134	70
47	1	55.0	1536	3.0	3.0	4.0	64	116	54
50	43	70.0	1630	4.0	6.0	11.7	72	132	90
54	40	87.0	1542	11.3	11.7	11.3	92	152	88

Trees

People in forestry need to be able to estimate the amount of timber in a given area of a forest. Therefore, they need a quick and easy way to determine the volume of any given tree. Of course, it is difficult to measure the volume of a tree directly. But it is not too difficult to measure the height, and even easier to measure the diameter. Thus, the forester would like to develop an equation or table that makes it easy to estimate the volume of a tree from its diameter and/or height. A sample of trees of various diameters and heights were cut, and the diameter, height, and volume recorded. Below are the results of one such sample. This sample is for black cherry trees in Allegheny National Forest, Pennsylvania. (Of course, different varieties of trees and different locations will yield different results. So separate tables are prepared for each species and each location.)

Description of Tree Data

	Description
Diameter	Diameter in inches at 4.5 feet above ground level
Height	Height of tree in feet
Volume	Volume of tree in cubic feet

Diameter	Height	Volume
8.3	70	10.3
8.6	65	10.3
8.8	63	10.2
10.5	72	16.4
10.7	81	18.8
10.8	83	19.7
11.0	66	15.6
11.0	75	18.2
11.1	80	22.6
11.2	75	19.9
11.3	79	24.2
11.4	76	21.0
11.4	76	21.4
11.7	69	21.3

Diameter	Height	Volume
12.0	75	19.1
12.9	74	22.2
12.9	85	33.8
13.3	86	27.4
13.7	71	25.7
13.8	64	24.9
14.0	78	34.5
14.2	80	31.7
14.5	74	36.3
16.0	72	38.3
16.3	77	42.6
17.3	81	55.4
17.5	82	55.7
17.9	80	58.3
18.0	80	51.5
18.0	80	51.0
20.6	87	77.0

Grades

Scholastic Aptitude Tests (SAT) are often used as a criterion for admission to college, or as predictors of college performance, or indicators for placement in courses. The data below are a sample of SAT scores and freshman year grade point averages (GPA) from a northeastern university. (The university wishes to remain anonymous.) Students who did not take the SAT tests, or who did not complete their freshman year, were omitted from the sample. The remaining sample of 200 students was randomly broken down into 4 samples of size 50 for ease of use in this handbook. These samples can be used separately or combined to make larger samples for analysis.

Description of Grades Data

	Description
Verb	Score on verbal aptitude test
Math	Score on mathematical aptitude test
GPA	Grade point average (0 to 4, with 4 the best grade)

Sample A

Verb	Math	GPA
623	509	2.6
454	471	2.3
643	700	2.4
585	719	3.0
719	710	3.1
693	643	2.9
571	665	3.1
646	719	3.3
613	693	2.3
655	701	3.3
662	614	2.6
585	557	3.3
580	611	2.0
648	701	3.0
405	611	1.9
506	681	2.7
669	653	2.0
558	500	3.3
577	635	2.0
487	584	2.3
682	629	3.3
565	624	2.8
552	665	1.7
567	724	2.4
745	746	3.4
610	653	2.8
493	605	2.4
571	566	1.9
682	724	2.5
600	677	2.3
740	729	3.4
593	611	2.8
488	683	1.9
526	777	3.0
630	605	3.7
586	653	2.3
610	674	2.9
695	634	3.3
539	601	2.1
490	701	1.2
509	547	3.3
667	753	2.0
597	652	3.1
662	664	2.6

Sample A (Cont'd)

Verb	Math	GPA
566	664	2.4
597	602	2.4
604	557	2.3
519	529	3.0
643	715	2.9
606	593	3.4

Sample B

Verb	Math	GPA
500	661	2.8
460	692	1.4
717	672	2.8
592	441	2.4
752	729	3.4
695	681	2.5
610	777	3.6
620	638	2.6
682	701	3.6
524	700	2.9
552	692	2.6
703	710	3.8
584	738	3.0
550	638	2.5
659	672	3.5
585	605	2.0
578	614	3.0
533	630	2.0
532	586	1.8
708	701	2.3
537	681	2.1
635	647	3.0
591	614	3.3
552	669	3.0
557	674	3.2
599	664	2.3
540	658	3.3
752	737	3.3
726	800	3.9
630	668	2.1
558	567	2.6
646	771	2.4

Sample B (Cont'd)

Verb	Math	GPA
643	719	3.3
606	755	3.1
682	652	3.6
565	672	2.9
578	629	2.4
488	611	1.8
361	602	2.4
560	639	2.9
630	647	3.5
666	705	3.4
719	668	2.3
669	701	2.9
571	647	1.8
520	583	2.8
571	593	2.3
539	601	2.5
580	630	2.4
629	695	2.9

Sample C

Verb	Math	GPA
545	643	3.0
558	602	2.3
544	665	2.0
646	573	2.0
655	719	3.8
585	602	3.4
634	515	2.9
759	734	2.8
532	653	2.5
653	668	2.8
682	764	2.9
641	605	2.1
547	602	1.4
634	602	2.4
609	695	3.0
620	773	3.1
634	710	3.0
585	556	3.4
558	656	2.0
689	614	2.8

Sample C (Cont'd)

Verb	Math	GPA
780	692	1.3
448	645	2.0
523	614	2.1
571	674	1.6
680	490	2.0
550	782	2.5
544	575	1.4
580	677	2.1
626	724	2.0
617	621	2.0
578	609	0.3
430	710	2.4
662	621	2.6
494	561	2.5
520	618	2.3
760	710	1.1
604	700	3.0
523	643	2.3
484	620	2.0
584	567	2.7
613	626	3.3
696	620	2.0
649	621	2.6
649	665	3.6
578	635	2.9
585	710	3.1
610	634	2.6
641	656	3.1
465	683	2.4
667	611	2.3

Sample D

Verb	Math	GPA
578	584	2.1
564	575	1.8
578	665	3.0
539	586	2.5
495	748	2.8
537	638	2.3
558	557	2.3
564	593	2.9

Sample D (Cont'd)

Verb	Math	GPA
648	611	3.3
673	748	2.6
666	621	2.9
571	729	3.1
487	686	2.1
659	575	2.3
649	746	3.0
675	629	3.0
552	662	2.7
636	592	2.7
580	624	2.8
643	583	2.3
688	643	2.6
620	555	2.7
523	737	3.0
727	602	3.7
502	528	2.3
686	800	3.4
547	649	3.0
481	575	2.0
600	621	3.1
604	719	2.4
573	526	2.5
558	576	3.2
586	677	2.0
597	737	3.6
545	692	2.4
547	724	3.3
601	682	2.9
659	649	2.4
544	629	2.4
507	624	2.3
641	764	2.5
585	576	2.6
630	624	3.4
613	677	2.3
710	647	3.0
509	538	3.0
480	526	2.4
487	672	2.9
526	796	1.8
532	710	2.1

Pulse

Students in an introductory statistics course participated in an "in class" experiment. The students took their own pulse rate (which is easiest to do by holding the thumb and forefinger of one hand on the pair of arteries on the side of the neck). They then were asked to flip a coin. If their coin came up heads, they were to run in place for one minute. Then everyone took their own pulse again. The pulse rates and some other data are given below.

Description of Pulse Data

Variable	Description
1	First pulse rate
2	Second pulse rate
3	1 = ran in place; 2 = did not run in place
4	1 = smokes regularly; 2 = does not smoke regularly
5	1 = male; 2 = female
6	Height in inches
7	Weight in pounds
8	Usual level of physical activity: 1 = slight; 2 = moderate; 3 = a lot

					Variable		
1	*2*	*3*	*4*	*5*	*6*	*7*	*8*
64	88	1	2	1	66.00	140	2
58	70	1	2	1	72.00	145	2
62	76	1	1	1	73.50	160	3
66	78	1	1	1	73.00	190	1
64	80	1	2	1	69.00	155	2
74	84	1	2	1	73.00	165	1
84	84	1	2	1	72.00	150	3
68	72	1	2	1	74.00	190	2
62	75	1	2	1	72.00	195	2
76	118	1	2	1	71.00	138	2
90	94	1	1	1	74.00	160	1
80	96	1	2	1	72.00	155	2
92	84	1	1	1	70.00	153	3
68	76	1	2	1	67.00	145	2
60	76	1	2	1	71.00	170	3
62	58	1	2	1	72.00	175	3
66	82	1	1	1	69.00	175	2

					Variable		
1	*2*	*3*	*4*	*5*	*6*	*7*	*8*
70	72	1	1	1	73.00	170	3
68	76	1	1	1	74.00	180	2
72	80	1	2	1	66.00	135	3
70	106	1	2	1	71.00	170	2
74	76	1	2	1	70.00	157	2
66	102	1	2	1	70.00	130	2
70	94	1	1	1	75.00	185	2
96	140	1	2	2	61.00	140	2
62	100	1	2	2	66.00	120	2
78	104	1	1	2	68.00	130	2
82	100	1	2	2	68.00	138	2
100	115	1	1	2	63.00	121	2
68	112	1	2	2	70.00	125	2
96	116	1	2	2	68.00	116	2
78	118	1	2	2	69.00	145	2
88	110	1	1	2	69.00	150	2
62	98	1	1	2	62.75	112	2
80	128	1	2	2	68.00	125	2
62	62	2	2	1	74.00	190	1
60	62	2	2	1	71.00	155	2
72	74	2	1	1	69.00	170	2
62	66	2	2	1	70.00	155	2
76	76	2	2	1	72.00	215	2
68	66	2	1	1	67.00	150	2
54	56	2	1	1	69.00	145	2
74	70	2	2	1	73.00	155	3
74	74	2	2	1	73.00	155	2
68	68	2	2	1	71.00	150	3
72	74	2	1	1	68.00	155	3
68	64	2	2	1	69.50	150	3
82	84	2	1	1	73.00	180	2
64	62	2	2	1	75.00	160	3
58	58	2	2	1	66.00	135	3
54	50	2	2	1	69.00	160	2
70	62	2	1	1	66.00	130	2
62	68	2	1	1	73.00	155	2
48	54	2	1	1	68.00	150	0
76	76	2	2	1	74.00	148	3
88	84	2	2	1	73.50	155	2
70	70	2	2	1	70.00	150	2
90	88	2	1	1	67.00	140	2
78	76	2	2	1	72.00	180	3
70	66	2	1	1	75.00	190	2
90	90	2	2	1	68.00	145	1

				Variable			
1	*2*	*3*	*4*	*5*	*6*	*7*	*8*
92	94	2	1	1	69.00	150	2
60	70	2	1	1	71.50	164	2
72	70	2	2	1	71.00	140	2
68	68	2	2	1	72.00	142	3
84	84	2	2	1	69.00	136	2
74	76	2	2	1	67.00	123	2
68	66	2	2	1	68.00	155	2
84	84	2	2	2	66.00	130	2
61	70	2	2	2	65.50	120	2
64	60	2	2	2	66.00	130	3
94	92	2	1	2	62.00	131	2
60	66	2	2	2	62.00	120	2
72	70	2	2	2	63.00	118	2
58	56	2	2	2	67.00	125	2
88	74	2	1	2	65.00	135	2
66	72	2	2	2	66.00	125	2
84	80	2	2	2	65.00	118	1
62	66	2	2	2	65.00	122	3
66	76	2	2	2	65.00	115	2
80	74	2	2	2	64.00	102	2
78	78	2	2	2	67.00	115	2
68	68	2	2	2	69.00	150	2
72	68	2	2	2	68.00	110	2
82	80	2	2	2	63.00	116	1
76	76	2	1	2	62.00	108	3
87	84	2	2	2	63.00	95	3
90	92	2	1	2	64.00	125	1
78	80	2	2	2	68.00	133	1
68	68	2	2	2	62.00	110	2
86	84	2	2	2	67.00	150	3
76	76	2	2	2	61.75	108	2

Integration

A researcher at Columbia University was interested in the effect of school integration on racial attitudes. He gave an "ethnocentricism" test to four groups of children: black children in a segregated school, white children in a segregated school, black children in an integrated school, and white children in an integrated school. Here *ethnocentricism* is defined as the tendency of children to prefer to associate with, and respect, other children of the same ethnic group to those of another ethnic group. Thus, students who score high on this test have a stronger preference for their own race.

The results he got are given below. There are 50 students in each group.

Integrated Blacks	Integrated Whites	Segregated Blacks	Segregated Whites
15	12	11	23
12	12	11	17
14	13	13	14
15	11	13	18
22	16	9	16
21	12	21	18
18	19	21	15
18	12	9	21
23	5	13	22
22	8	13	20
14	20	11	10
22	7	10	18
15	12	12	16
7	24	18	13
17	13	19	10
12	18	18	19
18	14	12	10
17	18	18	15
19	8	17	22
18	16	19	15
14	9	21	12
19	19	22	11
13	9	22	9
21	1	17	14
21	9	12	21
12	11	13	10
16	9	21	15
14	17	14	14
22	16	20	7
16	16	19	14
17	12	15	21
20	7	19	10
18	9	12	14
22	24	12	10
20	13	16	24
23	15	14	24
20	20	16	12
14	14	11	9
20	17	15	14

Integrated Blacks	Integrated Whites	Segregated Blacks	Segregated Whites
17	8	12	13
13	15	9	14
17	16	15	16
14	6	11	12
16	5	11	14
15	14	10	22
15	7	10	21
12	12	14	15
17	22	12	9
13	14	11	9
24	11	13	9

Cancer

Cancer is one of the most feared diseases in the United States today. Billions of dollars have been spent on cancer research, but progress has been frustratingly slow. Even the smallest bit of new evidence relating to cancer and its causes or diagnosis is given the greatest attention. Thus, considerable interest was generated in August 1975 when a University of Wisconsin medical chemist happened to notice that a small "band" appeared in a chemical spectrum analysis of blood (alkalin phosphatase) when the blood sample came from the cancer wing of the hospital, but didn't appear when the sample came from other parts of the hospital.

The key question was, Could this finding be duplicated in a controlled study? A team of researchers was quickly assembled and a small but intensive data collection program was begun. One of the authors of this book, Brian L. Joiner, was a member of this team and helped decide what data to collect, how to collect it, and how to analyze it. Another member of the team studied patient records and recorded pertinent information. Three others independently judged each specimen by looking at the spectrum and writing down what they saw—no band, possibly a faint band, a definite band, or a very strong band.

A portion of the data is given on the following pages. At this point no thorough analysis has been done on these data. Some suggested exercises are given in the book, but these are not sufficient to tell us all we would like to know. Perhaps you can think of some other things to try yourself. Here are some of the most important questions:

(a) Does this band seem to help identify which patients have cancer and which do not?

(b) Is the band a better predictor for some types of patients (e.g., males, or older people)?

(c) Is the band better for some types of cancer?

(d) Is there any way to use some of the other data to help the band make better predictions (e.g., by also looking at some of the lab data)?

(e) Do there appear to be any errors in the data?

Some of the variables involved in this study are described in Exhibit A.1. A very useful additional variable can be created by adding the two variables, cancer and band. This new variable, let's call it "result," will have four values as follows:

0 = False negative (patient has cancer, but judges didn't see band)
1 = True negative (patient does not have cancer and judges didn't see band)
2 = True positive (patient has cancer and judges saw band)
3 = False positive (patient doesn't have cancer, but judges saw band)

For convenience, the data have been divided into four sets corresponding to these four groups.

Further Comments.   The scaling on the judges' opinions is somewhat arbitrary and it is felt that scores of 2 and 3 are further apart than are 1 and 2 or 3 and 4. Adding them up to get a total is also a bit arbitrary, as is cutting them off at 7 or above to get a "positive" test result. Work is underway to develop a device that will read the spectrum directly, bypassing the need for the judges.

  Some cleaning has already been done on the data to simplify its use in this book. For example, several types of patients have been totally excluded from the data presented here. These include all diabetics, and all patients with renal disease or hepatitis.

Analyzing the Data on Minitab.   This data set is the largest in this book. It contains 362 observations (patients) of 18 variables each for a total of 362 × 18 = 6516 numbers. On many computers the worksheet will not hold 6516 numbers. There are several things you can do.

(1)   You can analyze each of the four groups separately. Most of the exercises in this book analyze the groups separately.

(2)   You can read into the worksheet only the first few variables. For example, suppose you say READ C1-C10, and follow this by the whole set of data (362 lines). Then only the first 10 variables will be read into the worksheet, the other 8 will be ignored. This gives a total of $362 \times 10 = 3620$ numbers. Of course, you need a worksheet that has 362 rows. If your worksheet normally has only 200 rows, then you must redimension it (see page 314). To do this, use the command DIMENSION 365 ROWS before you type the READ command.

(3)   The technique in part (2) works if you want to analyze only the first few variables. Suppose you want to analyze variables 3, 10, and 15. You could use the command

READ C1 C1 C1, C2 C2 C2 C2 C2 C2 C2, C3 C3 C3 C3 C3

followed by the data. When several variables are read into the same column (e.g., variables 1, 2, and 3 are all read into c1) only the last variable read will be in the column at the end (here variable 3). In general, whenever a column is reused, all previous contents are first erased. So, at the end of reading the **Cancer** data, you will have variable 3 in c1, variable 10 in c2 and variable 15 in c3. (This technique is simply a "computer trick" that happens to work in Minitab.)

EXHIBIT A.1

Description of Cancer Data

(Wherever a value was not recorded, or the question did not apply to the patient, a zero was entered.)

Variable	Description
1	Sex of patient: 1 = male; 2 = female
2	Age of patient
3	Cancer: 1 = patient has (or has had) cancer; 2 = isn't known to have (or have had) cancer
4	Band: 1 = test is positive; − 1 = test is negative. The band test is considered positive if the sum of the three judges' scores

EXHIBIT A.1 (Cont'd)

Variable	Description
	was 7 or more. If the sum was less than 7, the test is considered negative.
5	Alkaline phosphatase (AKP), the chemical that was being measured when the new band was discovered. There may be some positive (or negative) correlation between the appearance of the band and the AKP value.
6	Phosphate (P) concentration in blood.
7	Lactate dehydrogenase (LDH), an enzyme used for general screening of patients. High values are usually caused by some type of cellular destruction in the liver, heart, muscle, etc.
8	Albumin as a percent of total protein in blood, indicator of liver or kidney malfunction. Status of liver may be an indicator of whether cancer has spread to liver.
9	Blood urea nitrogen. High levels indicate poor kidney functioning.
10	Glucose, amount of sugar in the blood. May correlate with the appearance of the band. (Note: All known diabetics have been removed from the data since they almost always had the band.)
11	Success of treatment: 1 = presumed cure; 2 = possible cure; 3 = tumor remaining; 0 = unknown or does not apply
12	Judge A
13	Judge B } For each judge: 1 = no band was seen; 2 = possibly a faint band; 3 = a definite band; 4 = very strong band
14	Judge C
15	Metastasis: 1 = cancer has spread to other organs; 2 = cancer has not spread; 0 = unknown or does not apply
16	Lymph: 1 = cancer in lymph nodes; 2 = no cancer in lymph nodes; 0 = unknown or does not apply
17	Liver: 1 = cancer in liver; 2 = no cancer in liver; 0 = unknown or does not apply
18	Organ. In patients with cancer, a code number for organ where cancer began (see Exhibit A.2 for codes). Patients without cancer were assigned a zero.

EXHIBIT A.2

Code Number for Organ First Having Cancer (Variable 8)

Code Number	Organ	Code Number	Organ
0	No answer, or no cancer	20	Small intestine
1	Bladder	21	Stomach
2	Breast	23	Uterus
3	Cervix	24	Esophagus
4	Colon	25	Testis
6	Fallopian tubes	26	Vagina
7	Gallbladder	27	Liver
9	Kidney	29	Myeloma
10	Larynx	30	Thyroid
11	Lung	31	Brain or nerve tissue
12	Lymph nodes	32	Smooth muscle
14	Mouth	33	Striated muscle
15	Ovary	34	Other
17	Rectum	35	Unknown or multiple
18	Sinus	36	Prostate
19	Skin	37	Leukemia

Note: Codes 5, 8, 13, 16, 22, and 28 are not assigned.

Group A
False Negative (Cancer and No Band)

1	2	3	4	5	6	7	8	9	10	11	12	13	14	15	16	17	18
1	71	1	−1	8.0	3.2	7.8	62	6	113	3	1	1	1	1	1	0	10
1	66	1	−1	10.5	5.1	50.1	57	9	93	4	1	1	2	1	3	3	0
1	83	1	−1	8.5	3.3	15.3	53	21	109	1	1	1	2	0	0	0	4
2	52	1	−1	12.8	3.2	18.8	45	14	91	3	1	1	2	0	0	0	31
1	61	1	−1	7.4	4.3	12.9	69	19	78	2	1	1	2	3	0	0	34
2	54	1	−1	8.1	2.7	15.9	57	10	122	3	2	2	2	1	0	1	4
1	27	1	−1	3.8	3.2	24.9	64	14	88	3	1	1	1	1	1	2	30
2	91	1	−1	7.8	3.5	30.1	61	28	104	3	1	1	1	1	1	3	12
2	74	1	−1	8.2	3.2	20.7	66	21	91	3	1	1	1	2	2	2	11
2	67	1	−1	14.0	2.9	15.8	60	15	103	2	1	1	1	1	1	2	2
2	43	1	−1	7.3	3.9	11.8	68	15	93	4	1	1	1	1	1	3	2
1	40	1	−1	5.5	2.8	18.1	63	16	96	3	1	1	1	3	0	0	0
2	64	1	−1	6.3	3.2	22.4	56	14	127	3	1	1	1	1	0	0	2

Group A (Cont'd)

1	2	3	4	5	6	7	8	9	10	11	12	13	14	15	16	17	18
2	23	1	−1	3.3	2.4	24.2	61	13	93	1	1	2	1	2	2	2	23
1	58	1	−1	10.3	3.0	14.9	62	14	102	3	1	1	1	1	1	3	12
2	18	1	−1	9.3	2.7	12.5	55	6	99	3	2	3	1	2	2	2	15
1	63	1	−1	13.3	3.7	14.0	68	21	105	3	1	1	1	1	3	2	1
1	34	1	−1	1.7	3.0	23.2	48	9	116	3	1	1	1	0	0	0	37
1	34	1	−1	7.1	3.5	16.7	72	20	91	2	1	1	1	0	0	0	12
2	25	1	−1	5.3	3.6	13.6	56	9	79	2	1	1	2	2	0	0	3
2	82	1	−1	7.5	2.9	14.3	61	12	153	3	1	1	2	0	0	0	24
1	42	1	−1	4.2	4.5	52.2	52	11	83	3	1	1	1	0	0	0	37
2	55	1	−1	5.8	3.1	12.2	63	16	93	1	1	1	1	2	2	2	3
2	58	1	−1	9.2	2.0	17.9	48	7	88	3	2	2	2	3	3	3	3
2	86	1	−1	9.5	3.4	13.4	64	17	93	3	1	1	1	3	3	2	23
1	66	1	−1	5.0	2.6	13.6	65	17	85	3	1	1	1	1	1	3	34
1	25	1	−1	15.9	3.0	99.9	58	18	94	4	1	1	2	1	1	2	25
2	62	1	−1	8.1	3.1	18.6	67	13	99	3	1	1	1	1	1	2	2
2	54	1	−1	12.7	2.2	2.2	60	21	152	2	1	1	1	0	0	0	4
1	63	1	−1	6.8	3.5	21.6	59	4	72	3	2	1	2	3	3	3	4
2	36	1	−1	6.9	4.1	14.0	69	8	92	1	1	1	2	3	3	3	23
1	31	1	−1	13.1	3.3	12.8	60	14	134	3	1	1	1	2	0	0	31
2	63	1	−1	11.4	2.9	14.9	67	13	83	3	1	1	1	3	3	3	0
1	40	1	−1	6.6	3.2	15.5	66	13	109	4	1	1	1	1	3	3	34
2	56	1	−1	7.4	3.2	16.1	59	11	93	3	1	1	2	1	3	3	6
2	31	1	−1	8.9	2.4	12.6	66	9	90	2	1	1	1	1	1	3	19
2	50	1	−1	9.2	3.4	12.7	52	12	101	3	1	2	2	1	1	2	2
1	101	1	−1	6.4	2.3	14.5	57	12	106	1	1	1	1	2	2	2	1
2	25	1	−1	5.7	3.7	15.8	60	9	91	4	1	3	2	2	2	2	3
2	28	1	−1	6.5	2.8	14.4	60	8	92	2	1	1	1	2	2	2	3
2	55	1	−1	10.6	3.5	21.6	54	14	109	4	1	1	2	3	3	3	11
2	65	1	−1	13.7	3.5	24.0	54	19	100	3	1	1	1	1	1	0	2
2	63	1	−1	9.8	3.6	10.4	66	16	117	3	1	1	1	2	0	0	14
2	50	1	−1	9.3	2.2	10.7	59	10	94	2	1	1	1	0	0	0	15
2	61	1	−1	11.2	4.2	13.5	61	14	102	2	1	1	1	1	1	2	12
1	68	1	−1	10.0	4.3	15.1	59	19	96	3	1	1	1	3	3	3	17
1	70	1	−1	10.1	2.9	12.2	70	16	101	2	1	1	1	1	1	2	12
2	41	1	−1	8.9	3.3	12.6	55	9	92	3	1	1	1	1	1	1	4
2	73	1	−1	9.9	3.4	25.9	65	10	124	3	1	1	1	1	3	3	2
2	46	1	−1	11.3	3.7	29.3	55	9	99	4	2	2	2	1	1	3	12
2	43	1	−1	9.7	3.2	14.4	66	10	96	3	1	1	1	1	1	1	2
1	37	1	−1	8.0	2.1	15.5	65	13	101	2	1	1	1	1	1	0	19
1	62	1	−1	10.9	3.3	11.9	60	14	100	1	1	1	1	1	3	2	19
2	66	1	−1	19.5	3.9	31.5	53	37	73	3	1	1	1	1	0	0	2
1	29	1	−1	7.9	2.9	11.6	63	14	111	3	1	1	2	3	0	0	12
2	52	1	−1	8.4	3.9	12.1	60	13	91	3	1	1	1	1	1	2	2

Group B
True Negative (No Cancer and No Band)

1	2	3	4	5	6	7	8	9	10	11	12	13	14	15	16	17	18
2	72	2	−1	6.2	2.8	12.8	66	28	101	4	1	1	1	0	0	0	0
1	72	2	−1	5.3	2.6	12.0	64	23	180	4	1	1	1	0	0	0	0
2	58	2	−1	7.4	3.4	15.3	76	17	142	4	1	1	1	0	0	0	0
2	58	2	−1	5.4	3.4	12.4	63	17	83	4	1	2	2	0	0	0	0
2	70	2	−1	9.8	4.2	18.3	62	13	91	4	1	1	1	0	0	0	0
2	78	2	−1	10.9	3.5	30.2	67	20	89	4	1	1	1	0	0	0	0
2	24	2	−1	6.3	3.2	15.1	67	10	83	4	1	1	1	0	0	0	0
2	54	2	−1	7.9	3.6	16.1	66	19	98	4	1	2	1	0	0	0	0
1	41	2	−1	11.8	3.5	14.9	54	19	86	4	1	1	1	0	0	0	0
1	70	2	−1	7.0	2.7	12.8	51	21	93	4	1	1	1	0	0	0	0
1	19	2	−1	8.9	2.8	15.7	65	13	122	4	1	1	1	0	0	0	0
2	44	2	−1	6.9	3.2	17.6	64	11	97	4	1	1	1	0	0	0	0
1	58	2	−1	7.2	3.4	12.2	55	19	90	4	1	1	1	0	0	0	0
1	75	2	−1	12.0	2.2	17.5	69	19	95	4	1	1	2	0	0	0	0
1	21	2	−1	10.0	3.6	13.8	73	14	85	4	1	1	1	0	0	0	0
2	65	2	−1	7.5	3.0	14.9	64	13	85	4	1	1	1	0	0	0	0
1	60	2	−1	8.4	3.4	21.0	64	7	81	4	1	1	2	0	0	0	0
1	81	2	−1	7.3	3.1	17.3	54	18	122	4	1	1	1	0	0	0	0
2	76	2	−1	10.9	3.1	17.2	61	13	97	4	1	1	1	0	0	0	0
2	14	2	−1	9.4	4.1	12.5	65	5	75	4	1	1	2	0	0	0	0
1	76	2	−1	6.0	2.9	12.4	64	16	72	4	1	1	1	0	0	0	0
2	49	2	−1	6.9	3.9	16.9	64	11	99	4	2	1	1	0	0	0	0
2	69	2	−1	14.9	2.4	18.6	59	15	172	4	2	2	2	0	0	0	0
2	50	2	−1	8.4	2.3	32.4	59	17	116	4	2	1	2	0	0	0	0
2	51	2	−1	11.8	3.0	16.6	58	16	114	4	2	3	1	0	0	0	0
2	24	2	−1	6.5	3.0	14.3	65	10	84	4	1	1	1	0	0	0	0
1	80	2	−1	6.2	2.9	11.2	66	11	92	4	1	1	2	0	0	0	0
1	47	2	−1	4.9	2.7	13.4	68	18	117	4	1	1	1	0	0	0	0
1	71	2	−1	9.0	2.7	19.3	57	25	132	4	1	2	1	0	0	0	0
1	26	2	−1	6.7	2.8	21.0	61	14	98	4	1	1	1	0	0	0	0
1	24	2	−1	7.5	2.4	12.5	61	12	95	4	1	2	1	0	0	0	0
1	29	2	−1	7.5	2.8	9.7	65	15	108	4	1	1	1	0	0	0	0
1	22	2	−1	5.4	2.9	13.0	65	10	101	4	1	1	1	0	0	0	0
2	54	2	−1	17.2	3.5	19.4	50	14	66	4	1	1	2	0	0	0	0
2	37	2	−1	8.5	2.9	14.4	28	12	92	4	1	1	2	0	0	0	0
2	32	2	−1	12.8	4.0	17.6	51	9	84	4	1	1	1	0	0	0	0
2	41	2	−1	4.8	3.2	14.2	66	16	108	4	1	1	2	0	0	0	0
2	48	2	−1	5.5	3.6	13.8	64	16	93	4	1	1	1	0	0	0	0
2	41	2	−1	6.8	2.7	14.1	66	6	107	4	1	1	1	0	0	0	0
1	54	2	−1	7.5	3.2	18.4	65	15	105	4	1	1	1	0	0	0	0
1	63	2	−1	12.6	3.1	15.0	54	16	101	4	1	1	1	0	0	0	0
1	63	2	−1	6.8	3.4	15.8	59	18	104	4	1	1	1	0	0	0	0
2	34	2	−1	5.2	3.5	14.5	60	17	92	4	1	1	1	0	0	0	0

Group B (Cont'd)

1	2	3	4	5	6	7	8	9	10	11	12	13	14	15	16	17	18
2	33	2	−1	6.2	3.2	14.1	57	9	91	4	2	1	2	0	0	0	0
2	35	2	−1	8.9	2.6	12.6	64	14	101	4	1	1	1	0	0	0	0
1	42	2	−1	5.4	3.1	13.1	70	11	156	4	1	1	1	0	0	0	0
1	25	2	−1	10.7	3.6	18.7	63	16	105	4	1	1	1	0	0	0	0
2	69	2	−1	6.8	3.1	13.4	58	17	89	4	1	2	2	0	0	0	0
1	51	2	−1	5.4	2.7	15.7	65	13	150	4	1	2	1	0	0	0	0
2	32	2	−1	4.9	3.7	14.8	56	10	82	4	1	1	1	0	0	0	0
2	35	2	−1	6.5	2.7	13.7	64	11	99	4	1	1	1	0	0	0	0
2	57	2	−1	7.0	3.1	9.4	63	14	106	4	1	1	1	0	0	0	0
2	62	2	−1	12.8	2.5	16.5	62	11	80	4	1	1	1	0	0	0	0
2	40	2	−1	9.9	2.7	16.3	58	11	93	4	1	1	1	0	0	0	0
1	40	2	−1	7.7	3.7	18.4	60	17	106	4	2	2	1	0	0	0	0
2	80	2	−1	5.7	3.1	15.5	56	12	111	4	1	1	1	0	0	0	0
2	28	2	−1	8.2	2.7	13.7	66	14	83	4	1	1	1	0	0	0	0
2	27	2	−1	8.8	4.0	15.6	53	9	89	4	1	1	2	0	0	0	0
1	57	2	−1	6.2	3.6	15.0	65	17	94	4	1	2	2	0	0	0	0
2	61	2	−1	8.4	2.7	12.6	66	15	107	4	1	1	1	0	0	0	0
1	48	2	−1	6.9	2.5	11.6	65	15	102	4	1	2	2	0	0	0	0
1	43	2	−1	7.1	2.2	13.1	62	13	143	4	1	1	1	0	0	0	0
1	17	2	−1	6.4	4.1	16.9	61	11	70	4	1	1	1	0	0	0	0
2	75	2	−1	9.5	3.1	14.6	40	44	110	4	2	2	1	0	0	0	29
1	39	2	−1	7.8	1.8	15.7	52	14	105	4	1	2	1	0	0	0	0
1	57	2	−1	6.1	2.9	25.7	64	17	89	4	1	1	1	0	0	0	0
1	58	2	−1	6.3	2.4	16.1	55	17	153	4	1	2	1	0	0	0	0
2	15	2	−1	12.4	3.7	13.4	69	18	135	4	1	1	1	0	0	0	0
1	23	2	−1	6.6	3.2	74.1	63	19	161	4	1	1	1	0	0	0	0
1	40	2	−1	10.6	4.1	13.0	58	10	91	4	1	1	1	0	0	0	0
1	17	2	−1	9.6	3.5	11.1	64	15	94	4	1	1	1	0	0	0	0
2	20	2	−1	5.3	3.1	11.8	61	9	89	4	1	1	1	0	0	0	0
1	29	2	−1	7.9	2.2	19.0	59	15	151	4	1	1	1	0	0	0	0
1	39	2	−1	9.1	3.0	12.1	63	13	98	4	1	2	1	0	0	0	0
1	61	2	−1	12.8	2.6	13.6	58	15	95	4	1	2	1	0	0	0	0
1	67	2	−1	8.1	2.5	15.5	62	13	104	4	1	2	1	0	0	0	0
1	17	2	−1	9.3	3.4	14.3	63	19	90	4	1	1	1	0	0	0	0
1	31	2	−1	6.0	2.8	12.8	61	15	95	4	1	1	1	0	0	0	0
1	34	2	−1	9.7	3.2	17.4	63	18	102	4	1	1	1	0	0	0	0
1	65	2	−1	9.2	3.5	14.0	60	13	119	4	1	2	2	0	0	0	0
1	58	2	−1	5.5	3.3	14.8	60	31	103	4	1	1	1	0	0	0	0
1	70	2	−1	9.2	3.0	16.4	63	22	101	4	1	2	2	0	0	0	0
1	48	2	−1	6.8	3.2	16.2	64	15	114	4	1	1	1	0	0	0	0
1	80	2	−1	11.8	4.1	21.5	56	24	131	4	1	1	1	0	0	0	0
1	49	2	−1	10.8	3.0	14.9	57	16	89	4	1	1	1	0	0	0	0
2	70	2	−1	5.3	3.1	14.1	60	19	101	4	1	1	1	0	0	0	0
1	65	2	−1	7.1	3.8	10.1	63	33	117	4	1	1	1	0	0	0	0
2	59	2	−1	9.5	2.9	17.2	69	21	92	4	1	1	1	0	0	0	0

Group B (Cont'd)

1	2	3	4	5	6	7	8	9	10	11	12	13	14	15	16	17	18
1	19	2	−1	8.5	3.1	13.6	65	17	95	4	1	1	1	0	0	0	0
1	30	2	−1	9.0	3.3	12.0	60	15	89	4	1	1	1	0	0	0	0
1	46	2	−1	6.4	2.9	14.0	66	22	99	4	1	1	1	0	0	0	0
1	52	2	−1	5.4	3.5	13.3	59	5	83	4	1	1	1	0	0	0	0
1	59	2	−1	5.7	2.9	23.6	69	34	86	4	2	2	2	0	0	0	0
1	39	2	−1	11.3	3.2	14.6	63	13	112	4	2	2	2	0	0	0	0
1	36	2	−1	6.9	3.2	13.5	57	14	77	4	1	1	2	0	0	0	0
1	23	2	−1	6.8	2.7	12.5	65	16	110	4	1	1	2	0	0	0	0
1	78	2	−1	10.1	4.1	9.4	62	14	85	4	1	2	2	0	0	0	0
2	54	2	−1	8.2	3.4	15.1	49	10	105	4	2	2	2	0	0	0	0
2	68	2	−1	6.2	3.2	17.8	48	19	83	4	1	1	2	0	0	0	0
1	37	2	−1	13.2	3.0	21.1	65	12	105	4	1	1	2	0	0	0	0
1	26	2	−1	6.0	2.0	11.9	69	14	103	4	1	1	1	0	0	0	0
1	55	2	−1	13.6	2.9	25.6	59	15	70	4	1	1	1	0	0	0	0
1	38	2	−1	9.7	3.2	12.7	61	15	102	4	1	1	1	0	0	0	0
2	36	2	−1	5.3	2.9	12.9	60	10	100	4	1	1	1	0	0	0	0
2	66	2	−1	11.2	2.6	16.9	59	12	101	4	1	1	1	0	0	0	0
1	22	2	−1	4.6	3.5	14.2	69	17	106	4	1	1	1	0	0	0	0
2	85	2	−1	10.6	3.3	14.0	58	19	96	4	1	3	2	0	0	0	0
1	39	2	−1	10.9	3.5	17.3	63	5	81	4	1	2	2	0	0	0	0
1	56	2	−1	6.7	3.2	11.8	62	21	88	4	1	1	1	0	0	0	0
2	80	2	−1	4.5	3.0	17.3	67	39	60	4	1	1	2	0	0	0	0
1	24	2	−1	6.4	3.5	10.2	68	15	89	4	1	1	1	0	0	0	0
2	21	2	−1	3.2	3.3	15.5	59	11	140	4	1	1	1	0	0	0	0
1	18	2	−1	7.6	3.2	32.0	60	17	140	4	1	2	2	0	0	0	0
2	41	2	−1	4.0	3.7	13.3	59	12	85	4	1	1	1	0	0	0	0
1	51	2	−1	7.1	2.4	14.7	65	16	153	4	1	2	1	0	0	0	0
1	22	2	−1	5.6	3.2	11.4	73	15	102	4	1	1	2	0	0	0	0
1	17	2	−1	26.6	4.2	12.8	67	17	91	4	1	1	1	0	0	0	0
1	24	2	−1	7.2	3.0	13.2	72	15	83	4	1	2	1	0	0	0	0
1	23	2	−1	8.0	2.7	13.7	59	9	94	4	1	1	1	0	0	0	0
1	17	2	−1	10.2	3.0	26.7	59	12	118	4	1	1	1	0	0	0	0
2	18	2	−1	7.3	3.5	12.3	64	10	96	4	1	1	1	0	0	0	0
2	30	2	−1	3.9	3.2	15.8	70	13	96	4	1	1	1	0	0	0	0
1	24	2	−1	7.5	4.0	15.3	59	9	87	4	1	1	1	0	0	0	0
1	74	2	−1	12.2	1.9	9.0	59	15	88	4	1	1	2	0	0	0	0
1	60	2	−1	5.5	3.4	13.4	59	16	125	4	1	1	1	0	0	0	0
2	26	2	−1	10.1	5.6	15.9	51	13	106	4	1	1	1	0	0	0	0
2	26	2	−1	10.1	2.4	18.5	58	3	91	4	1	2	3	0	0	0	0
1	48	2	−1	7.8	3.1	14.2	66	9	97	4	1	2	2	0	0	0	0
2	25	2	−1	2.3	2.3	11.5	66	8	95	4	1	1	2	0	0	0	0
1	51	2	−1	9.2	3.1	15.0	66	13	96	4	1	1	1	0	0	0	0
2	51	2	−1	5.4	2.8	16.3	65	12	105	4	2	2	1	0	0	0	0
1	61	2	−1	5.3	1.9	12.9	66	18	98	4	1	1	1	0	0	0	0
2	26	2	−1	5.0	3.4	11.8	67	14	93	4	1	2	1	0	0	0	0

Group B (Cont'd)

1	2	3	4	5	6	7	8	9	10	11	12	13	14	15	16	17	18
1	42	2	−1	8.4	2.7	18.5	67	11	128	4	2	2	2	0	0	0	0
2	46	2	−1	6.0	4.7	13.9	54	12	106	4	1	2	2	0	0	0	0
1	44	2	−1	13.8	3.3	17.2	59	16	97	4	1	1	1	0	0	0	0
2	72	2	−1	9.2	3.4	17.8	58	12	104	4	1	1	1	2	0	0	0
2	76	2	−1	5.7	3.1	0.0	62	19	0	4	1	1	1	0	0	0	0
2	38	2	−1	5.4	3.0	13.4	63	11	87	4	1	1	1	0	0	0	0
1	34	2	−1	9.3	3.2	15.5	70	11	91	4	1	1	1	0	0	0	0
2	18	2	−1	7.1	3.6	13.6	64	10	91	4	1	1	2	0	0	0	0
2	69	2	−1	13.8	3.0	14.9	53	17	93	4	1	2	1	0	0	0	0
1	40	2	−1	7.5	4.4	15.9	59	15	96	4	1	1	1	0	0	0	0
1	57	2	−1	6.3	2.8	12.8	68	12	96	4	1	1	1	2	0	0	0
1	23	2	−1	7.7	3.4	17.3	58	15	102	4	1	1	1	0	0	0	0
1	25	2	−1	6.7	3.2	14.1	66	18	104	4	1	1	1	0	0	0	0

Group C
True Positive (Cancer and Band)

1	2	3	4	5	6	7	8	9	10	11	12	13	14	15	16	17	18
2	59	1	1	14.2	3.7	11.8	46	15	112	3	4	4	4	1	1	3	3
2	80	1	1	6.3	2.4	15.6	72	21	94	3	3	3	3	1	1	1	4
2	73	1	1	6.0	2.6	17.4	58	19	120	4	3	3	3	0	0	0	31
2	67	1	1	11.5	4.4	20.7	57	18	186	2	3	3	3	1	1	3	2
2	58	1	1	8.7	2.8	12.8	54	9	87	3	2	3	2	1	1	2	15
2	69	1	1	11.5	3.6	14.4	62	11	91	3	4	3	4	1	3	3	15
2	63	1	1	6.8	3.4	11.9	64	9	95	3	3	3	3	3	0	0	14
2	52	1	1	8.0	3.1	19.2	64	21	120	3	2	3	2	1	1	2	23
2	25	1	1	8.1	3.2	11.8	66	14	106	3	3	3	2	0	0	0	37
2	66	1	1	8.6	3.3	20.9	61	13	100	1	2	2	3	2	2	2	2
1	63	1	1	50.0	3.3	15.2	51	26	95	2	4	4	4	2	2	2	19
2	58	1	1	9.5	3.4	18.2	65	11	104	3	3	3	3	1	1	1	4
1	59	1	1	14.3	3.6	15.4	55	12	89	3	3	3	3	3	3	3	11
2	45	1	1	25.4	3.5	35.4	54	9	80	3	3	3	3	1	0	0	2
1	67	1	1	10.1	3.9	23.5	20	58	120	3	3	3	2	0	0	0	29
2	37	1	1	6.1	3.1	30.4	56	10	86	3	2	3	2	1	1	2	2
2	55	1	1	18.4	2.5	18.2	51	19	129	3	4	4	4	1	2	2	4
2	45	1	1	14.9	3.6	12.8	56	12	96	3	3	4	3	1	3	2	34
2	68	1	1	10.9	2.5	13.6	54	14	99	3	2	3	2	1	1	0	2
2	42	1	1	25.4	3.6	15.2	60	10	93	4	3	3	3	1	1	3	2
1	65	1	1	7.0	3.2	14.7	48	15	97	3	3	3	3	1	1	0	35

Group C (Cont'd)

1	2	3	4	5	6	7	8	9	10	11	12	13	14	15	16	17	18
2	42	1	1	11.6	3.7	18.6	53	11	144	2	2	3	3	1	1	0	2
1	58	1	1	27.9	3.0	69.1	45	18	135	3	4	4	4	1	3	1	4
2	60	1	1	7.6	3.4	11.5	62	15	89	3	3	3	3	1	1	0	19
1	64	1	1	9.8	3.7	15.4	58	16	119	3	2	3	2	3	0	0	14
2	46	1	1	19.3	3.6	59.4	52	18	202	3	3	3	3	1	1	2	2
1	70	1	1	8.5	3.1	12.2	61	11	94	3	3	3	2	1	3	3	34
2	54	1	1	16.9	2.6	26.5	59	11	98	2	3	3	3	1	1	2	2
1	78	1	1	10.5	3.2	17.5	55	17	89	3	3	3	3	1	1	3	34
1	66	1	1	10.2	3.1	13.1	56	18	94	3	2	3	3	2	0	0	11
1	61	1	1	14.9	1.8	99.9	57	17	100	3	4	4	4	1	3	1	4
2	22	1	1	9.2	3.1	17.1	54	14	105	4	3	2	2	1	1	3	12
1	47	1	1	30.2	4.9	12.4	44	12	124	4	4	4	4	1	1	3	11
2	71	1	1	10.2	2.9	18.4	46	12	142	3	3	4	4	2	0	0	3
2	72	1	1	8.9	3.7	28.7	47	30	138	3	4	3	3	1	3	2	6
2	21	1	1	5.2	3.4	20.0	60	7	104	3	3	3	3	1	0	3	32
1	36	1	1	5.6	1.2	15.6	62	10	131	4	2	3	2	1	1	2	25
2	33	1	1	2.8	3.5	16.7	53	20	83	2	4	4	4	1	0	0	3
2	70	1	1	8.3	2.0	17.7	66	4	101	3	3	3	3	2	0	0	26
2	86	1	1	6.3	3.2	19.0	55	12	111	3	3	3	2	3	3	3	23
1	25	1	1	7.0	3.6	15.1	68	14	120	2	2	3	2	0	0	0	25
1	67	1	1	13.4	3.0	11.3	56	11	116	3	4	4	4	1	2	2	11
2	91	1	1	8.5	3.4	19.8	51	15	117	4	2	3	2	3	2	3	24
2	65	1	1	7.1	3.3	20.1	66	19	95	4	4	3	3	3	0	0	37
1	71	1	1	10.4	3.0	12.4	51	17	113	4	3	3	3	3	3	3	11
2	52	1	1	6.1	3.1	16.4	68	8	117	4	3	3	3	2	2	2	23
2	57	1	1	9.4	3.2	11.8	46	13	102	4	3	3	3	3	3	3	4
2	72	1	1	15.8	2.3	10.7	52	15	107	4	3	3	2	3	3	3	4
2	22	1	1	7.7	3.6	19.6	62	8	83	4	3	3	2	1	2	2	15
1	54	1	1	10.8	3.8	23.5	65	14	105	4	2	3	2	0	0	0	37
2	39	1	1	5.7	1.8	11.8	57	12	110	3	2	3	2	2	2	2	3
2	44	1	1	10.1	3.3	13.5	58	6	89	2	3	3	2	1	2	2	15
1	72	1	1	11.4	3.1	14.4	46	12	100	3	2	3	2	0	0	0	12
2	69	1	1	7.1	4.1	69.9	69	29	121	4	3	3	3	0	0	0	37
2	81	1	1	13.8	2.8	99.9	51	12	80	3	3	4	4	3	3	3	35
1	81	1	1	17.5	2.3	14.6	59	12	133	3	3	3	3	0	0	0	34
1	26	1	1	6.6	3.7	21.4	68	18	99	4	2	3	2	0	0	0	37
1	77	1	1	14.9	2.6	13.2	42	15	125	3	3	3	3	1	1	3	11
2	52	1	1	10.8	3.6	15.5	63	15	93	1	3	3	3	3	3	3	2
1	87	1	1	13.7	3.3	10.4	54	14	111	3	3	3	3	2	2	2	4
2	62	1	1	5.4	2.6	17.4	63	9	86	3	2	3	2	0	0	0	4
1	74	1	1	6.3	2.2	49.8	53	23	192	4	3	3	3	0	0	0	37
2	66	1	1	7.9	2.9	30.3	62	16	112	4	3	3	2	0	0	0	12
1	60	1	1	5.6	3.1	18.6	60	11	138	4	3	3	3	1	1	3	18
2	65	1	1	19.7	3.4	24.1	59	21	92	3	4	4	4	1	1	2	19

Group C (Cont'd)

1	2	3	4	5	6	7	8	9	10	11	12	13	14	15	16	17	18
1	66	1	1	10.0	2.6	18.7	57	20	112	3	3	3	4	1	3	2	36
·2	103	1	1	26.4	4.7	26.9	66	15	114	2	2	3	3	2	0	0	31
2	60	1	1	7.0	3.5	40.4	65	17	97	4	3	3	3	1	1	3	2
1	23	1	1	7.8	4.0	48.9	53	14	97	4	4	3	4	1	0	0	20
2	82	1	1	7.9	2.3	8.9	54	14	127	3	2	3	2	1	1	3	2
1	47	1	1	12.7	3.2	17.7	61	16	147	3	4	3	3	3	3	3	17
1	57	1	1	10.0	3.2	31.6	48	18	87	3	4	4	4	1	0	1	4
2	39	1	1	27.6	4.9	19.5	45	9	104	3	4	4	4	1	3	2	37
2	59	1	1	12.4	3.1	15.1	57	4	108	2	4	3	3	1	1	0	2
2	56	1	1	9.0	2.8	15.0	56	17	82	4	3	3	3	1	1	3	1
1	50	1	1	8.2	2.7	31.6	50	14	133	3	3	3	2	1	0	0	9
2	72	1	1	8.6	3.7	30.2	47	14	107	3	4	4	4	1	3	1	7
1	61	1	1	8.6	3.2	14.8	52	21	94	2	3	4	3	2	1	2	4
1	74	1	1	9.1	3.2	16.4	47	20	113	3	3	3	3	1	1	3	21
1	68	1	1	18.5	3.7	41.4	48	19	93	3	4	4	4	1	2	3	11
2	35	1	1	10.8	3.6	11.1	67	11	115	4	4	3	3	1	1	2	14
2	35	1	1	8.8	2.8	14.4	62	11	97	4	3	3	3	1	2	2	4
2	59	1	1	16.2	3.1	14.2	53	15	105	4	3	3	4	1	1	1	2
2	63	1	1	8.6	3.3	29.7	51	18	117	4	4	4	4	2	2	2	37
1	56	1	1	10.8	3.9	69.0	45	10	100	3	3	4	3	1	3	3	35
2	49	1	1	12.4	3.7	33.5	61	15	177	3	4	4	4	1	2	1	4
2	68	1	1	12.4	2.7	14.0	58	13	247	2	3	3	3	1	0	3	2
2	54	1	1	10.7	2.8	17.2	59	15	104	3	3	3	3	1	1	3	15
1	59	1	1	36.8	2.9	42.5	50	14	97	3	4	4	4	1	3	1	4
1	58	1	1	12.7	3.6	16.7	58	15	121	3	3	3	3	3	0	0	11
2	52	1	1	34.9	4.9	28.6	50	33	79	3	4	4	4	1	1	3	2
1	100	1	1	10.9	3.5	11.7	62	15	131	3	3	3	4	1	1	3	12
1	48	1	1	9.7	3.4	17.0	57	12	117	3	3	3	2	3	3	3	11
2	60	1	1	13.9	3.4	20.4	66	16	72	2	4	4	4	1	1	3	2
2	59	1	1	11.8	3.6	12.1	58	10	109	4	3	3	3	1	1	1	2

Group D
False Positive (No Cancer and Band)

1	2	3	4	5	6	7	8	9	10	11	12	13	14	15	16	17	18
2	59	2	1	8.8	3.4	14.8	58	11	107	4	3	3	3	0	0	0	0
1	57	2	1	10.5	2.9	23.0	60	20	111	4	2	3	2	0	0	0	0
2	69	2	1	7.2	3.2	18.5	67	11	104	4	3	3	2	0	0	0	0
2	56	2	1	12.5	3.6	14.3	55	10	98	4	3	3	2	0	0	0	0
1	84	2	1	10.8	2.2	15.5	55	31	99	4	3	3	3	0	0	0	0
2	51	2	1	8.2	2.7	59.7	67	16	88	4	3	3	3	0	0	0	0
1	66	2	1	20.6	2.1	27.4	55	15	298	4	3	3	3	0	0	0	0

Group D (Cont'd)

1	2	3	4	5	6	7	8	9	10	11	12	13	14	15	16	17	18
1	49	2	1	7.4	2.7	13.4	66	14	106	4	3	3	3	0	0	0	0
2	88	2	1	10.0	3.5	18.0	62	43	98	4	2	3	2	0	0	0	0
1	65	2	1	11.5	2.3	14.1	61	17	124	4	3	3	3	0	0	0	0
2	50	2	1	7.2	2.8	13.0	70	19	128	4	2	3	2	0	0	0	0
2	44	2	1	7.1	2.7	13.1	59	8	88	4	3	3	3	0	0	0	0
2	60	2	1	4.8	2.9	14.4	61	11	108	4	2	2	3	0	0	0	0
1	68	2	1	7.4	3.3	13.2	61	20	93	4	3	3	3	0	0	0	0
2	67	2	1	6.8	3.4	21.6	64	18	79	4	3	2	3	0	0	0	0
1	66	2	1	12.9	3.7	8.7	42	21	99	4	4	4	4	0	0	0	0
2	9	2	1	2.0	4.9	20.5	58	16	91	4	2	2	3	0	0	0	0
2	51	2	1	5.7	2.9	12.1	59	10	102	4	2	3	2	0	0	0	0
2	67	2	1	8.1	2.6	14.2	61	17	89	4	3	3	2	0	0	0	0
1	39	2	1	22.6	2.8	16.2	61	15	86	4	4	4	4	0	0	0	0
2	45	2	1	10.6	2.5	17.2	62	14	111	4	3	3	3	0	0	0	0
1	66	2	1	12.8	2.4	15.0	54	22	117	4	3	3	3	0	0	0	0
1	65	2	1	8.8	1.9	16.6	60	12	106	4	3	3	3	0	0	0	0
2	54	2	1	8.4	3.8	12.4	58	9	103	4	2	3	3	0	0	0	0
1	49	2	1	8.7	2.7	15.4	63	16	110	4	2	3	2	0	0	0	0
2	68	2	1	8.7	2.7	16.7	61	22	96	4	3	3	3	0	0	0	0
1	42	2	1	8.3	3.4	23.6	63	16	93	4	3	3	3	0	0	0	0
1	80	2	1	9.9	2.7	19.7	56	36	86	4	3	3	3	0	0	0	0
1	79	2	1	8.3	2.9	16.5	65	12	114	4	3	3	3	0	0	0	0
1	37	2	1	10.5	2.9	17.0	56	21	96	4	3	3	3	0	0	0	0
2	54	2	1	13.7	3.7	12.0	61	6	101	4	3	3	3	0	0	0	0
1	51	2	1	9.0	3.6	16.4	65	13	110	4	3	3	2	0	0	0	0
2	54	2	1	10.7	3.5	15.3	59	9	99	4	2	3	2	0	0	0	0
1	83	2	1	8.6	2.6	6.4	54	9	102	4	3	3	3	0	0	0	0
2	19	2	1	12.4	3.0	12.4	57	10	76	4	3	3	2	3	3	3	-2
1	53	2	1	7.6	3.2	17.0	63	7	98	4	2	3	2	2	2	2	0
1	61	2	1	10.3	3.3	19.0	55	25	128	4	2	3	2	0	0	0	0
2	42	2	1	14.7	3.8	13.8	52	12	86	4	4	4	3	0	0	0	0
2	56	2	1	10.6	3.5	12.6	62	10	92	4	4	3	3	0	0	0	0
1	25	2	1	12.1	3.2	17.2	58	15	76	4	3	3	3	0	0	0	0
2	41	2	1	12.7	3.2	15.2	46	9	73	4	2	3	3	0	0	0	0
1	70	2	1	14.2	2.6	15.5	59	12	90	4	3	3	2	0	0	0	0
2	31	2	1	6.0	2.5	20.0	58	8	91	4	3	3	3	0	0	0	0
1	22	2	1	10.9	3.2	12.5	66	14	103	4	3	3	3	0	0	0	0
2	51	2	1	6.5	4.0	20.0	54	12	195	4	4	4	4	0	0	0	0
1	69	2	1	11.2	3.9	26.2	52	38	117	4	3	3	2	0	0	0	0
1	48	2	1	10.1	3.8	20.6	51	14	119	4	3	4	4	0	0	0	0
1	47	2	1	10.6	3.2	14.6	58	17	100	4	3	3	3	0	0	0	0
2	54	2	1	8.7	3.6	16.2	67	11	91	4	3	3	3	0	0	0	0
2	58	2	1	10.5	3.3	14.8	64	22	107	4	3	3	3	0	0	0	0
1	48	2	1	11.9	2.6	13.3	65	12	87	4	2	3	2	0	0	0	0

Group D (Cont'd)

1	2	3	4	5	6	7	8	9	10	11	12	13	14	15	16	17	18
2	18	2	1	7.0	3.0	15.1	62	7	72	4	4	3	4	0	0	0	0
2	33	2	1	10.3	3.0	14.6	67	15	115	4	3	3	3	0	0	0	0
1	17	2	1	23.6	3.6	19.7	65	13	75	4	3	3	3	0	0	0	0
2	19	2	1	11.7	3.3	13.5	63	6	94	4	3	3	3	0	0	0	0
1	22	2	1	6.6	4.3	11.9	63	13	100	4	3	3	3	0	0	0	0
1	47	2	1	7.0	3.1	10.2	61	15	121	4	2	3	2	0	0	0	0
2	31	2	1	6.0	2.6	13.6	58	10	95	4	2	3	2	0	0	0	0
2	24	2	1	8.2	2.9	12.6	64	9	92	4	3	3	3	0	0	0	0
1	46	2	1	5.9	3.7	15.2	48	7	121	4	3	3	3	0	0	0	0
1	16	2	1	16.1	3.5	13.3	66	13	106	4	2	3	2	0	0	0	0
1	63	2	1	11.0	3.2	15.0	60	20	158	4	3	3	3	0	0	0	0
2	56	2	1	13.2	3.4	14.2	56	19	99	4	3	3	3	0	0	0	0
1	49	2	1	5.8	4.0	12.1	68	11	129	4	3	3	3	0	0	0	0
2	83	2	1	17.0	4.2	18.0	56	18	124	4	2	3	3	0	0	0	0

APPENDIX B
Preparing Data for Computer Analysis

A student named Christy A. once did a small survey for an introductory statistics course. We will use her results to illustrate the methods used to prepare data for computer analysis. Christy was a nutrition major, and wanted to find out why college students drink the type of milk they drink. She was also interested in looking for relationships between milk consumption and other variables, such as sex, height, and major. The questions she used are listed in Exhibit B.1 and the results she obtained are in Exhibit B.2. It is possible to do some preliminary analyses of these data by hand. But in order to do more advanced analyses using the computer, the data must be put in a form which can be read by the computer. Most computer systems, including Minitab, require that the data be converted to numbers. (There is a way around this in Minitab, but it requires advanced procedures. See page 323.)

We could begin by coding the answers to question 1, using 1 for female and 0 for male. The results for the second question, major, are slightly more difficult. We could give a different number to each of the majors. A few decisions must be made. Should the major listed as "business admin." be given a separate code from "business"? From "account-

EXHIBIT B.1

**Milk Consumption Survey Done
by Christy A.**

QUESTIONNAIRE

1. Sex: _____ male _____ female
2. Major: _____
3. Height: _____
4. On the average, how many glasses of milk do you drink per day? ____
5. What kind of milk do you drink most often at school?
    a. Pasteurized homogenized or whole milk
    b. Skim or low-fat milk
    c. Chocolate milk
    d. Other
6. What is the major reason you drink this kind of milk more than the others?
    a. Health reasons
    b. Weight reasons
    c. Taste
    d. Other
7. What kind of milk do you drink most often at home?
    a. Pasteurized homogenized or whole milk
    b. Skim or low-fat milk
    c. Chocolate milk
    d. Other

ing"? Perhaps it would be useful if we grouped some majors together. Otherwise we will have too few people in each category to draw any conclusions. We decided to code the results of the second question as follows:

Code for Question 2

Major: Business = 1
        Education and related areas = 2
        Social Sciences and related areas = 3
        Liberal Arts = 4
        Agriculture and related areas = 5
        Engineering, Physical and Mathematical Sciences = 6
        Biological Sciences = 7

EXHIBIT B.2

Results of Milk Consumption Survey

Respondant No.	Sex	Major	Height	Avg Glasses of Milk/Day	Question 5	Question 6	Question 7
1	F	Business	5'2"	2	b	b	a
2	F	Business	5'2"	6	b	b	a
3	F	Business	5'5"	0	—	—	—
4	F	Education	5'6"	2	a	c	a
5	F	Education	5'2½"	1	a	c	d
6	F	Social Welfare	5'7½"	5	a	c	b
7	F	Health & Phys Ed	5'4"	4	c	c	c
8	F	French	5'9"	4	b	a	b
9	F	IFS	5'6"	1	b	c	a
10	F	Health & Phys Ed	5'6"	4	a	c	a
11	F	Nursing	5'7"	3	a	c	b
12	F	Speech Pathology	5'10"	2	a	c	a
13	F	IFS	5'4½"	1	b	c	b
14	F	French	5'6"	2	b	c	b
15	F	Pre-Med	5'8"	2	b	a	b
16	F	Art	5'3"	0	—	—	—
17	F	IFS	5'8"	4	b	d	a
18	F	Forestry Science	5'2"	3	b	a	a
19	F	IFS	5'5"	4	a	c	a
20	F	Nursing	5'4"	3	a	a	a
21	F	Animal Science	5'6"	2	b	c	b
22	F	MER	5'10"	2	a	c	a
23	F	Math	5'3"	0	—	—	—
24	F	Business Admin	5'4"	1	a	c	a
25	F	Speech Pathology	5'2"	2	a	c	a
26	M	Electrical Engineering	6'0"	3	c	c	a
27	M	Poli Sci	5'10"	4	b	c	a
28	M	Accounting	6'2"	9	a	c	a

IFS = Individual and Family Studies
MER = Man-Environment Relations

EXHIBIT B.2 (Cont'd)

Respondant No.	Sex	Major	Height	Avg Glasses of Milk/Day	Question 5	Question 6	Question 7
29	M	Poli Sci	5'11½"	5	a	c	a
30	M	Journalism	5'11"	4	a	c	a
31	M	Rec Park	6'4"	3	a	c	a
32	M	Accounting	5'6½"	2	a	c	a
33	M	Theatre	6'1"	1	c	a	a
34	M	Business	5'7"	5	a	a	a
35	M	Science	5'9"	4	a	a	a
36	M	Accounting	6'2"	1	a	c	a
37	M	Accounting	6'2"	2	a	c	a
38	M	Bio Physics	5'8"	6	b	a	a
39	M	Accounting	5'8"	2	a	a	a
40	M	Business Mg't	6'1"	4	a	c	a
41	M	Health & Phys Ed	6'3"	4	c	c	a
42	M	Pre-Med	6'0"	2	c	c	a
43	M	Rec Park	6'0"	4	a	a	b
44	M	Biology	6'0"	7	a	c	a
45	M	Ceramic Science	5'10"	7	a	c	a
46	M	Business	6'1"	3	a	d	a
47	M	Econ	6'3½"	10	a	c	a
48	M	Chemistry	6'0"	3	a	a	a
49	M	Arch Engineering	5'9"	4	a	c	a
50	M	Engineering	6'3"	6	a	c	a

Rec Park = Recreation and Parks

It may be necessary to group these even further when we get into the analysis. But this seems to be a reasonable place to start.

The other variables in Christy's study are easier to code. For question 3, height, we could by hand convert all heights to inches, for example 5 feet 5 inches into 65 inches. Another alternative is to use the number of inches above 5 feet. For example, convert 5 feet 6 inches into 6 inches and 6 feet 2 inches into 14 inches. A third alternative is to read both the feet and inches into the computer and then use the computer to calculate the height in inches. For example, if the number of feet had been read into column c8 and the number of inches into c9, then the following two instructions would compute height in inches:

MULTIPLY C8 BY 12., PUT IN C10
ADD C10 TO C9, PUT IN C3

The best method of coding these or any other data will depend upon many things, such as the total amount of data, the way in which it is recorded, and your familiarity with the computer.

The other questions in Christy's study are easy to code. Question 4 is okay as it is. Questions 5, 6, and 7 can be coded by using "1" for "a," "2" for "b," "3" for "c," and "4" for "d." When there is no response to a question, we could use "—1" as a missing value code.

Closed Response Versus Open Response

In general, open response questions such as Christy's question 2 are more difficult to code than closed response questions such as the following:

2. What is your major? (1) Business or related area
(2) Education or related area
(3) Social Sciences or related area
(4) Liberal Arts
(5) Agriculture or related area
(6) Engineering, Physical and Mathematical Sciences
(7) Biological Sciences

In a closed response question, only certain answers that have been specified in advance are possible. Closed response questions simplify the analysis of the results, but sometimes make it difficult for the respondant to know how to answer. For example, an architecture major might have a difficult time deciding how to answer the above closed response question.

Open response questions are often preferred if you do not know what sort of responses to expect in a preliminary survey, or if listing responses would make the question difficult to answer.

As an illustration of coding open response questions, suppose Christy's survey had included the open-ended question,

Why do you drink milk?

We might try to code answers which indicate health as 1, habit as 2, and so on. Now what do we do if an answer indicates several reasons, or falls between categories? The problem is multiplied in large surveys where the responses must be coded by several different people, or in interview-type surveys where the interviewer codes the answers as he conducts the interview.

Another point to notice is that a code must be made for missing data. Data can be missing because a respondent refused to reply, or because a question did not apply to some people, such as questions 5, 6, and 7 in Christy's survey.

Finally, we should point out that we have not considered here some of the most important aspects of doing a survey. These include selecting a sample, designing unambiguous questions which can get the desired information, and dealing with results where a significant number of people refuse to respond or are not at home. While these issues are very important, they are beyond the scope of this handbook.

APPENDIX C
Difference Between Interactive and Batch Computing

Minitab is designed to run in both batch and interactive modes. (A given computer center, however, may have it available in just one of these modes.)

In *batch* computing, you write a program, punch it onto cards (or type it on a typewriter-like keyboard), then submit the *entire* program at once, wait a short while, and then get all your answers back at once.

Interactive computing is always done sitting at a typewriter-like terminal. You type in one command and get back the results of that command before you type in the next command. For example, suppose C1 contains the numbers 4, 2, 2, 5. If you type AVERAGE C1 and then push the "carriage return" key, the terminal immediately responds with the answer, AVERAGE = 3.25.

One of the practical consequences of this difference for Minitab is in how much output to print. With batch computing, you usually have to wait a few minutes (or a few hours) for your output. In addition, output is usually printed on a fairly high speed printer. Therefore, it is usually desirable to get a moderately large amount of output from each command. With interactive computing, however, you must sit at a terminal while your output is being printed. If the output is very long, this can be a nuisance. In addition, any time you decide you need some further analysis, you can easily type in another command or two. Therefore, with interactive computing it is usually desirable to get just a small amount of output from each command. Minitab has been designed to take this into consideration. Ordinarily, if you are using an interactive terminal, Minitab will curtail its output by using the BRIEF command (see pages 193 and 327 for more details). But if you want to, you can use the NOBRIEF command to get more extensive output when using a computer interactively. Or conversely, you can use the BRIEF command to get less output when using a computer in the batch mode.

Both the NOPRINT command (see page 22) and the END OF DATA command (see page 21) are useful when using a computer in the interactive mode.

APPENDIX D
How Minitab Works

This appendix need be read only by those curious about the internal operations of Minitab. The information in this section is not required for successful operation of the system.

The flow chart in Exhibit D.1 summarizes the internal workings of Minitab. First a line is read character by character. Then any letters at the beginning of the line are assembled into a "word" and checked against the Minitab dictionary. All numerical characters in the line are assembled into numbers. If the "word" is not found in the dictionary, an error message is printed.

When a READ or SET command is encountered, control is transferred to the SETRD subroutine and subsequent numbers are read, counted, and stored as data until another legitimate command is encountered. At that time, control is transferred back to the main program.

When a legitimate command other than READ or SET is found, the main program calls the appropriate subroutine. That subroutine does the error checking appropriate for the command and then carries out the operations requested. For example, the instruction

ADD C12 TO C5 IN C7

EXHIBIT D.1

Flowchart of Minitab System

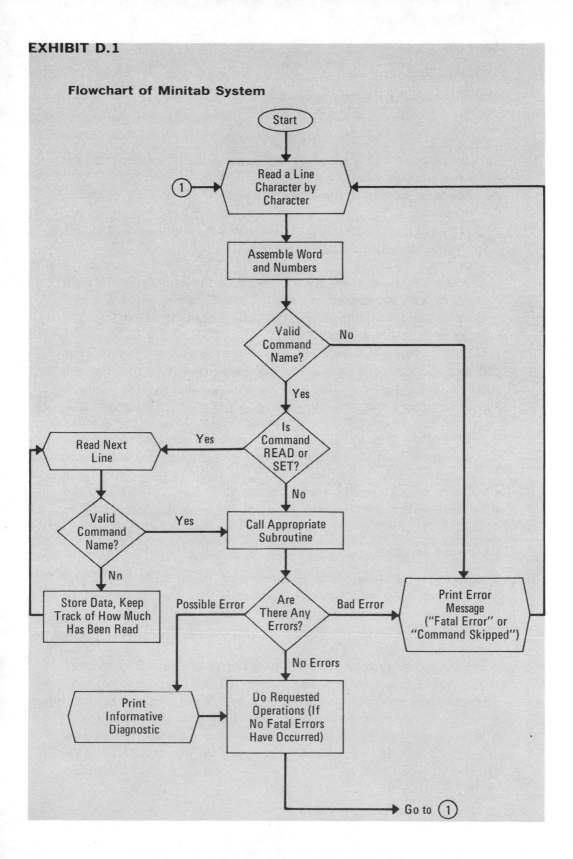

causes the main program to call a subroutine named ARITH which checks to make sure everything seems reasonable. Specifically, it checks the following:

(a) Are columns c12, c5, and c7 legitimate column numbers? (Print error message if not.)

(b) Are there data in both columns c12 and c5? (Print error message if not.)

(c) Are there the same number of data points in columns c12 as in c5? (Print informative diagnostic if not.)

If no bad error has occurred, ARITH then adds the numbers in columns c12 and c5, and stores their sums in column c7 as requested. Control is then returned to the main program which reads the next line and begins the cycle again.

If you are using Minitab on an interactive system, and you make a bad error, Minitab tells you so. You can then correct your mistake and continue. But suppose you are working with a batch system. Then, if you make a bad error on a command and the command is supposed to store numbers in the worksheet, this error could mess up later computations. Therefore, Minitab calls this a *fatal error.* When a fatal error has occurred, the rest of the commands are checked for obvious errors, but no further calculations are performed. If, on a batch system, you make a bad error on a command which does not store numbers in the worksheet, then that command is skipped but later commands are carried out.

Column Lengths

Minitab automatically keeps track of how many numbers have been put into each column and, in virtually all cases, it uses this information in exactly the way you want. Most users will thus never need to think about "bookkeeping." However, advanced or curious readers might find this section interesting or helpful.

For commands such as READ, SET, BRANDOM, where a definite amount of data is put into a column, Minitab records and keeps track of that amount. Using this information, commands operate in a natural way. For example, when two columns are added (row by row) and stored in a third column, the resulting column has the same length as the two original columns. However, a problem arises if the two original columns are of unequal lengths. In this case, Minitab sets the length of the third column equal to the length of the shorter of the two original columns.

And, since addition of unequal length columns is unusual and may be an error, an informative diagnostic is printed.

For some other types of commands, such as AVERAGE OF C3 PUT IN C5, it is not always clear how much of the storage column should be filled with the answer. In such cases, where there is no natural length to the column, Minitab fills the entire column and sets a "flag" to indicate that the column is an artificially long constant column. No diagnostic message is generated if an artificially long constant column is used with a column of a different length (e.g., added to another column) since this is a very natural operation.

Internal Storage

Minitab does not actually store the numbers in a rectangular array as we show in our diagrams. In reality, numbers are stored in one long array. Columns are stored in the order in which they are first used. For example, the array which stores the worksheet might look like this:

C1		C4		C2	C8	C3	

Minitab keeps "pointers" to tell where each column begins. Artificially long constant columns are actually stored in only one space.

In some large problems there may not be enough room in the computer to store all the columns if they are all in use at the same time. In other cases, if there is room for all the columns, there may not be enough extra room for Minitab to use as working or "scratch" area. If either of these situations arises, Minitab will tell you to erase any unnecessary columns so that everything will fit.

Limitations

Two problems can occur when using any computer program. The first is *round-off error*. This is caused by the fact that the computer does not store all numbers exactly, but rounds them off. These errors can add up in certain calculations, even though the best known methods have been used in Minitab's subroutines.

Another type of problem is caused by undetected errors ("bugs") in the program. Minitab has been extensively checked by the authors and their colleagues and has been used by students for some time. However, in programs as complex as this and during revisions of Minitab, un-detected programming errors can be made. Output from this program, and any other program, should be checked to see if it is reasonable. The authors cannot take responsibility for any errors. They would very much appreciate having any apparent errors called to their attention, prefera-bly with the output and/or card deck in question.

APPENDIX E
Other Features of Minitab

A full listing of all of Minitab's present capabilities is given in Appendix F (pages 318 to 328). This appendix discusses a few features of Minitab that, while useful, are not ordinarily necessary for doing elementary statistics.

Stored Constants

Whenever we wish to store a single number, we can use Minitab's *stored constants*. Stored constants are referenced just like columns, except a K is used instead of a C. At most installations, 50 stored constants, called K1, K2,...,K50, are available. When we first start a program, K49=2.7183... (the base of the natural logarithms) and K50=3.14159... (π). Any com-mand which has a single-number answer can store that answer in a stored constant (e.g., COUNT, AVERAGE, SUM). For example, we could use

```
COUNT C6, PUT COUNT INTO K1
GENERATE THE FIRST K1 INTEGERS INTO C7
PLOT C6 VS C7
```

We can also put numbers into stored constants with the DEFINE command.

DEFINE K INTO STORED CONSTANT **K**

DEFINE THE VALUE IN ROW **K** OF COLUMN **C** INTO STORED

CONSTANT **K**

Example

DEFINE 6.5 INTO K12
DEFINE VALUE IN ROW 3 OF C5 INTO K8

A stored constant may be used in any place, in any command, where a regular constant can be used. Thus, in the general command descriptions, stored constants can be used in any place K or E appears.

Continuation onto a Second Line

Occasionally a Minitab command may be too long to fit all on one line. In that case put an asterisk (*) in the last allowable space on the line, then continue on the next line. (Ordinarily, the last allowable space is space 80, but this can be changed with the SCAN command.) For example, we could write

AVERAGE C8 PUT AVERAGE INCOME FOR NON-WHITE   *

INTO C9 AMERICANS

More Than 200 Rows of Data

If a data set has more than 200 rows, you must increase the length of the worksheet by using the DIMENSION command before data are read into the computer.

DIMENSION THE WORKSHEET TO HAVE **K** ROWS

Changes the number of rows in the worksheet. However, the total amount of storage you are allowed remains fixed. This total amount is decided by your computer center. It may be as low as 1,000 numbers, or as high as 100,000, or even more. The maximum number of columns is 50 (on most computers), and you *cannot* increase this.

Suppose your computer center allows you a total of 5000 spaces. You could use DIMENSION to ask for 1000 rows. You would then have a worksheet of 1000 rows by 50 columns. But, at any given time you could fill no more than 5000 of these spaces.

As an example, if you have about 275 rows of data you might say

DIMENSION WORKSHEET TO 300 ROWS

before reading the data.

DIMENSION is needed only if you use READ or SET to enter more than 200 rows. If you simulate more than 200 observations, or create a long column through a command such as JOIN, then Minitab automatically redimensions the worksheet for you.

FORTRAN Formatted Input and Output

Minitab has five commands that allow us to use FORTRAN capabilities for reading and writing data: FREAD, FSET, TAPEREAD, FPRINT, and FPUNCH. Here is a very brief overview of how these are used.

FREAD and FSET

There are two main reasons for using FREAD rather than READ: (1) It is the only way to read data that have been prepared without separators between numbers. (2) It is faster and saves computer time for larger data sets.

For example, suppose we have the following data:

$$23161548254.360821$$
$$554312994938.41283$$

We want these numbers "separated" and read into c1-c6 as follows:

c1	c2	c3	c4	c5	c6
231	615	4	82.5	4.36	821
554	312	9	94.9	38.4	1283

The procedure for telling the computer how to read the numbers is this. First note how wide each field is. In this case, the first field on each card is 3 spaces wide, the second is also 3 spaces wide, the third is 1, the fourth is 3, and the next two are 4. If we want to insert decimal points in the middle of numbers where none are punched, note how many digits should be on the right of the decimal point. In c4 we want a decimal point inserted with one digit to the right of the decimal. In c5 we want the decimal points left where they are.

Bearing this information in mind, the following format may be obvious:

$$(F3.0, F3.0, F1.0, F3.1, F4.0, F4.0)$$

In F3.0, for example, the 3 tells the computer that the number to be read is in a field which is 3 spaces wide, and the 0 indicates there are no digits to the right of the decimal point. The F1.0 and F4.0 are similar. In the F3.1, the field is 3 spaces wide and there is 1 digit to the right of the decimal point. Notice in c5 that a decimal point is present in each number (e.g., in 38.4). The decimal point in a number always takes precedence over the value specified in the format statement. Thus, for the specification for c5, we could have used F4.0, F4.1, F4.2, etc. The format specifications must be separated by commas, and the entire list enclosed in parentheses.

To save writing, we could replace the F3.0, F3.0 in the above format with 2F3.0. The 2 says to use the F3.0 twice. Similarly, F1.0, F1.0, F1.0

could be replaced by 3F1.0, etc. Using this convention, the format could be rewritten as

$$(2F3.0, F1.0, F3.1, 2F4.0)$$

Skipping Some Numbers

Suppose we want to read only the second and fifth variables in the preceding example. Then we would want to skip over the first 3 spaces on each card, read the number in the next 3 spaces into, say, $c1$, then skip the next 4 spaces, and read the numbers in the next 4 spaces into, say, $c7$. To do this, we could use the format (3X, F3.0, 4X, F4.0). Notice that to skip 3 spaces all we need to write is 3X, to skip 4 spaces use 4X, and so on. Also note that if we don't want to read a number at the end of a line, we can just ignore it. So we didn't need to put 4X after the F4.0.

More Than One Card

If a row of data is to be read from more than one card, a slash (/) is used to indicate a new card. For example, if our data deck has 3 cards for each subject, our format might look like

$$(F4.0,F5.0/8X,F1.0/F2.0,F5.0)$$

For each row of the worksheet, we would read two numbers from a card into two columns, go to the next card and read one number, then go to the third card for the last two numbers. This would be repeated (starting with the next card) for the next row. Unlike other format specifications, do not put commas around the slash.

For more details concerning format specifications, consult a FORTRAN manual.

FREAD K ROWS INTO C,...,C

This command is followed by a FORTRAN format specification. The data follow the format. Note that, unlike the READ command, you must specify the number of rows to be read into the worksheet.

Example

```
FREAD 3 ROWS INTO C1-C6
(2F3.0, F1.0, F3.1, 1F4.0)
```

Note that the K in FREAD says how many rows of the worksheet are to be filled with numbers, not how many data cards are to be read.

FSET K NUMBERS INTO C

This command is followed by a FORTRAN format specification, which is followed by data. This command is like SET in that all numbers go into one column, and more than one number can be read on each line. Note that the number of rows to be read must be specified. Also note that the FSET command must appear on one line, the format on the next line, and the data on following lines.

Example

```
FSET 10 VALUES INTO C3
(8X,4F2.0)
SARAH      123456789012
BETTY      943851680327
VERONICA 635419837656
```

This formatted set tells the computer that, on each line, it should skip the first 8 spaces, then read 4 fields each of which is 2 spaces wide. This will put the following values into c3: 12, 34, 56, 78, 94, 38, 51, 68, 63, 54.

Other formatted reading and writing commands are TAPEREAD, which is used to read data from tape (or other devices), FPUNCH, which is used to put data on cards (or tape or other devices), and FPRINT.

APPENDIX F
List of Commands

Notation

K   denotes a constant (such as 8.3 or 21).
C   denotes a column number (such as c12).
E   denotes either a constant or a column number (Minitab looks for a c and acts accordingly).
[ ] denotes an optional argument.

Entering Numbers

READ THE FOLLOWING DATA INTO **C,...,C**

Data lines follow - one line per row.

SET THE FOLLOWING DATA INTO COLUMN **C**

All numbers go into the same column. Data must begin on the line following SET, not on the same line as the SET command.

END OF DATA

Follows data. For use on interactive computers.

DEFINE THE CONSTANT **K** INTO COLUMN **C**

Puts the specified number into all rows of the column.

DEFINE THE NUMBER IN ROW **K** OF **C** INTO COLUMN **C**

Puts the indicated number into all rows of the column.

SUBSTITUTE THE NUMBER **K** INTO ROW **K** OF COLUMN **C**

The number previously in the specified location is replaced.

SUBSTITUTE THE NUMBER IN ROW **K** OF **C** INTO ROW **K** OF **C**

The number previously in the specified location is replaced.

GENERATE THE FIRST **K** INTEGERS INTO COLUMN **C**

Puts 1, 2, 3, ..., K into the column.

GENERATE THE INTEGERS FROM **K** TO **K**, PUT INTO **C**

GENERATE VALUES FROM **K**, IN STEPS OF **K**, TO **K**, PUT IN **C**

Example

GENERATE FROM 1, STEPS OF −.5, TO −3.5, PUT IN C5

PRINT, NOPRINT, see page 327.

Printing and Punching

PRINT THE VALUES IN COLUMNS **C**,...,**C**

PUNCH THE VALUES IN COLUMNS **C**,...,**C**

From 1 to 4 columns may be punched onto computer cards. If 1 column is punched, there are 4 numbers per card. Otherwise, there is 1 row per card.

COLUMNS, see page 327.

FORTRAN Formatted Input and Output

Each of these commands must be followed by a line with a FOR-TRAN format specification, enclosed in parentheses. Data lines, if any, follow the format line. Integer, or I, format cannot be used (e.g., use F4.0 in place of I4).

FREAD K ROWS INTO **C,...,C**

Similar to READ. Note that the number of rows of data must be specified.

FSET K VALUES INTO **C**

Similar to SET. Note that the number of data values must be specified.

FPRINT C,...,C

FPUNCH C,...,C

TAPEREAD K ROWS INTO **C,...,C**

Reads from unit 8. Similar to FREAD (or FSET if one column is specified).

Plots and Histograms

HISTOGRAM OF COLUMN C

HISTOGRAM OF COLUMN C, FIRST MIDPOINT **K,** INTERVAL WIDTH **K**

PLOT Y IN **C** VS X IN **C**

PLOT Y IN **C** FROM **K** TO **K** VS X IN **C** FROM **K** TO **K**

Plot with scales specified.

TPLOT Y IN **C** VS X IN **C** VS Z IN **C**

Pseudo 3-dimensional plot with different symbols indicating the value of the third (z) dimension.

TPLOT C FROM **K** TO **K** VS **C** FROM **K** TO **K** VS **C**

MPLOT C VS **C** AND **C** VS **C** AND ...

Multiple plots on the same axes.

LPLOT C VS **C** USING LETTERS CORRESPONDING TO **C**

Letters which correspond to the numerical values in the third column are used as plotting symbols. The following correspondence is used:

$$... -2 \; -1 \; 0 \; 1 \; 2 \; 3 \; ... \; 25 \; 26 \; 27 \; 28 \; ...$$
$$... \; X \; \; Y \; Z \; A \; B \; C \; ... \; Y \; \; Z \; \; A \; \; B \; ...$$

LPLOT C FROM K TO K VS C FROM K TO K, LETTERS IN C

WIDTH, see page 327.

Random Data Generation

NRANDOM K NORMAL OBS. WITH MU = K, SIGMA = K, PUT INTO C

BTRIALS K BERNOULLI TRIALS WITH P = K, PUT INTO C

Random sequence of 0 and 1, with p = probability of 1.

BRANDOM K BINOMIAL EXPERIMENTS, N = K, P = K, PUT INTO C

IRANDOM K RANDOM INTEGERS BETWEEN K AND K, PUT INTO C

PRANDOM K POISSON OBS. WITH POP. MEAN = K, PUT INTO C

DRANDOM K OBS. USING VALUES IN C, PROB. IN C, PUT INTO C

Generates random observations from a discrete distribution specified by the first 2 columns.

SAMPLE K ROWS FROM C, PUT INTO C (WITHOUT REPLACEMENT)

SAMPLE K ROWS FROM C,...,C, PUT INTO C,...,C

URANDOM K UNIFORM OBS., PUT INTO C

BASE FOR RANDOM NUMBER GENERATOR = K

PRINT, NOPRINT, see page 327.

Sorting

ORDER COL **C** [AND **C**,...] PUT INTO **C** [AND PUT INTO **C**,...]

Each column is ordered separately, with the smallest number in the first row.

SORT THE VALUES IN **C** [CARRY ALONG CORRESP. ROWS OF **C**,...,**C**] PUT INTO **C**
[AND INTO **C**,...,**C**]

Sorted all together, according to first column.

RANK THE VALUES IN **C**, PUT RANKS INTO **C**

Puts 1 by the smallest value, 2 by next smallest value, and so on.

Manipulations

JOIN E TO BOTTOM OF **E** [TO **E**,..., TO **E**] PUT INTO **C**

Puts columns and/or constants together to form a new column.

PICK ROWS **K** TO **K** OF **C**, PUT INTO **C**

PARSUMS (PARTIAL SUMS) OF **C**, PUT INTO **C**

PARPRODUCT OF **C**, PUT INTO **C**

The product of the first i rows of the first column is put in the i-th row of the second column.

Editing

OMIT ROWS WITH **K** IN **C** [CORRESP. ROWS OF **C**,...,**C**] PUT INTO **C** [CORRESP. ROWS
INTO **C**,...,**C**]

OMIT ROWS WITH VALUES BETWEEN **K** AND **K** IN **C** [CORRESP. ROWS OF **C**,...,**C**],
PUT INTO **C** [CORRESP. ROWS INTO **C**,...,**C**]

CHOOSE ROWS WITH **K** IN **C** [CORRESP. ROWS OF **C**,...,**C**] PUT INTO **C** [CORRESP.
ROWS INTO **C**,...,**C**]

CHOOSE ROWS WITH VALUES BETWEEN **K** AND **K** IN **C** [CORRESP. ROWS OF **C**,...,**C**]
PUT INTO **C** [CORRESP. ROWS INTO **C**,...,**C**]

RECODE THE VALUE **K** IN **C** TO **K**, PUT INTO **C**

Copies the column, making the indicated changes.

RECODE VALUES FROM **K** TO **K** IN **C** TO **K**, PUT INTO **C**

CONVERT USING CONVERSION TABLE IN **C**, **C**, CONVERT **C** INTO **C**

Used primarily to convert character data to numbers.

Arithmetic

ADD   E TO   E, PUT INTO **C**
SUBTRACT E FROM E, PUT INTO **C**
MULTIPLY E BY   E, PUT INTO **C**
DIVIDE   E BY   E, PUT INTO **C**
RAISE   E TO   E, PUT INTO **C**
RMAX (ROW-BY-ROW) OF E AND E, PUT INTO **C**
RMIN (ROW-BY-ROW) OF E AND E, PUT INTO **C**

The following four commands allow operation on more than two
items:

ADD   E TO   E,..., TO   E, PUT INTO **C**
MULTIPLY E BY   E,..., BY   E, PUT INTO **C**
RMAX   OF E,   E,..., AND E, PUT INTO **C**
RMIN   OF E,   E,..., AND E, PUT INTO **C**

Functions

SIGNS OF **E** [PUT INTO **C**]

Gives −1 for negative, +1 for positive, and 0 for 0.

ABSOLUTE VALUE OF **E**, PUT INTO **C**
ROUND E TO NEAREST INTEGER, PUT INTO **C**
SQRT (SQUARE ROOT)   OF **E**, PUT INTO **C**
LOGE (NATURAL LOG)   OF **E**, PUT INTO **C**
LOGTEN (LOG TO BASE TEN) OF **E**, PUT INTO **C**
EXPONENTIAL   OF **E**, PUT INTO **C**
    Raises e to the E power.
ANTILOG (TEN TO THE POWER) OF **E**, PUT INTO **C**
NSCORES (NORMAL SCORES)   OF **E**, PUT INTO **C**

The six trigonometric functions below use angles in radians. Note that to convert from radians to degrees, multiply by 57.297. To convert from degrees to radians, multiply by 0.017453.

SIN (SINE)   OF **E**, PUT INTO **C**
COS (COSINE)   OF **E**, PUT INTO **C**
TAN (TANGENT)   OF **E**, PUT INTO **C**
ASIN (ARCSINE)   OF **E**, PUT INTO **C**
ACOS (ARCCOSINE)   OF **E**, PUT INTO **C**
ATAN (ARCTANGENT)   OF **E**, PUT INTO **C**

Column Operations

In the following commands, the results are printed automatically and the storage is optional:

COUNT   THE NUMBER OF VALUES IN **C** [PUT COUNT   INTO **C**]
SUM   THE VALUES   IN **C** [PUT SUM   INTO **C**]
AVERAGE   THE VALUES   IN **C** [PUT AVERAGE INTO **C**]
STANDARD   DEVIATION   OF **C** [PUT S. D.   INTO **C**]
MEDIAN   OF THE VALUES   IN **C** [PUT MEDIAN   INTO **C**]
MAXIMUM   OF THE VALUES   IN **C** [PUT MAXIMUM INTO **C**]
MINIMUM   OF THE VALUES   IN **C** [PUT MINIMUM INTO **C**]

General Statistics

BINOMIAL PROBABILITIES FOR N = **K**, P = **K** [PUT INTO **C**]
POISSON PROBABILITIES FOR MEAN **K**

RUNS ABOVE AND BELOW **K** FOR DATA IN COLUMN **C**
ZINTERVAL **K** PERCENT CONFIDENCE, ASSUMING SIGMA = **K**, ON **C**

ZTEST OF MU = **K** [ALT. **K**] ASSUMING SIGMA = **K**, ON **C**

TINTERVAL WITH **K** PERCENT CONFIDENCE FOR DATA IN COLUMN **C**
TTEST OF MU = **K** [ALT. **K**] ON DATA IN COLUMN **C**

WILCOXON ONE-SAMPLE RANK TEST OF MEDIAN = **K** AND C.I. FOR DATA IN **C**
WALSH AVERAGES OF **C**, PUT INTO **C** [INDICES INTO **C**, **C**]

TWOSAMPLE T [ALTERNATIVE **K**] [PERCENT CONFIDENCE **K**] FOR DATA IN **C** AND **C**

>   Test and confidence interval. Population variances are not assumed
>   to be equal.

POOLED T [ALTERNATIVE **K**] [PERCENT CONFIDENCE **K**] FOR DATA IN **C** AND **C**

>   Test and confidence interval. Assumes the two populations have
>   equal variances.

MANN-WHITNEY [ALTERNATIVE **K**] [PERCENT CONFIDENCE **K**] FOR DATA IN **C** AND **C**

>   Does a two-sample rank test and corresponding confidence interval.

DIFFERENCES (ALL POSSIBLE) BETWEEN **C** AND **C**, PUT INTO **C** [PUT INDICES INTO **C**
>   AND **C**]

DESCRIBE THE DATA IN **C**,...,**C**

>   Gives various descriptive statistics on each column.

CHISQUARE TEST ON TABLE STORED IN COLUMNS **C**,...,**C**

CONTINGENCY TABLE ANALYSIS FOR DATA IN **C** VS. **C**

TABLE FOR DATA IN **C** VS. **C**

Correlation, Regression, and Analysis of Variance

CORRELATION COEFFICIENT BETWEEN DATA IN COLUMNS **C** AND **C**

CORRELATION COEFFICIENTS FOR DATA IN **C**,...,**C**

REGRESS Y IN **C** USING **K** PREDICTORS IN **C**,...,**C**

REGRESS Y IN **C**, **K** PREDICTORS IN **C**,...,**C** [STORE STD. RES. IN **C** [PRED. VALUES IN **C** [COEF. IN **C**]]]

REGRESS Y IN **C** [WEIGHTS IN **C**] **K** PRED. IN **C**,...,**C** [STORE STD. RES. IN **C** [PRED. IN **C** [COEF. IN **C**]]]

NOCONSTANT

Fits equation with no intercept. Applies to all REGRESS commands which follow.

CONSTANT

Cancels out NOCONSTANT.

AOVONEWAY ON DATA IN COLUMNS **C**,...,**C**

Does a one-way analysis of variance. Each level (group, cell) must be in a separate column.

ONEWAY AOV, DATA IN **C**, LEVEL IN **C**

One-factor analysis of variance, where the factor levels are given by codes in the second column.

TWOWAY AOV, DATA IN **C**, LEVELS IN **C** AND **C**

Balanced two-factor analysis of variance.

INDICATOR VARIABLES FOR VALUES IN **C**, PUT IN **C**, ..., **C**

Useful in regression approach to analysis of variance.

BRIEF

Brief output from all regression and analysis of variance commands which follow.

NOBRIEF

Restores full output from regression and analysis of variance.

BRIEF OUTPUT CODE **K** FOR REG. AND AOV.

K can be from 1 to 6. The higher the number, the more output.

Miscellaneous

STOP
NOTE PRINT OUT COMMENTS PUT ON THIS LINE
ERASE COLUMNS **C,...,C**
RESTART

Erases worksheet, sets error counters to 0, etc.

NEWPAGE

Prints output from the next command on a new page when using a batch computer.

Use of the following two commands (not available on some computers) varies from computer to computer:

SAVE THE WORKSHEET
RETRIEVE STORED COPY OF THE WORKSHEET

Control

The control commands below apply to commands which follow them, until they are over-ridden.

NOPRINT

Suppresses automatic printing of data from READ, SET, FREAD, FSET, TAPEREAD, and random data generators.

PRINT (WITHOUT ANY COLUMN NUMBERS)

Restores automatic printing.

WIDTH OF PLOTS = **K** SPACES
WIDTH OF PLOTS = **K** SPACES, HEIGHT **K** LINES
COLUMNS PRINTED = **K**

> K may be between 4 and 10. K = 6 is useful to fit output on a regular sheet of paper.

DIMENSION THE WORKSHEET TO **K** ROWS
SCAN ONLY THE FIRST **K** SPACES ON COMMAND AND DATA LINES
INUNIT = **K**

> Redirects all reading to another unit.

OUTUNIT = **K**

> Redirects all printing to another unit.

BATCH

> Makes Minitab suitable for batch operation. Not available on some computers.

TSHARE

> Makes Minitab suitable for interactive (time-shared) operation. Not available on some computers.

CONSTANT, NOCONSTANT, BRIEF, NOBRIEF, see page 326.

References

Chapter 1

The data in Exercise 1-4 were obtained from

The World Almanac & Book of Facts, 1976 (New York: Newspaper Enterprise Association, Inc., 1975).

More details about Minitab are given in

T. Ryan, B. Joiner, and B. Ryan, *Minitab II, Reference Manual*, preliminary ed. (University Park: Department of Statistics, The Pennsylvania State University, 1975).

An advanced, general introduction to statistical computing is given in

A. A. Afifi and S. P. Azen, *Statistical Analysis, A Computer Oriented Approach* (New York: Academic Press, 1972).

The following are some of the major statistical computing systems presently available:

W. J. Dixon, editor, *BMDP, Biomedical Computer Programs* (Los Angeles: University of California Press, 1975).

D. Hogben, S. Peavy, and R. Varner, *Omnitab II, User's Reference Manual* (Washington, D.C.: National Bureau of Standards, Technical Note 552, 1971).

J. Service, *SAS, A User's Guide to the Statistical Analysis System* (Raleigh: Student Supply Stores, North Carolina State University, 1972).

N. Nie, C. H. Hull, J. Jenkins, K. Sternbrenner, and D. Bent, *SPSS, Statistical Package for the Social Sciences*, 2nd ed. (New York: McGraw-Hill, 1975).

W. Klecka, N. Nie, and C. H. Hull, *SPSS Primer* (New York: McGraw-Hill, 1975).

Chapter 2

The data in Exercise 2-22 were brought to our attention by John J. Wiorkowski. For a related discussion, see

John J. Wiorkowski, "The Wind Chill Index—A Case Study in Table Sleuthing," *The American Statistician* (November, 1975).

The data in Exhibit 2.4 are from

The World Almanac & Book of Facts, 1976 (New York: Newspaper Enterprise Association, Inc., 1975).

A very interesting four volume collection of data and elementary analyses is

Frederick Mosteller, William H. Kruskal, Richard F. Link, Richard S. Pieters, and Gerald R. Rising, editors, *Statistics by Example* (Reading, Massachusetts: Addison-Wesley, 1973).

The creative use of descriptive statistics is nicely treated in

Edward R. Tufte, *Data Analyses for Politics and Policy* (Englewood Cliffs, New Jersey: Prentice-Hall, 1974).

The following are some texts in general statistics:

W. Mendenhall, *Introduction to Probability and Statistics*, 4th ed. (North Scituate, Massachusetts: Duxbury Press, 1975).

D. V. Huntsberger and P. Billingsley, *Elements of Statistical Inference*, 3rd ed. (Boston: Allyn and Bacon, 1973).

T. H. Wonacott and R. J. Wonacott, *Introductory Statistics*, 2nd ed. (New York: Wiley, 1973).

P. G. Hoel, *Elementary Statistics*, 3rd ed. (New York: Wiley, 1971).

R. R. Johnson, *Elementary Statistics*, 2nd ed. (North Scituate, Massachusetts: Duxbury Press, 1976).

J. E. Freund, *Modern Elementary Statistics,* 4th ed. (Englewood Cliffs, New Jersey: Prentice-Hall, 1973).

G. E. Noether, *Introduction to Statistics: A Nonparametric Approach,* 2nd ed. (Boston: Houghton-Mifflin, 1976).

Chapter 3

An advanced treatment of the winning streaks example of Section 3.6 is given in

W. Feller, *An Introduction to Probability Theory and Its Application,* 3rd ed. (New York: John Wiley, 1968) pp. 78-88.

A good general introduction to simulation is given in

W. Freiberger and V. Grenander, *A Short Course in Computational Probability and Statistics* (New York: Springer-Verlag, 1971).

Chapter 4

A very nice introduction to confidence intervals, that provided the motivation for Section 4.2, is given in

Peter Nemenyi, Sylvia K. Dixon, and Nathaniel B. White, Jr., *Statistics From Scratch* (San Francisco: Holden-Day, 1976).

Chapter 8

The cholesterol data are from a study conducted by a major northeastern medical center.

The method for comparing two means, when the population variances are not assumed equal, is concisely discussed in

K. A. Brownlee, *Statistical Theory and Methodology in Science and Engineering,* 2nd ed. (New York: John Wiley, 1965) pp. 299-303.

Chapter 9

The Olympic races data in Exercise 9-5 were obtained from

The World Almanac & Book of Facts, 1976 (New York: Newspaper Enterprise Association, Inc., 1975).

The Pendulum data for Exercise 9-23 were obtained from John Mandel. These data also appear in his article

Frederick Mosteller, William H. Kruskal, Richard S. Pieters, Gerald R. Rising, and Richard F. Link, editors, "The Acceleration of Gravity," *Statistics by Example: Detecting Patterns* (Reading, Massachusetts: Addison-Wesley, 1973).

More advanced treatments of regression analysis and related topics are given in the following books:

N. R. Draper and H. Smith, *Applied Regression Analysis* (New York: John Wiley, 1966).

Cuthbert Daniel and Fred Wood, *Fitting Equations to Data* (New York: Wiley-Interscience, 1971).

John Neter and W. Wasserman, *Applied Linear Statistical Models* (Homewood, Illinois: Richard D. Irwin, Inc., 1974).

Chapter 10

The fabric flammability test in Section 10.1 was conducted by the American Society for Testing Materials. Related analyses are

"ASTM Studies DOC Standard FF-3-71 on Flammability of Children's Sleepwear," *Materials Research Standards* (May, 1972) pp. 38-39.

John Mandel, Mary N. Steel, and L. James Sharman, "National Bureau of Standards Analysis of the ASTM Interlaboratory Study of DOC/FF 3-71 Flammability of Children's Sleepwear," *ASTM Standardization News* (May, 1973) pp. 9-12.

The meat loaf data were obtained in a study at the University of Wisconsin conducted by Barbara J. Bobeng and Beatrice David.

The oxygen in steel data in Exercise 10-4 have also been reported by

Brian L. Joiner and Cathy Campbell, "Designing Experiments When Run Order May be Important," *Technometrics* (Summer, 1976).

The mean annual income table was taken from

The World Almanac and Book of Facts, 1975 (New York: Newspaper Enterprise Association, Inc., 1975).

Useful general treatments of analysis of variance appear in the following books:

O. J. Dunn and V. A. Clark, *Applied Statistics: Analysis of Variance and Regression* (New York: John Wiley, 1974).

Charles R. Hicks, *Fundamental Concepts in the Design of Experiments* (New York: Holt, Rinehart & Winston, 1973).

John Neter and W. Wasserman, *Applied Linear Statistical Models* (Homewood, Illinois: Richard D. Irwin, Inc., 1974).

Chapter 11

The data on migratory geese given in Exhibit 11.1 are also discussed in

R. K. Tsutakawa, "Chi-Square Distribution by Computer Simulation," in *Statistics by Example: Detecting Patterns*, Frederick Mosteller, William H. Kruskal, Richard S. Pieters, Gerald R. Rising, and Richard F. Link, editors (Reading, Massachusetts: Addison-Wesley, 1973).

The penny tossing data in Exercise 11-4 are described in

W. F. Youden, *Risk, Choice and Prediction* (North Scituate, Massachusetts: Duxbury Press, 1974).

Further discussions of the ESP data of Section 11.2 are given in

Marvin Lee Moon, "Extrasensory Perception and Art Experience," Doctoral thesis, The Pennsylvania State University, 1973.

Marvin Lee Moon, article in *American Journal of Psychical Research* April, 1975.

The Harrisburg, Pennsylvania infant mortality data in Exercise 11-6 are given in

Vilma Hunt and William Cross, "Infant Mortality and the Environment of a Lesser Metropolitan County: A Study Based on Births in One Calendar Year," *Environmental Research* 9 (1975) pp. 135-151.

The Mark Twain data in Exercise 11-7 are given in

Claude Brinegar, "Mark Twain and the Quintus Curtius Snodgrass Letters: A Statistical Test of Authorship," *Journal of the American Statistical Association* 58 (1963) pp. 85-96.

A useful general exposition of chi-square tests is given in

Joseph Fleiss, *Statistical Methods for Rates and Proportions* (New York: John Wiley, 1973).

Chapter 12

The data for Exercises 12-8 and 12-9 were obtained from

The World Almanac & Book of Facts, 1976 (New York: Newspaper Enterprise Association, Inc., 1975).

The Parkinson's disease data in Exhibit 12.5 were obtained by Gastone Celesia in a study at the University of Wisconsin.

The azalea data in Exercise 12-12 are from a study done at Penn State by Professor Stanley Pennypacker, Department of Plant Pathology.

The bird fat data in Exercise 12-14 were obtained from

Jack Hailman, "Notes on Quantitative Treatments of Subcutaneous Lipid Data," *Bird Banding* 36 (1965) pp. 14-20.

Useful books on nonparametric statistics include

Peter Nemenyi, Sylvia K. Dixon, Nathaniel B. White, Jr., *Statistics From Scratch* (San Francisco: Holden-Day, 1976).

W. F. Conover, *Practical Nonparametric Statistics* (New York: John Wiley, 1971).

Myles Hollander and Douglas Wolfe, *Nonparametric Statistical Methods* (New York: John Wiley, 1973).

Eric Lehmann, *Nonparametrics: Statistical Methods Based on Ranks* (San Francisco: Holden-Day, 1975).

Appendix A

Cartoon Data

Stephen Kauffman, "An Experimental Evaluation of the Relative Effectiveness of Cartoons and Realistic Photographs in Both Color and Black and White Visuals in In-Service Training Programs," Master's thesis, The Pennsylvania State University, 1973.

Peru Data

Edward P. Davin, "Blood Pressure Among Residents of the Tambo Valley," Master's thesis, The Pennsylvania State University, 1975.

Trees Data

H. Arthur Meyer, *Forest Mensuration* (State College, Pennsylvania: Penns Valley Publishers, Inc., 1953).

Grades Data

A university that wishes to remain anonymous.

Pulse Data

A classroom experiment conducted by Brian L. Joiner.

Integration Data

Milton Hinton, Doctoral thesis (New York: Teachers College, Columbia University, 1968).

Cancer Data

A study conducted at the University of Wisconsin by L. Kahan, R. N. Carey, S. S. Ehrmeyer, B. L. Joiner, F. C. Larson, R. L. Metzenberg, and W. H. Wolberg.

Index